Contents

How to Use This Book

Learning Objectives

These tell you exactly what you need to learn, or be able to do, for the exam.

Examples

- These are here to help you understand the theory.
- You don't need to learn them unless it says so in the text.

Tips

These are here to help you understand the theory.

[Sample page — Correlations]

Learning Objectives:
Know about the following features of data analysis, presentation and interpretation:
- Analysis and interpretation of correlational data
- Positive and negative correlations and the interpretation of correlation coefficients

9. Correlations

There's a bit more maths here so brace yourself...

Correlation between variables

Correlation is a measure of the relationship between two variables.

Examples

Correlation can tell you how closely exam grades are related to the amount of revision that someone's done, or how the number of fillings a person has relates to how many sweets they eat.

In a correlational study, data is collected for some kind of correlational analysis.

The correlation coefficient

The **correlation coefficient** is a number between −1 and +1. To find the correlation between two variables, you first have to collect some data. For example, you could ask every student in a class how many hours of study they did each week, and note their average test result.

Figure 1: You can use the correlation coefficient to see if there's a relationship between the hours spent studying per week and a person's test scores.

Student	Hours of study	Average test score — %
A	4	58
B	1	23
C	7	67
D	15	89
E	2	34
F	11	78
G	8	60
H	18	98
I	12	86
J	5	45

You can then work out a correlation coefficient (e.g. Spearman's rho — see page 96). This is a number between −1 and +1, and shows:
- How closely the variables are linked. This is shown by the size of the number — if it's close to +1 or −1, then they are very closely related, while a smaller number means the relationship is less strong (or maybe not there at all if it's close to 0).
- The type of correlation — a positive correlation coefficient (i.e. between 0 and +1) means that the variables rise and fall together, while a negative correlation coefficient (i.e. between −1 and 0) means that as one variable rises, the other falls.

Tip: If you work out a correlation coefficient and get a value that doesn't fall between +1 or −1 then you know that you've gone wrong somewhere.

Perfect Negative Correlation	Moderate Negative Correlation	No Correlation	Moderate Positive Correlation	Perfect Positive Correlation
−1.0	−0.5	0	+0.5	+1.0

Figure 2: Scale showing correlation coefficients and their meanings.

The correlation coefficient for the data above is around 0.97. This means that there is a strong positive correlation coefficient — as hours of study increase,

---

[Sample page — Short-Term and Long-Term Memory]

2. Short-Term and Long-Term Memory

Learning Objectives:
- Understand encoding, capacity and duration

Memory is usually divided into two parts — long-term memory and short-term memory.

Types of memory

Memory is a process in which information is retained about the past. Memories are thought to have a physical basis or 'trace'. Most psychologists agree that there are three types of memory — sensory memory (SM), short-term memory (STM) and long-term memory (LTM).

SM contains visual and auditory information that passes through our senses very briefly. Data disappears quickly in SM through spontaneous decay — the trace just fades. SM isn't around for very long, so most studies are on LTM and STM.

STM and LTM differ in terms of:
- **Duration** — How long a memory lasts.
- **Capacity** — How much can be held in the memory.
- **Encoding** — Transferring information into code, creating a 'trace'.

Figure 1: Diagram to show the three types of memory.

Research into STM and LTM

Duration

STM has a limited duration (i.e. we can remember information for a short time). LTM is theoretically permanent (i.e. the information is there forever).

Key study of the duration of STM — Peterson and Peterson (1959)

Method: Participants were shown nonsense trigrams (3 random consonants, e.g. CVM) and asked to recall them after either 3, 6, 9, 12, 15 or 18 seconds. During the pause, they were asked to count backwards in threes from a given number. This was an 'interference task' — it prevented them from repeating the letters to themselves.

Results:

Figure 2: Line graph to show the results of the study.

Exam Tip
In exam questions, always make sure you make it really clear whether you're talking about long-term memory or short-term memory.

Tip: Don't worry if this isn't the study you've learnt about in class — in psychology there are lots of different studies investigating the same thing. For the exam, as long as you know one, that's all that matters.

Exam Tips

There are tips throughout the book to help with all sorts of things to do with answering exam questions.

Studies

- There are lots of psychological studies throughout the book. There are plenty of details about the methods, results and conclusions, as well as some evaluation points.
- Some are labelled as 'key studies' and others as 'additional studies'. If you're pushed for time, just focus on the key studies.
- Also, don't worry if your teacher has taught you about different studies in your lessons — as long as they're on the right topic, using any studies in your exam answers is fine.

Worked Exam Questions

- These are the sorts of questions that could come up in the exams.
- There's an example answer, plus tips on answering the question (and other questions like it).
- Don't just learn these answers though — you'll need to tailor your exam answers to the specific questions asked in the exam.

2   (a) Outline the multi-store model of memory.   *(4 marks)*
2   (b) Evaluate the multi-store model of memory.   *(8 marks)*

(a)   Atkinson and Shiffrin developed the multi-store model. The model suggests that memory is made up of three stores — the sensory store, a short-term store and a long-term store. The sensory store is where information from the environment initially goes. Not much of this information is noticed, but if attention is paid to it, the information gets encoded and passes into short-term memory. If this information is rehearsed and processed even further, it will then be transferred to long-term memory.

(b)   There are many studies that have provided support for the multi-store model of memory. For example, research into the primacy effect (which means that people are able to recall the first few items of a list better than items from the middle) can be explained by the model. The earlier items will have been rehearsed better and transferred to long-term memory. However, if rehearsal is prevented using an interference task, then the primacy effect disappears, which is also predicted by the model.

The recency effect also supports the model. This effect is where people tend to recall the last few items from a list better than those in the middle. The multi-store model would suggest that these items are recalled easily because they're still in short-term memory.

People with Korsakoff's syndrome also provide support for the model. They can recall the last items in a list, suggesting that their short-term memory is unaffected. However, their long-term memory is very poor. This provides evidence that supports the model — long-term memory and short-term memory are shown to be separate stores.

However, the model has limitations. The model proposes that information is transferred from short-term memory to long-term memory through rehearsal. However, in real life, people don't always spend time rehearsing the information that they take in, yet some of it is stored in long-term memory. The model doesn't account for this. Also, it has been suggested that the model is oversimplified. It assumes that there is only one long-term memory store, and one short-term store. However, evidence from brain damaged patients has shown that this is not true. Evidence has suggested that there are several different short-term stores as well as different long-term stores.

Overall then, much research has supported the model, but other research cannot be explained using the model. This suggests that the model is not completely correct.

Summary Questions

Q1   Who came up with the multi-store model of memory?
Q2   What are the three stores in the multi-store model of memory?
Q3   a)   What is the primacy effect?
      b)   Why does it happen?
Q4   How does Korsakoff's syndrome support the multi-store model?
Q5   Who came up with the working memory model?
Q6   What are the three components of the working memory model?

Summary Questions

- There are a lot of facts to learn for AS Psychology — these questions are here to test that you know it all.
- All the answers are in the back of the book.

How Science Works

This book covers How Science Works. The scientific process is described at the front of the book and Unit 1: Section 3 is a whole section on research methods and experiment design.

Exam-style Questions

- Practising exam-style questions is really important — you'll find some at the end of each section.
- They're the same style as the ones you'll get in the real exams — some will test your knowledge and understanding, some will test that you can apply your knowledge and some will test How Science Works.
- In the back of the book you'll find loads of help with answering the questions. There are explanations of what you'll get marks for, and lots of hints and tips about what to include and how to structure your answers.

Exam Help

There's a section at the back of the book stuffed full of things to help with your exams.

Glossary

There's a glossary at the back of the book full of all the definitions you need to know for the exam, plus loads of other useful words.

Exam-style Questions

1   Rachel is conducting a questionnaire investigating how people comply to social influence in the workplace. Evaluate the method Rachel is using to collect her data.
    (4 marks)

2 (a)   Describe how normative social influence can explain why someone might conform.
    (2 marks)
2 (b)   Describe how informational social influence can explain why someone might conform.
    (2 marks)

3   Outline and evaluate research into the effects of informational social influence.
    (12 marks)

4 (a)   Outline what is meant by 'locus of control'.
    (6 marks)
4 (b)   Describe how locus of control can affect conformity and independent behaviour.
    (2 marks)

5   Describe how studies into minority influence have helped psychologists to understand social change.
    (12 marks)

6   Dave is carrying out an investigation into conformity.
    He has decided to test his participants in the laboratory.
6 (a)   State **two** advantages of carrying out an investigation in a laboratory.
    (2 marks)
6 (b)   State **two** disadvantages of carrying out an investigation in a laboratory.
    (2 marks)

7 (a)   Outline Milgram's work into obedience.
    (8 marks)
7 (b)   Consider reasons why someone might disobey an authority figure.
    (6 marks)

8   In Milgram's study, participant A couldn't see the learner.
    Participant B had to place the learner's hand on the electric shock pad.
    Describe and explain the difference you might see in their obedience levels.
    (4 marks)

9   Ben has very strong views against animal testing but his teacher at school has asked him to take part in the school debate team where he has to argue against his morals.
    Explain why Ben might obey his teacher despite it being against his views.
    (3 marks)

Introduction to Psychology

What is Psychology?

Psychology is made up of lots of different approaches. These pages will introduce you to them all so that you know what to expect through the book.

Theories and approaches in psychology

Psychology is "the scientific study of experience and behaviour."
This basically means that psychologists look at what people and animals do, why they do it, and how they feel. A lot of psychology sounds like common sense, but it's a science, so everything's got to be investigated. You've got to come up with a theory about something and then scientifically test it.

Psychology is a science with lots of theories and few 'facts' — it's difficult to prove things in psychology, so there are loads of disagreements and a lot of theories that sound rubbish. But you can't just say they're rubbish in your exam — that'd be too easy. No, you've got to use other theories and experiments to support your answer.

The different schools of thought are called approaches. Each approach has its own explanation for why we do what we do. You'll be looking at the cognitive, developmental, biological, social and psychodynamic approaches. Fortunately for you, they're split up into handy little sections.

The cognitive approach

Cognitive psychologists focus on internal processes to understand behaviour, such as how we perceive or remember things. They compare the human mind to a computer system, so they use computer models to try to understand human cognition (thinking). Using concepts from information processing, cognitive psychologists describe the brain as a processor — it receives input, processes it, and produces an output. Obviously it's ridiculously more complicated, but the general idea is the same.

Cognitive psychology studies are often laboratory-based and artificial, so they can lack validity in the real world. This is known as 'ecological validity' (see page 10).

A big part of research in the cognitive approach is into memory — for example, the differences between long-term memory and short-term memory. A lot of research has been carried out into how long these types of memory last, how much they can hold, and how information is transferred into them. For example, Peterson and Peterson looked into how long short-term memory lasts. Participants were shown 3 random consonants and had to recall them after either 3, 6, 9, 12, 15 or 18 seconds. During this time, they were prevented from practising the letters by doing a counting task. Memory was the best after 3 seconds, and got progressively worse up to 18 seconds.

Other research has tried to come up with a model of memory. For example, Atkinson and Shiffrin developed the multi-store model, and Baddeley and Hitch developed the working memory model.

Tip: You don't need to learn the stuff on these pages — it's just here as a good introduction to the things that you're going to be meeting during AS Psychology.

Tip: Psychology is a science so researchers have to follow the scientific process when they're coming up with new theories. See pages 5-6 for more about the scientific process.

Tip: The cognitive approach starts on page 9 — you'll be tested on it in your Unit 1 exam.

Figure 1: *A lot of studies into memory are carried out using computers, so they're not that representative of real-life situations.*

Developmental psychology

Developmental psychology is a bit of a jumble of ideas from different approaches... Developmental psychologists look at how people develop and change over their lifetime. They place emphasis on the importance of early experiences in shaping the rest of a person's life. Part of the approach looks at the importance of attachment — the emotional bond that infants form with their caregivers.

Some researchers, like Bowlby, believe that the attachment has to be with the mother. This is known as monotropy. Others have shown that infants will attach to their primary caregiver, even if that's not their biological mother. A big area of research looks at what can happen if attachments are broken (deprivation) or never form in the first place (privation). It ranges from studying things like the effect of being put into day care, where an infant is away from its caregiver for a few hours, to research on children who've had hardly any human contact their entire lives.

Because a lot of the research is done on children, one of the main research methods is observational research. This ensures that the children's behaviour is natural. Researchers have to be really careful about ethics, because people under 16 can't give informed consent. They have to get consent from the child's parents instead, and make sure that they use the least stressful procedure possible.

Tip: The developmental approach starts on page 34. You'll be tested on it in your Unit 1 exam, along with the cognitive approach and research methods. There's a big section on research methods starting on page 61.

Figure 2: Participants in psychological studies always have to give their consent first — it's very important that studies meet strict ethical guidelines.

The biological approach

The biological approach explains behaviour as a product of nature. There are three key assumptions:

- Human behaviour can be explained by looking at internal, biological stuff, like hormones and the nervous system.
- Experimental research that uses animals can tell us about human behaviour because we have similar biological make-ups.
- Unwanted behaviour can sometimes be changed for the better using biological treatments — e.g. medication for mental illness.

So, as far as this approach is concerned, it's what's inside that counts... Researchers look at genetics, the brain, hormones and the nervous system to explain behaviour. It's very scientific — research is mostly carried out in laboratory experiments. Common research techniques include brain scans and correlational studies.

A big area of research has looked into stress. Biological psychologists have tried to map the parts of the body that are activated in stressful situations, and have identified the sympathomedullary pathway and the pituitary-adrenal system. Research has also looked into the causes of stress, and the link between stress and illness. Biological psychology has proved helpful by discovering ways to manage and treat stress.

Biological psychology has also been valuable in identifying possible biological causes of many mental disorders, for example, depression, schizophrenia and anxiety disorders. This has led to biological treatments being developed which have helped many patients.

Tip: The section on the biological approach starts on page 106. This is examined in the Unit 2 exam.

Tip: Brain scanning allows the structure and functioning of the brain to be studied (see page 107).

Tip: Correlational studies identify relationships between variables (see page 63).

Social psychology

The social approach is all about how we interact with and influence each other. Major areas of research include conformity and obedience. Society needs people to conform and be obedient in order to function properly — e.g. if drivers didn't abide by the rules of the road there would be chaos. This can be a problem though, because people might be more likely to do something they think is wrong if they feel pressured by others.

Tip: You won't meet social psychology until you're preparing for your Unit 2 exam. It starts on page 138.

Probably the most famous experiment in social psychology is Milgram's Behavioural Study of Obedience (1963). In the experiment he tested people's obedience by asking participants to give someone electric shocks. Most of his participants carried on giving the shocks, even when they thought they were causing harm. He concluded that most people will follow orders even if it means doing something they don't think is right. Pretty scary stuff. You can find this study on pages 155-156.

There are a few very famous studies into conformity, including Asch's line judging study, Sherif's autokinetic effect study, and Zimbardo's Stanford Prison experiment. For example, Asch (1951) wanted to see whether his participants would give wrong answers to an unambiguous task if a majority of other people (who were actually confederates of the experiment — they were in on the whole thing) also gave the wrong answers. He found that the participants did conform and give the wrong answers, even though they were very obviously wrong. You'll find the details of this study on pages 142-143.

Figure 3: *A lot of what happens in daily life requires people to obey rules and conform to norms, such as when driving. A big area of research in social psychology is looking at what causes people to obey and conform.*

Individual differences

It's another one that's made up of bits from loads of approaches. The main thing that researchers want to find out is how and why we're all different from each other. You might think it's pretty obvious that we're all different, but psychologists have got to find something to fill the day.

Tip: Individual differences is the last approach that you'll meet. It starts on page 170, and it's tested in the Unit 2 exam along with biological psychology and social psychology.

In the individual differences approach, the theories of why we're all different come from various different approaches. For example, we might be depressed because of genetic factors (the biological approach), or it might be down to irrational or negative thoughts (the cognitive approach).

Other areas of psychology tend to assume that people are broadly the same — e.g. developmental psychologists assume that we all go through the same basic stages of development. A big area of research in the individual differences approach is abnormality. Deviation from the norm is okay to a point, but societies have difficulties dealing with people who are considered to be very abnormal.

Because of this, an important issue to bear in mind is how normality is defined, and whether anyone has the right to decide that someone else is abnormal. Several different definitions have been suggested — abnormality can be seen as a deviation from social norms, it could be a failure to function adequately in day-to-day life, or it could be defined by using a tick-list of symptoms. To complicate matters, culture and time often affect the way that things are defined. To some cultures, or in certain times, someone's behaviour could seem perfectly normal — however, to other cultures, or in other times, the same behaviour could be deemed to be abnormal.

1. The Scientific Process

Developing and testing scientific ideas is done in a certain way for all sciences. These pages will give you the low-down on everything you need to know.

What happens in the scientific process?

Science tries to explain how and why things happen — it answers questions. It's all about seeking and gaining knowledge about the world around us. Scientists do this by asking questions and suggesting answers and then testing them, to see if they're correct — this is the scientific process.

- Ask a question — make an observation and ask why or how it happens.
- Suggest an answer, or part of an answer, by forming a **theory** (a possible explanation of the observations).
- Make a prediction or **hypothesis** — a specific testable statement, based on the theory, about what will happen in a test situation.
- Carry out a test — to provide evidence that will support the prediction (or help to disprove it).

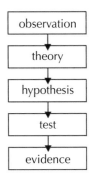

Figure 1: *The process of forming and testing a hypothesis.*

--- Example -------------

- You might have seen someone give an obviously wrong answer to a question in front of a group of people, just because everyone else in that group has already given that answer. So, your question could be, "Why do people sometimes give obviously wrong answers when they're in a group of people?"
- You might form a theory that they do this to appear normal, and to avoid being excluded or rejected from the group.
- Your hypothesis might then be, "People carrying out an unambiguous task will give an incorrect answer to be consistent with the majority."
- To test this, you might put a participant in a group with some confederates (people who are 'in' on the experiment) who give a deliberately wrong answer to an easy task. You would then observe whether the participant also gives the wrong answer, or whether they resist the influences of conformity.

Tip: Every single theory that you come across in books and journals has been through this process. Loads of evidence needs to be collected before a theory can be accepted.

Suggesting explanations is all very well and good, but if there's no way to test them then it just ain't science. A theory is only scientific if it can be tested.

Peer review

Peer review is a process used to ensure the integrity of published scientific work. Before publication, scientific work is sent to experts in that field (peers) so they can assess the quality of the work. This process helps to keep scientists honest — e.g. you can't 'sex-up' your conclusions if the data doesn't support it, because it won't pass peer review.

Tip: Peer review is an important part of the scientific process. It takes place in all areas of science, not just psychology.

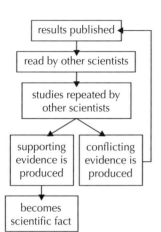

These pieces of research wouldn't pass peer review:

- 80% of schizophrenia patients show a significant improvement in their symptoms after using a new treatment for schizophrenia, so the researchers conclude that it'll help everyone with schizophrenia. However — the researchers can't conclude this because they'd be ignoring the 20% of patients who didn't show an improvement.

- A researcher conducting a survey into whether local people are for or against a new housing development carries out his survey at a meeting held by people campaigning against new housing developments. However — his results will be biased, so he can't draw any reliable conclusions from his data.

Figure 2: *The process of testing theories by collecting more evidence.*

Peer review helps to validate conclusions — it means published theories, data and conclusions are more trustworthy. But it can't guarantee that the conclusions are 100% right. More rounds of predicting and testing are needed before they can be taken as 'fact'.

Sometimes mistakes are made and bad science is published. Peer review isn't perfect but it's probably the best way for scientists to self-regulate their work and to ensure reliable scientific work is published.

Testing theories

Science is all about testing theories. It starts off with one experiment backing up a prediction and theory. It ends up with all the scientists in the world agreeing with it and you learning it. Stirring stuff. This is how the magical process takes place:

- The results are published — scientists need to let others know about their work, so they try to get their results published in **scientific journals**. These are just like normal magazines, only they contain scientific reports (called papers) instead of celebrity gossip. All work must undergo peer review before it's published.

- Other scientists read the published theories and results, and try to repeat them — this involves repeating the exact experiments, and using the theory to make new predictions that are tested by new experiments.

Figure 3: *Studies are replicated by other psychologists — if they come up with the same results, it provides more support for the conclusion.*

- If all the experiments in all the world provide evidence to back it up, the theory is thought of as scientific 'fact' (for now).

- If new evidence comes to light that conflicts with the current evidence the theory is questioned all over again. More rounds of testing will be carried out to see which evidence, and so which theory, prevails.

Accepting theories

If the evidence supports a theory, it's accepted — for now. Our currently accepted theories have survived this 'trial by evidence'. They've been tested over and over and over and each time the results have backed them up. BUT, and this is a big but (teehee), they never become totally undisputable fact. Scientific breakthroughs or advances could provide new ways to question and test a theory, which could lead to changes and challenges to it. Then the testing starts all over again...

Tip: The key thing to remember here is that just because theories are published in journals and books, they never become hard fact — there's always the chance that conflicting evidence could one day be found.

And this, my friend, is the tentative nature of scientific knowledge — it's always changing and evolving.

2. The Role of Science

Science isn't just done so that we know more and more stuff.
We can use the knowledge we gain to improve our lives.

Making decisions

Lots of scientific work eventually leads to important discoveries that could benefit humankind. Oh yes. These results are used by society (that's you, me and everyone else) to make decisions about the way we live. All sections of society use scientific evidence to make decisions:

- Politicians use science to devise policy.

> **Example**
>
> Cognitive behavioural therapy is available on the NHS because there's evidence to show it can help people with depression.

- Private organisations use science to determine what to make or develop.

> **Example**
>
> Evidence has shown that the number of people being diagnosed with depression is increasing, so drugs companies might put more money into this area of research.

- Individuals also use science to make decisions about their own lives.

> **Example**
>
> Government guidelines were changed in 2010 to reduce the maximum recommended amount of salt people should eat per day. This was due to the results of a study showing that reducing salt could significantly reduce heart disease. However, even if evidence suggests that we should eat less salt, it's up to individuals to decide whether they take that advice or not.

Influences on decision making

Making decisions in science isn't straightforward. Other factors can influence decisions about science or the way science is used.

Economic factors

Society has to consider the cost of implementing changes based on scientific conclusions.

> **Example**
>
> The NHS can't afford the most expensive drugs without sacrificing something else. Sometimes they decide to use a less expensive drug despite evidence showing there's a more effective one.

Scientific research is expensive so companies won't always be able to afford to develop new ideas.

> **Example**
>
> Developing new drugs is costly, so pharmaceutical companies often only invest in drugs that are likely to make money.

Social factors

Decisions affect people's lives. How psychologists decide what's normal and what's abnormal affects how people are treated.

Real World Connection

Psychologists don't just do research for the fun of it. For example, psychologists study mental disorders in order to try to discover the causes and also to develop effective treatments. Our knowledge of many disorders has been massively increased due to studies that have been carried out.

Figure 1: *Pharmaceutical companies will only mass produce drugs that are known to be effective and are likely to make money.*

Tip: The DSM is the Diagnostic and Statistical Manual of Mental Disorders. It contains details of all known mental disorders and includes criteria that must be present for a person to be diagnosed. There have been many versions of the DSM — it's updated and republished to include newly discovered disorders and also to remove others which are no longer considered to be disorders.

Figure 2: *A test tube containing the extract from a curare plant.*

Tip: There's more information about ethics in psychology on pages 81-83. The British Psychological Society have a very strict set of guidelines that all experiments and studies must stick to.

Example

Homosexuality was defined as an abnormal behaviour until fairly recently — it was included in the DSM-II, but removed and replaced with 'sexual orientation disturbance' when the manual was revised for a later printing. This was again changed for the publication of the DSM-III — a new category called 'ego dystonic homosexuality' was included. However, in 1986, the diagnosis was finally completely removed and replaced with a broader category called 'sexual disorders not otherwise specified'. This category was more in line with what's currently classed as abnormal behaviour, as symptoms include a very distressed state caused by an unwanted sexual orientation.

Environmental factors

Some scientific research and breakthroughs might affect the environment. Not everyone thinks the benefits are worth the possible environmental damage.

Example

Scientists have only tested a very small percentage of tropical plants for medicinal purposes, but many of them are already used in drugs. For example, a muscle relaxant used in Parkinson's disease is derived from a plant called curare liana. Scientists believe unexplored regions of the world like remote parts of rainforests might contain many more untapped drug resources. But some people think we shouldn't exploit these regions because any interesting finds may lead to deforestation and reduced biodiversity in these areas.

Being responsible

Science has to be responsible in many ways. Yes, you've guessed it — **ethics**. Scientists aren't allowed to test something just because they can. They have to think about the ethical considerations surrounding the experiment design and how the results could affect society.

Design

Experiments have to be carefully designed and run to avoid any ethical issues.

Examples

- Experiments involving animals are tightly controlled and monitored.
- Studies are checked to ensure they aren't placing individuals in unnecessary danger.
- If a study shows a drug has a highly beneficial effect, it's stopped and those in the placebo (negative) group are given the drug too.

Results

Psychologists have to be careful how they use the results of their studies.

Example

Scientists' understanding of some genetic disorders (e.g. autism) could lead to tests to detect members of the population that carry the genes for them. But would people want to know?

Society does have a say in what experiments take place. Controversial experiments involving ethical issues have to be approved by scientific and ethics councils before they are allowed to be carried out.

1. The Cognitive Approach

There are lots of different approaches to psychology.
So, first up — the cognitive approach.

Cognitive psychology

Cognitive psychology is all about how we think. Cognitive psychologists try to explain behaviour by looking at our thought processes, such as perception, language, attention and memory. Computers and computer models are often used to explain how we think and behave. Humans are treated as information processors (computers) and behaviour is explained in terms of information processing (how computers deal with information). Cognitive psychology is sometimes called the information processing approach.

But cognitive psychology has limitations. Research is often carried out in artificial situations (laboratories, using computer models) and the role of emotion and influence from other people is often ignored. For these reasons some argue that the results aren't valid in the real world. A second criticism is that cognitive psychology fails to take individual differences into account by assuming that all of us process stuff in exactly the same way.

Tip: Individual differences can be things like age, intelligence, motivation, etc.

The development of cognitive psychology

People began to see similarities in how computers and humans make sense of information. Computer terms are often used in cognitive psychology. The brain is described as a processor (the thing that makes things happen) — it has data input into it, and output from it. Some parts of the brain form networks (connections of bits). Other parts work in serial (info travels along just one path) or in parallel (info travels to and fro along lots of paths at the same time) — see Figure 1. Cognitive psychologists use computers to create computational models of the human mind — see Figure 2.

Tip: Information can either travel by serial pathways or in parallel:

Figure 1: *Diagrams showing a serial pathway (left) and a parallel pathway (right).*

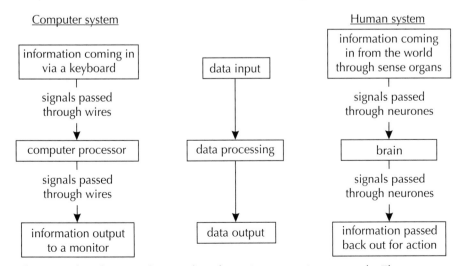

Figure 2: *Flow diagrams showing the information processing approach. The computer and human systems follow the same route — data input, processing and data output.*

Main research methods

Here's a snappy little phrase for you to learn before you read on: '**ecological validity**' — it's the measure of how much the result of an experiment reflects what would happen in natural settings. If a result has low ecological validity, it might work fine in the lab. But try and use it to explain real life behaviour, and you'll find yourself up the creek without a paddle. And no-one wants that. Coming up are six research methods frequently used in the cognitive approach:

1. Laboratory experiments

A lot of research in cognitive psychology happens in laboratories. This is very scientific and reliable as it is possible to have great control over variables in a lab. However, often this type of research doesn't tell us much about the real world — it has low ecological validity.

2. Field experiments

Field experiments take place in a natural situation (e.g. studies of memory or attention in a school environment), so they have more ecological validity, but there's less control of other variables.

3. Natural experiments

Natural experiments involve making observations of a naturally occurring situation. The experimenter has little control of the variables, and participants can't be randomly assigned to conditions. Natural experiments have high ecological validity, but they're not massively reliable, as uncontrolled (or confounding) variables can affect the results.

4. Brain imaging

Brain imaging can now be carried out during a cognitive task. For example, MRI scans have been used to show the blood flow in different brain areas for different types of memory tasks.

5. Case studies

Case studies provide support for the cognitive approach. Case studies use patients' behaviour to test a theory. Brain damaged patients are often studied — the damaged parts of the brain are linked to observed differences in behaviour. However, it's hard to make generalisations from the study of subjects with brain damage to 'normal' individuals. Also, individual differences between people mean that one subject may respond in a way that is totally different from someone else. Hmmm, tricky.

Cognitive psychologists believe that the different types of memory are separate systems in the brain. The case study of HM supported this by showing that short- and long-term memory must be based in different brain structures.

Key study of HM — Milner et al (1957)	
Diagnosis:	HM was a patient with severe and frequent epilepsy. His seizures were based in a brain structure called the hippocampus. In 1953, doctors decided to surgically remove part of the brain round this area.
Results:	The operation reduced his epilepsy, but led to him suffering memory loss. He could still form short-term memories (STMs), but was unable to form new long-term memories (LTMs). For example, he could read something over and

Figure 3: *A lot of lab research uses computers — studies of memory of words and pictures are often done this way.*

Tip: There's more about these research methods on pages 61-64 — they all have their own pros and cons.

Tip: Case studies aren't just used in cognitive psychology — for example, they're a useful research method in biological psychology too (see page 106).

Tip: Short-term memory and long-term memory are covered on page 13.

over without realising that he had read it before. He also moved house and had difficulty recalling the new route to his house. However, he could still talk and show previous skills (procedural memory). From tests, they found HM's episodic memory (for past events) and semantic memory (for knowledge, e.g. word meanings) was affected more than his procedural memory.

6. Animal research

The results of non-human studies can be applied to human cognitive abilities. For example, discovering whether chimpanzees can learn language helps psychologists develop theories about how humans learn language.

However, there are so many differences between humans and animals that results can be explained wrongly. For example, you might conclude that chimpanzees can't learn a spoken language because they lack the cognitive abilities. But it's actually more likely to be because they lack the physiological attributes, like a voice box.

Tip: There's a lot of debate about using animals in research. Have a look at some of the arguments on pages 82-83.

Key study of language in chimps — Gardner and Gardner (1969)

Method: Washoe, a chimpanzee, was raised like a human child and taught American Sign Language (ASL).

Results: By the end of the 22nd month of the project, Washoe had learnt at least 34 signs.

Conclusion: The development of language in the chimpanzee appeared to follow the same patterns as language development in children (both speaking children, and those using ASL). Washoe learnt language at similar rates to children of the same age. Additionally, language acquisition seemed to require interaction with caregivers and communication in everyday situations. However, she did not learn grammar.

Evaluation: There are ethical considerations, in that Washoe was taken from the wild and deprived of other chimpanzees for companionship. There are also issues of external validity — it is not possible to accurately generalise results from the study of a chimp to the study of human children.

Figure 4: A lot of psychology studies have used chimps and monkeys for their research.

Worked Exam-style Questions

1   Discuss the use of case studies on brain damaged patients to provide support for the cognitive approach.   *(8 marks)*

By studying brain damaged patients, the damaged parts of the brain ■ *can be linked to differences in the patients' behaviour. For example, cognitive psychologists have tried to link different types of memory with separate parts of the brain.*

*   A case study of a patient known as HM is one example of this.* ■ *HM had epileptic seizures which were based in a part of the brain called the hippocampus. His doctors decided to remove part of the brain around the hippocampus in order to stop his seizures. After the operation, HM*

Exam Tip
Start with an explanation of how case studies are used.

Exam Tip
Then it's always a good idea to give examples of the points you're making.

suffered memory loss. His short-term memory was fine, but he was unable to form new long-term memories. His procedural memory was unharmed, but his episodic memory and his semantic memory were affected. From this, cognitive psychologists were able to suggest that different types of memory are associated with different areas of the brain.

It would seem that case studies can provide good support for the cognitive approach. However, it's hard to be completely certain that particular behaviours are linked to specific parts of the brain because it's hard to make generalisations from studies of subjects with brain damage to people with no brain damage. Also, case studies only show the behaviour of one person — individual differences between people mean that one person may show behaviours that are totally different from another person.

2   Outline and evaluate three research methods used
    in the cognitive approach.   *(9 marks)*

Laboratory experiments are used in cognitive psychology. These are very scientific and reliable because the experimenters can have a lot of control over the variables in the study. However, these studies usually have low ecological validity because they don't really resemble the real world.

Another type of research method used in the cognitive approach is natural experiments. The problem with these is that they're not very reliable and the experimenter doesn't have much control over the variables. However, they do have very high ecological validity, which is an advantage over laboratory experiments.

A third research method used in cognitive psychology is field experiments. These take place in a natural situation, for example, in a school environment. Because they take place in a natural setting, they have good ecological validity. However, this also means that the experimenters have less control over the variables.

Summary Questions

Q1 How is cognitive psychology linked to a computer model?

Q2 Give two limitations of the cognitive approach.

Q3 Give one advantage and one disadvantage of field experiments.

Q4 Give one way in which natural experiments are better than laboratory experiments.

Q5 What were the results and conclusion of Gardner and Gardner's (1969) study of language in chimps?

Q6 Give one limitation of Gardner and Gardner's (1969) study.

2. Short-Term and Long-Term Memory

Learning Objectives:
- Understand encoding, capacity and duration

Memory is usually divided into two parts — long-term memory and short-term memory.

Types of memory

Memory is a process in which information is retained about the past. Memories are thought to have a physical basis or 'trace'. Most psychologists agree that there are three types of memory — sensory memory (SM), short-term memory (STM) and long-term memory (LTM).

SM contains visual and auditory information that passes through our senses very briefly. Data disappears quickly in SM through spontaneous decay — the trace just fades. SM isn't around for very long, so most studies are on LTM and STM.

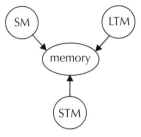

Figure 1: *Diagram to show the three types of memory.*

STM and LTM differ in terms of:

- **Duration** — How long a memory lasts.
- **Capacity** — How much can be held in the memory.
- **Encoding** — Transferring information into code, creating a 'trace'.

Research into STM and LTM

Duration

STM has a limited duration (i.e. we can remember information for a short time). LTM is theoretically permanent (i.e. the information is there forever).

Exam Tip
In exam questions, always make sure you make it really clear whether you're talking about long-term memory or short-term memory.

Key study of the duration of STM — Peterson and Peterson (1959)

Method: Participants were shown nonsense trigrams (3 random consonants, e.g. CVM) and asked to recall them after either 3, 6, 9, 12, 15 or 18 seconds. During the pause, they were asked to count backwards in threes from a given number. This was an 'interference task' — it prevented them from repeating the letters to themselves.

Results:

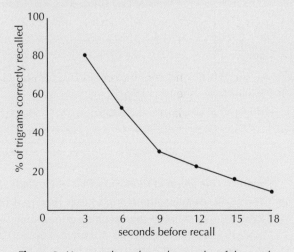

Figure 2: *Line graph to show the results of the study.*

Tip: Don't worry if this isn't the study you've learnt about in class — in psychology there are lots of different studies investigating the same thing. For the exam, as long as you know one, that's all that matters.

After 3 seconds, participants could recall about 80% of trigrams correctly. After 18 seconds, only about 10% were recalled correctly.

Conclusion: When rehearsal is prevented, very little can stay in STM for longer than about 18 seconds.

Evaluation: The results are likely to be reliable — it's a laboratory experiment where the variables can be tightly controlled. However, nonsense trigrams are artificial, so the study lacks ecological validity (see page 71 for more about reliability and validity). Meaningful or 'real-life' memories may last longer in STM. Only one type of stimulus was used — the duration of STM may depend on the type of stimulus. Also, each participant saw many different trigrams. This could have led to confusion, meaning that the first trigram was the only realistic trial.

Exam Tip
If you're asked to evaluate a lab study, you can usually say that it's reliable because the variables should have been tightly controlled (see page 71). However, they'll usually also lack ecological validity (see page 61).

Key study of very long-term memories (VLTMs) — Bahrick et al (1975)

Method: Bahrick et al (1975) investigated LTM in a natural setting. 392 people were asked to list the names of their ex-classmates. (This is called a 'free-recall test'.) They were then shown photos and asked to recall the names of the people shown (photo-recognition test) or given names and asked to match them to a photo of the classmate (name-recognition test).

Results: Within 15 years of leaving school, participants could recognise about 90% of names and faces. They were about 60% accurate on free recall. After 30 years, free recall had declined to about 30% accuracy. After 48 years, name-recognition was about 80% accurate, and photo-recognition about 40% accurate.

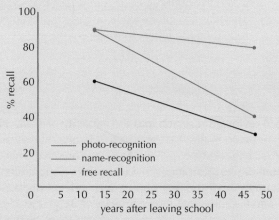

Figure 3: Line graph to show the results of the study.

Conclusion: The study shows evidence of VLTMs in a 'real-life' setting. Recognition is better than recall, so there may be a huge store of information, but it's not always easy to access all of it — you just need help to get to it.

> Evaluation: This was a field experiment and so had high ecological validity. However in a 'real-life' study like this, it's hard to control all the variables, making these findings less reliable — there's no way of knowing exactly why information was recalled well. It showed better recall than other studies on LTM, but this may be because meaningful information is stored better. This type of information could be rehearsed (if you're still in touch with classmates, or if you talk to friends about memories of classmates), increasing the rate of recall. This means that the results can't be generalised to other types of information held in LTM.

Capacity

STM has a limited capacity (i.e. we can only remember a little information). LTM has a pretty much unlimited capacity (i.e. lots of information).

Key study of the capacity of STM — Jacobs (1887)

Method: Participants were presented with a string of letters or digits. They had to repeat them back in the same order. The number of digits or letters increased until the participant failed to recall the sequence correctly.

Results: The majority of the time, participants recalled about 9 digits and about 7 letters. This capacity increased with age during childhood.

Conclusion: Based on the range of results, Jacobs concluded that STM has a limited storage capacity of 5-9 items. Individual differences were found, such as STM increasing with age, possibly due to increased brain capacity or use of memory techniques, such as chunking (see below). Digits may have been easier to recall as there were only 10 different digits to remember, compared to 26 letters.

Evaluation: Jacobs' research is artificial and lacks ecological validity — it's not something you'd do in real life. More meaningful information may be recalled better, perhaps showing STM to have an even greater capacity. Also, the previous sequences recalled by the participants might have confused them on future trials.

Tip: Studies of capacity nearly always look at STM, because it's generally thought that LTM is limitless.

Exam Tip
Ecological validity is a really good phrase to remember for the exam. If something's got high ecological validity, it means that the results are representative of what would happen in the real world. Don't mix it up with external validity, which means that the results can be generalised to other settings.

Miller (1956) reviewed research into the capacity of STM. He found that people can remember about seven items. He argued that the capacity of STM is seven, plus or minus two — 'Miller's magic number'. He suggested that we use '**chunking**' to combine individual letters or numbers into larger more meaningful units. So 2,0,0,3,1,9,8,7 is about all the digits STM can hold. 'Chunked' into the meaningful recent years of 2003 and 1987, it's much easier to remember. STM could probably hold about seven such pieces of chunked information, increasing STM's capacity.

┌─ Example ──
│ ▪ You might remember a mobile phone number by chunking it into
│   groups of two or three numbers.
└─

Additional studies of the capacity of STM

Research that has been done since Miller came up with his magic number has proposed that the number of items that we can remember in short-term memory is actually much less than seven. Other psychologists have suggested that the number is between three and five. For example, Cowan (2001) predicted the capacity to be more like four items. He believes that Miller's overestimation might be due to some rehearsal still happening, and therefore his experiment was also testing long-term memory. If rehearsal was completely prevented, Miller's number would be much less.

A lot of the research into capacity has used verbal stimuli — for example, word lists or strings of numbers. However, Vogel et al (2001) took another approach to the study of the capacity of short-term memory by using visual stimuli. Using this visual information, their results agreed with Cowan's results — they found that the capacity was also no more than four items.

Miller talked about the idea of chunking, but the size of the chunks could also have a big effect on how much is remembered. Simon (1974) found that the larger the chunks of information were, the fewer that could be remembered. For example, it would be easier to recall a list of words than a list of phrases each containing many words. However, the reliability of this study is quite low, as it only used a very small sample.

Encoding

Tip: Encoding can be visual (pictures), acoustic (sounds, e.g. 'chunky' and 'monkey' are acoustically similar) or semantic (meanings, e.g. 'chunky' and 'beefy' are semantically similar).

Encoding is about the way information is stored. In STM, we sometimes try to keep information active by repeating it to ourselves. This means it generally involves acoustic coding. In LTM, encoding is generally semantic — it's more useful to code words in terms of their meaning, rather than what they sound or look like (although encoding in LTM can also be visual or acoustic).

Key study of encoding in STM and LTM — Baddeley (1966)

Method:	Participants were given four sets of words that were either acoustically similar (e.g. man, mad, mat), acoustically dissimilar (e.g. pit, cow, bar), semantically similar (e.g. big, large, huge) and semantically dissimilar (e.g. good, hot, pig). The experiment used an independent groups design — participants were asked to recall the words either immediately or following a 20-minute task.
Results:	Participants had problems recalling acoustically similar words when recalling the word list immediately (from STM). If recalling after an interval (from LTM), they had problems with semantically similar words.
Conclusion:	The patterns of confusion between similar words suggest that LTM is more likely to rely on semantic encoding and STM on acoustic encoding.
Evaluation:	This is another study that lacks ecological validity. Also, there are other types of LTM (e.g. episodic memory, procedural memory) and other methods of encoding (e.g. visual) which this experiment doesn't consider. The experiment used an independent groups design, so there wasn't any control over participant variables.

Exam Tip
An independent groups design means that the participants are put into different groups — each group only experiences one of the conditions in the study. So here, one group did an immediate recall test and the other did a delayed recall test. See page 69 for more.

Additional studies of encoding

Conrad (1964) carried out a study to see whether encoding in short-term memory is acoustic even when information is presented to participants visually. Participants saw six consonants shown one after another very quickly on a screen. They were either acoustically similar letters (e.g. D and B) or acoustically dissimilar letters (e.g. H and P). The participants had to write down the letters in the order that they had been shown.

Conrad found that the majority of the errors were made by participants listing a wrong but similar sounding letter (e.g. D and P). Participants were worse at recalling lists of acoustically similar letters in the right order than acoustically dissimilar letters. Because the letters were produced visually but mistakes were made in terms of their sounds, Conrad concluded that items are encoded in STM as an acoustic code rather than a visual code.

However, other studies have shown that it's not just acoustic encoding that's used in STM. Brandimonte et al (1992) found that when participants weren't able to use acoustic encoding, visual encoding was used instead. Participants were shown six basic line drawings of familiar objects, like the one on the right. They had to memorise the drawings in order, and were then asked to imagine them one at a time and subtract a particular part of the drawing (as shown on the right). They were then asked to identify the resulting image. Another group were prevented from acoustically encoding the images by saying "la la la" during the memorising stage. It was found that this group of participants was actually better at identifying the subtracted picture.

So, it might be that the nature of the task has an effect on the type of encoding used — but that acoustic encoding is usually the one that is naturally used.

Features	STM	LTM
capacity	limited	unlimited
duration	limited	permanent
encoding	acoustic, visual	semantic

Figure 4: *Summary table of the features of STM and LTM.*

Worked Exam-style Questions

1   Outline and evaluate **one** study into the capacity of memory.   *(6 marks)* ■

Jacobs (1887) carried out a study into the capacity of short-term memory. He gave participants a list of letters or numbers. Participants were asked to repeat the list back in the same order. The number of letters or numbers was increased until the participant wasn't able to remember the list correctly.

Most of the time, participants recalled about 9 numbers and about 7 letters. This also increased with age during childhood. Jacobs was able to conclude that short-term memory has a capacity that is limited to between 5 and 9 items.

One problem with Jacob's study is that it lacked ecological validity — the lists of letters and numbers were very artificial. If the information had been more interesting or meaningful, more items might have been remembered. Also, the participants were tested with several lists, so earlier lists could have caused confusion on later trials.

Exam Tip
This sort of question gives you the freedom to pick what study you write about. However, think about it carefully — make sure you know enough about that study to get you all the marks.

However, Miller later reviewed a lot of research into the capacity of short-term memory, and he found that people can remember about 7 items. This provides support for Jacobs' study.

2   (a) What is meant by the duration of memory?   *(1 mark)*

2   (b) Outline and evaluate research into the duration of memory.   *(12 marks)*

(a) The duration of a memory is how long it lasts.

(b) Peterson and Peterson (1959) carried out a study into the duration of short-term memory using trigrams (3 random consonants). Participants were shown trigrams and had to recall them after either 3, 6, 9, 12, 15 or 18 seconds. During the pause, they were given an interference task to prevent them from repeating the letters to themselves. They found that after 3 seconds, participants could recall about 80% of the trigrams correctly. However, after 18 seconds, only 10% were recalled correctly. They concluded that when people can't rehearse things, very little can stay in their short-term memory for longer than 18 seconds.

This was a laboratory experiment, so the researchers could control the variables and the results are likely to be reliable. However, it's not a memory task that you'd be likely to meet in the real world, so the study lacks ecological validity.

Bahrick et al (1975) carried out an experiment into the duration of memory too. They looked at very long-term memories. They asked almost 400 people to list the names of their old classmates. They were also given a photo-recognition test, where they had to recall the names of people in photos. Lastly, they were given names and asked to match them to a photo. It was found that 15 years after leaving school, recognition of names and faces was at about 90%. They were about 60% accurate at recalling a list of names. However, after 30 years, free recall was down to 30%, and after 48 years, name recognition was at 80% and photo recognition was at about 40%.

The researchers used this as evidence of very long-term memories. Recognition was better than recall, so the information might all be there but might just need cues to get at it.

This was a field experiment so it had high ecological validity. However, it was hard to control the variables, reducing the reliability of the results. The type of memories that the study tested could be rehearsed if you're still in touch with classmates, so the results can't be generalised to other types of information.

Summary Questions

Q1 Why are most memory studies on short-term and long-term memory, rather than sensory memory?

Q2 What is Miller's 'magic number'?

Q3 Give three different ways that information can be encoded.

Q4 Summarise the differences between encoding in STM and LTM.

Q5 Name one psychologist who studied the encoding of memories.

3. Models of Memory

Several people have had a bash at suggesting models of memory.
These include the multi-store model and the working memory model.

Atkinson and Shiffrin's (1968) multi-store model

The multi-store model proposes that memory consists of three stores — a sensory store, a short-term store and a long-term store. Information from our environment (e.g. visual or auditory) initially goes into sensory memory. You don't really notice much of this stuff. However, if you pay attention to it, or think about it, the information will be encoded and will pass into short-term memory.

Short-term memory has a finite capacity and duration. But if information is processed further (rehearsed) then it can be transferred to long-term memory. In theory, the information can then remain there forever. (Unless you really really need to remember it, in which case it'll probably stay there until something more interesting comes along, like a bee or a cloud.)

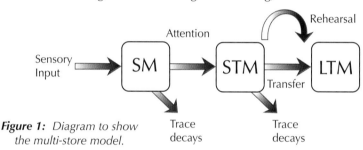

Figure 1: *Diagram to show the multi-store model.*

Support for the multi-store model

Several studies have been carried out that show that memory is made up of separate stores.

- **The Primacy Effect** — Research shows that participants are able to recall the first few items of a list better than those from the middle. The multi-store model explains this because earlier items will have been rehearsed better and transferred to LTM. If rehearsal is prevented by an interference task, the effect disappears, as the model predicts.

- **The Recency Effect** — Participants also tend to remember the last few items better than those from the middle of the list. Earlier items are rehearsed, so transfer to LTM, whilst later items are recalled because they're still in STM.

> **Example**
>
> | spoon | duck | house | fishing | night | trousers | excellent | mouse | cube |
>
> Primacy effect — these will have been rehearsed more and transferred to LTM.
>
> Recency effect — these will still be in STM.

- People with **Korsakoff's Syndrome** (amnesia that's mostly caused by chronic alcoholism) provide support for the model. They can recall the last items in a list (they show the recency effect), suggesting an unaffected STM. However, their LTM is very poor. This supports the model by showing that STM and LTM are separate stores.

Limitations of the model

Although there's lots of support for the model, there's plenty of criticism too. In the model, information is transferred from the STM to LTM through rehearsal. But in real life people don't always spend time rehearsing, yet they still transfer information into LTM. Rehearsal is not always needed for information to be stored and some items can't be rehearsed, e.g. smells.

The model is oversimplified. It assumes there is only one long-term store and one short-term store. This has been disproved by evidence from brain damaged patients, suggesting several different short-term stores, and other evidence suggesting different long-term stores.

Exam Tip
If you're asked to evaluate a model or theory in the exam, then don't forget that you need to talk about the weaknesses as well as the strengths.

Baddeley and Hitch's (1974) working memory model

Baddeley and Hitch developed a multi-store model of STM called the 'working memory model'. Their model proposed that STM is made up of several different stores.

Figure 2: Diagram to show the working memory model.

The **central executive** is in charge of attention. It has a limited capacity and controls two 'slave' systems that also have limited capacity:

- The articulatory-phonological loop holds speech-based information. It contains a phonological store (the inner ear) and an articulatory process (the inner voice).

- The visuo-spatial sketchpad deals with the temporary storage of visual and spatial information.

Baddeley and Hitch based their model on results from studies that used 'interference tasks'. If participants are asked to perform two tasks simultaneously that use the same system, their performance will be affected — e.g. saying 'the the the' while silently reading something is very difficult. According to the working memory model, both these tasks use the articulatory-phonological loop. This has limited capacity so it can't cope with both tasks. Performance on one, or both tasks, will be affected. However, if the two tasks involve different systems, performance isn't affected on either task (e.g. saying 'the the the' whilst tracking a moving object).

Tip: Using an interference task can also be known as a 'dual task method'.

Key study of STM using an interference task — Baddeley and Hitch (1974)

When developing their model, Baddeley and Hitch carried out a study which used an interference task. The participants had to carry out a reasoning task at the same time as saying aloud a list of six digits. If STM can only hold a certain amount of information (e.g. Miller's magic number — 7 plus or minus 2) then participants would perform badly on the reasoning task because their STM would already be at full capacity remembering the digits.

However, Baddeley and Hitch found that participants didn't make very many errors on either task. The only difference was that the reasoning task was done more slowly that when done on its own.

From this, Baddeley and Hitch were able to say that STM must be made up of more than one system and isn't just used for simple storage. The different systems can carry out different tasks at the same time — the reasoning task used the central executive and the digit task used the phonological loop.

Strengths and weaknesses of the model

Shallice and Warrington (1974) found support for the working memory model through their case study of KF. KF was a brain damaged patient who had an impaired STM. His problem was with immediate recall of words presented verbally, but not with visual information. This suggested he had an impaired articulatory loop, therefore providing evidence for the working memory model's view of STM.

However, many psychologists have criticised this model — they think that Baddeley and Hitch's idea of a central executive is simplistic and vague. Their model doesn't really explain exactly what the central executive is, apart from being involved in attention.

Worked Exam-style Questions

1   Outline and evaluate the working memory model.   *(12 marks)*

Baddeley and Hitch developed the working memory model. Their idea was that short-term memory is made up of three different stores called the central executive, the articulatory-phonological loop and the visuo-spatial sketchpad. The central executive is the key part. It is in charge of attention and it has a limited capacity. It controls the articulatory-phonological loop and the visuo-spatial sketchpad. The articulatory-phonological loop holds speech information. The visuo-spatial sketchpad holds visual and spatial information.

Baddeley and Hitch provided support for their model using studies. These studies all used interference tasks. They found that if two tasks were being performed at the same time that required the same system, then performance was affected. For example, silent reading and saying "the the the" both use the articulatory-phonological loop, so performance will be affected. Doing two tasks that involved different systems didn't affect performance. Therefore, a strength of the model is that it can explain parallel processing.

Shallice and Warrington also found support for the working memory model in a case study. They looked at a brain damaged patient who had problems with short-term memory. He was unable to recall words that were presented to him verbally, but he could recall visual information. This suggests that he had an impaired articulatory-phonological loop, but that this visuo-spatial sketchpad was unimpaired. This again shows that the model can explain parallel processing of different types of information.

However, there has been criticism of the working memory model. ■ *Many psychologists think that the idea of a central executive is too simplistic, and that their model doesn't properly explain what the central executive actually is and does.*

2   (a) Outline the multi-store model of memory.   *(4 marks)*

2   (b) Evaluate the multi-store model of memory.   *(8 marks)*

(a)   Atkinson and Shiffrin developed the multi-store model. The model suggests that memory is made up of three stores — the sensory store, a short-term store and a long-term store. The sensory store is where information from the environment initially goes. Not much of this information is noticed, but if attention is paid to it, the information gets encoded and passes into short-term memory. If this information is rehearsed and processed even further, it will then be transferred to long-term memory.

(b)   There are many studies that have provided support for the multi-store model of memory. For example, research into the primacy effect (which means that people are able to recall the first few items of a list better than items from the middle) can be explained by the model. The earlier items will have been rehearsed better and transferred to long-term memory. However, if rehearsal is prevented using an interference task, then the primacy effect disappears, which is also predicted by the model.

The recency effect also supports the model. This effect is where people tend to recall the last few items from a list better than those in the middle. The multi-store model would suggest that these items are recalled easily because they're still in short-term memory.

People with Korsakoff's syndrome also provide support for the model. They can recall the last items in a list, suggesting that their short-term memory is unaffected. However, their long-term memory is very poor. This provides evidence that supports the model — long-term memory and short-term memory are shown to be separate stores.

However, the model has limitations. The model proposes that information is transferred from short-term memory to long-term memory through rehearsal. However, in real life, people don't always spend time rehearsing the information that they take in, yet some of it is stored in long-term memory. The model doesn't account for this. Also, it has been suggested that the model is oversimplified. It assumes that there is only one long-term memory store, and one short-term store. However, evidence from brain damaged patients has shown that this is not true. Evidence has suggested that there are several different short-term stores as well as different long-term stores.

■ *Overall then, much research has supported the model, but other research cannot be explained using the model. This suggests that the model is not completely correct.*

Summary Questions

Q1 Who came up with the multi-store model of memory?

Q2 What are the three stores in the multi-store model of memory?

Q3 a) What is the primacy effect?

     b) Why does it happen?

Q4 How does Korsakoff's syndrome support the multi-store model?

Q5 Who came up with the working memory model?

Q6 What are the three components of the working memory model?

4. Eyewitness Testimony

There's been a lot of research into eyewitness testimony. The results have even influenced techniques used in police questioning.

Eyewitness testimony

Eyewitness testimony (EWT) is the evidence provided by people who witnessed a particular event or crime. It relies on recall from memory. EWT includes, for example, descriptions of criminals (e.g. hair colour, height) and crime scenes (e.g. time, date, location).

Witnesses are often inaccurate in their recollection of events and the people involved. As you can probably imagine, this has important implications when it comes to police interviews. Many cognitive psychologists focus on working out what factors affect the accuracy of eyewitness testimony, and how accuracy can be improved in interviews.

Factors that affect the accuracy of eyewitness testimony

There are many factors that can affect the accuracy of eyewitness testimony:

Misleading information

Loftus and Palmer (1974) investigated how EWT can be distorted. They used **leading questions**, where a certain answer is subtly implied in the question.

> **Example**
>
> An example of a misleading question is:
> "What colour was the woman's coat?"
>
> This implies that the woman was definitely wearing a coat.
> It would be better to ask: "Was the woman wearing a coat?"

Figure 1: *The accuracy of eyewitness testimony has a big impact in the courtroom.*

Key study of misleading information — Loftus and Palmer (1974)

Loftus and Palmer carried out two experiments in their study.

Experiment 1:

Method:	Participants were shown a film of a multiple car crash. They were then asked a series of questions including 'About how fast were the cars going when they hit each other?' In different conditions, the word 'hit' was replaced with 'smashed', 'collided', 'bumped' or 'contacted'.
Results:	It was seen that participants given the word 'smashed' estimated the highest speed (an average of 41 mph), and those given the word 'contacted' gave the lowest estimate (an average of 32 mph).

Experiment 2:

Method:	The participants were split into three groups. One group was given the verb 'smashed', another 'hit', and the third, control group wasn't given any indication of the vehicles' speed. A week later, the participants were asked

Figure 2: *The effect of leading questions was highlighted by Loftus and Palmer's (1974) study.*

'Did you see any broken glass?'

Results: Although there was no broken glass in the film, participants were more likely to say that they'd seen broken glass in the 'smashed' condition than any other.

Conclusion: Leading questions can affect the accuracy of people's memories of an event.

Evaluation: This has implications for questions in police interviews. However, this was an artificial experiment — watching a video is not as emotionally arousing as a real-life event, which potentially affects recall. In fact, a later study found that participants who thought they'd witnessed a real robbery gave a more accurate description of the robber. The experimental design might lead to demand characteristics (see page 79), where the results are skewed because of the participants' expectations about the purposes of the experiment. For example, the leading questions might have given participants clues about the nature of the experiment (e.g. they could have realised that the experiment was about susceptibility to leading questions), and so participants might have acted accordingly. This would have reduced the validity and reliability of the experiment.

Tip: Validity and reliability are key words when it comes to evaluating a study — see page 71.

Additional study of misleading information — Loftus and Zanni (1975)

Loftus and Zanni (1975) showed participants a film of a car accident, then asked them either 'Did you see **the** broken headlight?' or 'Did you see **a** broken headlight?' There was no broken headlight, but 7% of those asked about 'a' broken headlight claimed they saw one, compared to 17% in the group asked about 'the' broken headlight. So, the simple use of the word 'the' is enough to affect the accuracy of people's memories of an event.

Real World Connection
The discovery of these factors has made people aware that heavily relying on eyewitness testimony is not always totally safe. Innocent people have been incorrectly convicted of crimes due to errors in eyewitness testimony.

Age
Studies have shown that the age of the witness can have an effect on the accuracy of eyewitness testimony.

Key study of the effect of age on EWT — Valentine and Coxon (1997)

Method: Three groups of participants (children, young adults and elderly people) watched a video of a kidnapping. They were then asked a series of leading and non-leading questions about what they had seen.

Results: Both the elderly people and the children gave more incorrect answers to non-leading questions. Children were misled more by leading questions than adults or the elderly.

Conclusion: Age has an effect on the accuracy of eyewitness testimony.

Evaluation: This has implications in law when children or elderly people are questioned. However, the experiment was artificial and so wasn't as emotionally arousing as the same situation would have been in real life — the study lacks external validity. The study could be considered more like an experiment into how well people remember things from watching them on TV, which isn't the same as real life.

Tip: External validity means that the results of the study can be generalised to different people or places — see page 71.

Anxiety

Psychologists tend to believe that small increases in anxiety and arousal may increase the accuracy of memory, but high levels have a negative effect on accuracy. In violent crimes (where anxiety and arousal are likely to be high), the witness may focus on central details (e.g. a weapon) and neglect other peripheral details.

Figure 3: High anxiety and arousal levels may cause victims to focus on central details and neglect peripheral details.

Key study of anxiety in EWT — Loftus (1979)

Method: In a study with an independent groups design (see page 69), participants heard a discussion in a nearby room. In one condition, a man came out of the room with a pen and grease on his hands. In the second condition, the man came out carrying a knife covered in blood. Participants were asked to identify the man from 50 photographs.

Results: Participants in condition 1 were 49% accurate. Only 33% of the participants in condition 2 were correct.

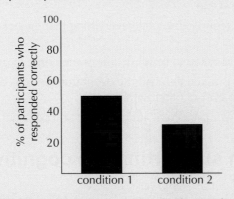

Figure 4: Graph to show the results of Loftus' study.

Conclusion: When anxious and aroused, witnesses focus on a weapon at the expense of other details.

Evaluation: The study has high ecological validity, as the participants weren't aware that the study was staged. However, this means that there are also ethical considerations, as participants could have been very distressed at the sight of the man with the knife.

Tip: In these sorts of studies, the participants can't give informed consent beforehand (see page 81). So, they have to be debriefed afterwards — this is where they're told about the aims of the experiment.

Additional studies of anxiety in EWT

Not all studies have found that anxiety reduces accuracy of EWT. Some psychologists have looked at evidence in real-life settings. For example, Yuille and Cutshall (1986) carried out interviews with 13 people who had witnessed a shooting. The people that were nearest to the incident were

Figure 5: *Diagram to show the factors that can affect eyewitness testimony.*

able to give the most detail, and those who had been more distressed by the event had more accurate recall five months later. Also, misleading questions (see page 76) had no effect on accuracy.

A natural experiment was carried out by Christianson and Hubinette (1993). They interviewed 110 people who had previously witnessed bank robberies. Some of the participants had just been witnesses, but others had actually been threatened by the robbers. The researchers found that the people who'd been threatened actually had the most accurate and detailed recall of events. These results make the results of the artificial lab studies seem less reliable.

The cognitive interview

Cognitive psychologists have played a big part in helping to increase the accuracy of eyewitness testimony. As you've seen, research shows that the accuracy of eyewitness testimony is affected by many factors. The cognitive interview technique was developed by Geiselman et al (1984) to try to increase the accuracy of witnesses' recall of events during police questioning.

Here's basically what happens in cognitive interviews:

- The interviewer tries to make the witness relaxed and tailors his/her language to suit the witness.
- The witness recreates the environmental and internal (e.g. mood) context of the crime scene.
- The witness reports absolutely everything that they can remember about the crime.
- The witness is asked to recall details of the crime in different orders.
- The witness is asked to recall the event from various different perspectives, e.g. from the eyes of other witnesses.
- The interviewer avoids any judgemental and personal comments.

Research supporting the cognitive interview

Research has shown that people interviewed with the cognitive interview technique are much more accurate in their recall of events. For example:

Key study of the cognitive interview — Geiselman et al (1986)
Method: In a staged situation, an intruder carrying a blue rucksack entered a classroom and stole a slide projector. Two days later, participants were questioned about the event. The study used an independent groups design — participants were either questioned using a standard interview procedure or the cognitive interview technique. Early in the questioning, participants were asked 'Was the guy with the green backpack nervous?'. Later in the interview, participants were asked what colour the man's rucksack was.

Results: Participants in the cognitive interview condition were less likely to recall the rucksack as being green than those in the standard interview condition.

Conclusion: The cognitive interview technique enhances memory recall and reduces the effect of leading questions.

Evaluation: The experiment was conducted as though a real crime had taken place in the classroom — it had high ecological validity. The experiment used an independent groups design. The disadvantage of this is that the participants in the cognitive interview condition could have been naturally less susceptible to leading questions than the other group.

Additional studies of the cognitive interview

A study by Fisher et al (1990) provided some support for the usefulness of the cognitive interview. The researchers trained American detectives to use the cognitive interview technique. The detectives then used the technique to interview witnesses to crimes. They found that using the cognitive interview increased the amount of information that the witnesses reported.

On the other hand, some studies have found problems with the cognitive interview technique. A study by Koehnken et al (1999) compared witnesses questioned with the cognitive interview technique with witnesses questioned using a standard technique. They found that those questioned with the cognitive interview technique recalled more incorrect details than with the standard technique. However, this could be due to the cognitive interview causing witnesses to recall more information in the first place than the standard procedure, therefore there is more opportunity to make mistakes.

Worked Exam-style Question

1 (a) Shona was a witness to a robbery. She reported feeling very anxious. Explain why the accuracy of her eyewitness testimony might have been affected. Use psychological research in your answer. *(6 marks)*

1 (b) Give two other factors that can affect the accuracy of eyewitness testimony. *(2 marks)*

(a) Psychologists have found that small amounts of anxiety may increase the accuracy of memory, but that high levels can have a negative effect on accuracy. As Shona was anxious during the robbery, she may have focused on central details (e.g. a weapon being used) and may be unable to recall peripheral details (e.g. the robber's appearance).

Loftus carried out a study which provides support for this idea. The study had an independent groups design. Participants heard a discussion in a nearby room. In one condition, a man came out of the room with a pen and grease on his hands. In the second condition, the man came out carrying a knife covered in blood. Participants were then asked to identify the man from 50 photographs.

Tip: When an exam question refers to a scenario it's a good idea to make reference to it in your answer — it shows that you have a good understanding of the situation, and that you can apply your psychological knowledge appropriately.

Exam Tip
You won't get all 6 marks unless you've supported your answer using a piece of research. Make sure you do everything that the question asks.

Loftus found that almost half of the participants in the first condition recalled the man accurately. However, in the second condition, only a third of the participants recalled the man correctly. Loftus concluded that when people are anxious, they focus on a weapon at the expense of other details.

(b) The age of the witness and misleading information can also affect the accuracy of eyewitness testimony.

Summary Questions

Q1 Say whether the questions below are leading or not. For the questions that are leading, write a new non-leading version.

a) Did you see the two children?

b) How many bikes did you see?

c) Was there anybody in the restaurant?

Q2 a) How did Loftus and Zanni (1975) investigate leading questions?

b) What did they find?

Q3 Who were the participants in Valentine and Coxon's (1997) study?

Q4 What effect does the age of a witness have on the accuracy of recall?

Q5 Who developed the cognitive interview technique?

Q6 Outline what happens in a cognitive interview.

Q7 a) Describe the methodology used in the study by Geiselman et al (1986).

b) What were the results of this study?

c) Give one disadvantage of this study.

5. Strategies for Memory Improvement

There are some little tricks for improving memory — could be useful for those exams of yours...

Mnemonics

We often avoid having to remember things by making notes and lists. However, sometimes this isn't possible — say, when you're learning stuff for an exam. This is where mnemonics come in useful. These are internal memory strategies and they use things like visual imagery and associations to cue your recall.

Tip: Recall is where you list everything that you can remember.

Examples of mnemonics

Here are just a few...

Organising material

Research has shown that when we're learning something, we often automatically organise the material in a way that makes it easier to remember. For example, Jenkins and Russell (1952) studied the recall of word lists. The word lists contained words that were highly associated (e.g. knife and fork). They found that participants tended to group the associated words together in recall even though they'd been separated in the original presentation. So, if 'knife' and 'fork' had been separated by other words in the original list, they'd be recalled together.

> **Example**
>
> A list of words might be:
>
> shoes
> day
> king
> night
> socks
> queen
>
> It's likely that they'd be recalled as:
>
> king
> queen
> shoes   associated
> socks   words
> day
> night

Tulving (1962) repeatedly gave his participants a list of words to learn. He found that the order of the participants' recall became increasingly consistent — they were organising and chunking the material to be learnt into easily remembered groups. E.g. if the word list contained cat, daisy, sock, giraffe, shoe, scarf, dog and rose, it's likely that no matter what order they were presented in, the words would be grouped together into categories for recall — animals, clothes and flowers.

Tip: This is like Miller's idea of chunking — grouping pieces of information together into meaningful units in order to make them easier to remember (see page 15).

> **Example**
>
> A list of words might be:
>
> blue
> tennis
> red
> squash
> snooker
> purple
>
> It's likely that they'd be recalled as:
>
> blue
> red   colours
> purple
> tennis
> squash   sports
> snooker

The method of loci

The method of loci is a strategy that uses imagery. It's useful for remembering a list of words or objects. The items to be remembered are associated with locations (loci) in a well-known place, e.g. your house:

> **Example**
>
> Say the shopping list contains milk, chocolate, apples, bananas and bread.
>
> - You'd take a mental tour around your house, visually placing each object at a specific place.
> - You could place the bottle of milk at your front door, put the chocolate on a table in the hall, put the apples on the sofa in the living room, put the bananas in the kitchen sink and, finally, put the bread on the stairs.
> - When you get to the shop, all you'd need to do is mentally repeat the tour around your house, remembering which items were placed where.

Figure 1: *These memory strategies can be useful for things like remembering shopping lists.*

The peg-word technique

This is another technique that uses imagery to remember a set of objects or words.

> **Example**
>
> Take the shopping list again — milk, chocolate, apples, bananas and bread.
>
> 1. First of all, you use a set of peg-words which are already stored in memory.
> 2. So, for this list of five objects, you'd need five peg-words:
>
>   One is a bun   Two is a shoe   Three is a tree
>   Four is a door   Five is a hive
>
> 3. Then, each item on the shopping list is linked to a number. So, you could imagine a bar of chocolate inside a bun, bananas poking out of a shoe, apples hanging on a tree, and so on...
> 4. In the supermarket, you'd just need to remember each peg-word and picture the item associated with it.

Tip: The peg-words rhyme with the numbers — this helps you to remember them.

The first letter mnemonic

The first letter mnemonic helps with learning something's order. The trick here is to use the first letter of each word to create a new sentence.

> **Example**
>
> Say you're trying to learn the order of the planets:
>
> **M**ercury, **V**enus, **E**arth, **M**ars, **J**upiter, **S**aturn, **U**ranus, **N**eptune
>
> You could turn this into...
>
> **M**y **V**olkswagen **E**ats **M**ouldy **J**am **S**andwiches **U**ntil **N**oon

Exam Tip
An exam question might ask you to describe how someone could apply these strategies to something that they need to memorise. So, you need to know how they work.

Mnemonic verses

Mnemonic verses are little poems that help you remember facts. Mnemonic verses help you remember information by encoding it acoustically (by sound, see page 16). There are loads of really famous ones...

> **Examples**
>
> ...like the one to help you remember what happened to Henry VIII's six wives...
>
> Divorced, beheaded, died,
> Divorced, beheaded, survived.

...and the one to help you remember how many days are in each month...

> Thirty days has September,
> April, June, and November,
> All the rest have thirty-one,
> Except February alone,
> Which has twenty-eight days clear,
> And twenty-nine each leap year.

Narrative stories

This method involves linking together all the items into a story.

Tip: You might even find some of these strategies useful in your revision...

Example

So, say the list of words to be learnt is bicycle, duck, ice cream, tree and house — you could turn this into...

Bob got onto his bicycle and rode down to the duck pond at the park. He bought an ice cream and sat under a tree to eat it. After a while, he cycled back to his house. That's Bob for you — he lives on the edge. He's a crazy guy.

Key study of narrative stories — Bower and Clark (1969)

Method:	The study used an independent groups design — participants were split into two conditions. Each group was given 12 lists, each containing 10 words. In one condition, the participants were advised to come up with stories to link the 10 words together. The second group of participants was a control group — they were simply asked to learn the word lists.
Results:	Both groups recalled the lists equally well immediately after learning each one. However, when it came to recalling all 12 lists at the end of the session, recall was much better in the group that had created stories.
Conclusion:	Creating narrative stories aids recall from LTM.
Evaluation:	This links to the multi-store model — the words are moving into long-term memory because they are being rehearsed during the creation of stories. The study used a control condition, which meant that the effect of the independent variable (the stories) could be measured. However, it lacks ecological validity — learning word lists isn't something that you'd normally do in real life.

Limitations of mnemonic strategies

The above strategies work best when you're learning a list, or trying to learn the order of something. This isn't much use if it's equally important to understand something whilst you're learning it. You've still got to be able to remember the mnemonic — e.g. the peg-words. If you forget those, you've got no link to the stuff you were trying to remember.

Tip: Don't forget, there are always limitations to think about.

Worked Exam-style Question

1 (a)   Helen is going shopping, and needs to remember a list of ten items. Describe two mnemonic strategies that she could use to help her remember what she needs to buy. *(6 marks)*

1 (b)   Outline **one** problem that Helen might have when using the mnemonic strategies you suggested.   *(2 marks)*

(a) Helen could use the peg-word technique or the method of loci. The peg-word technique uses imagery to remember a set of objects. Helen would need to start with a set of ten peg-words already stored in memory. For example, 'one is a bun', 'two is a shoe', 'three is a tree', 'four is a door', and so on. Then she would need to link each item on the shopping list to a number, e.g. by imagining the first item inside a bun, the second item inside a shoe, and so on. At the shop, she would then just need to remember each peg-word, and then picture the item associated with it.

Exam Tip
Don't forget that you've been asked to write about two strategies. The question is worth 6 marks overall, so each strategy could get you up to 3 marks. So, don't spend ages writing loads about each one, and don't write loads about one and forget to cover the second.

The method of loci is also useful for remembering items in a list. Helen would need to associate the items on her shopping list with locations in a well-known place (e.g. her house). She would take a mental tour around her house, placing each object in a specific place. Then at the shop, she would just need to mentally repeat the tour around her house, remembering which items were placed where.

(b) Helen still needs to remember the mnemonic, for example, the peg-words or the locations in the method of loci. If she forgets these, then she has no link to the items she was trying to remember. So, the strategies still require the use of memory.

Summary Questions

Q1   What did Jenkins and Russell find about the recall of word lists?

Q2   What is the first letter mnemonic?

Q3   Give an example of a mnemonic verse.

Q4   a)   What did Bower and Clark (1969) find out about narrative stories?

       b)   How does this link to the multi-store model?

Section Summary

- The cognitive approach is all about how we think — it looks at things like perception, language, attention and memory.

- Cognitive psychologists use laboratory, field and natural experiments, brain imaging, case studies and animal research.

- The main types of memory are short-term and long-term — they're different in terms of capacity, duration and encoding.

- Atkinson and Shiffrin came up with the multi-store model of memory. It proposed that memory consists of a sensory store, a short-term store and a long-term store.

- Baddeley and Hitch proposed the working memory model. They thought memory is made up of the central executive, the articulatory-phonological loop and the visuo-spatial sketchpad.

- Both models have strengths and weaknesses.

- The accuracy of eyewitness testimony can be affected by misleading information, age and anxiety.

- The development of the cognitive interview has helped to increase the accuracy of witness recall during police questioning.

- There are lots of mnemonics that can be used to improve memory — for example, organising material into groups, the method of loci, the peg-word technique, the first letter mnemonic, mnemonic verses and narrative stories.

Exam-style Questions

1   Outline and evaluate **one** research method used in the cognitive approach.

(4 marks)

2   Describe how short-term memory and long-term memory differ in terms of duration and capacity.

(4 marks)

3 (a)   What is meant by encoding?

(2 marks)

3 (b)   Outline and evaluate research into the encoding of memory.

(8 marks)

4   Using the working memory model, explain why performance might be affected if two speech-based tasks are carried out simultaneously.

(4 marks)

5 (a)   David was being interviewed by the police after witnessing a car crash.
The police officer asks him, "Did you see the man pull out of the junction?"
Suggest how this question might have a negative effect on the accuracy
of David's eyewitness testimony.

(4 marks)

5 (b)   Suggest how this question could be phrased differently to avoid this problem.

(1 mark)

5 (c)   Describe how the use of the cognitive interview could help David to give
a more accurate witness statement.

(6 marks)

6   Two people were witnesses to a crime.
One was a boy aged eight.
The other was a woman aged thirty.
Discuss how their age might affect the accuracy of their eyewitness testimonies.

(8 marks)

7   Outline and evaluate two strategies that could be used to improve the recall of a list
of words.

(8 marks)

Learning Objective:

- Know about and understand the research methods used in developmental psychology.

Tip: You came across the term 'ecological validity' in Unit 1: Section 1 (see page 10). It's just a measure of how much the results of an experiment reflect what would happen in a natural setting.

Tip: Some of the advantages of naturalistic observations are disadvantages of controlled observations and vice versa. For example, naturalistic observation has high ecological validity, whereas it's very low in controlled observation.

Figure 1: Children are often given specific toys to play with in controlled observations.

1. The Developmental Approach

Getting your head around cognitive psychology is one thing — but you've got to know all about the developmental approach too.

Main research methods

(There's more general stuff on research methods on pages 61-64, for those of you who can't get enough of 'em...)

Observational studies

Observational studies can be naturalistic or controlled.

Naturalistic observation takes place in the child's own environment and none of the variables are manipulated — e.g. a parent might note down their child's behaviour in a diary.

<u>Advantage</u>

- Ecological validity — behaviour will be natural because the subject is in a real-life, familiar setting.

<u>Disadvantage</u>

- Extraneous variables — there's no control over the variables, so you can't be sure what caused your results.

With **controlled observation** the child is observed by a researcher, usually in a laboratory setting. Some of the variables are controlled — e.g. a child might be given a certain toy to play with and observed through a one-way mirror.

<u>Advantage</u>

- Control — the effect of extraneous variables is minimised, so you're more likely to be able to establish cause and effect.

<u>Disadvantage</u>

- Observer bias — the observer's expectations may affect what they focus on and record, so the reliability of the results might be a problem. Another observer might have come up with very different results.

Correlational studies

Correlational studies look for relationships between variables. Variables often rise and fall together.

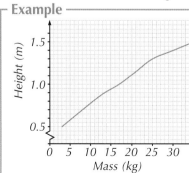

Figure 2: This graph shows a correlation between mass and height in children.

But this doesn't mean that one variable causes the other to change — that's pretty important to remember.

> **Example**
>
> There's a correlation between height and vocabulary, but neither of them causes the other one to change. Instead, they're linked by a third variable — age (the older you get, the taller you get and also the more you learn which extends your vocabulary).

Tip: Correlation and cause are different things. Even if two variables show a strong correlation, you can't assume that one of them is actually influencing the other one.

The data for correlational studies often comes from surveys, questionnaires and interviews.

<u>Advantage</u>

- Ethical — you can study variables that would be unethical to manipulate, e.g. whether there's a relationship between smoking during pregnancy and low birthweight.

<u>Disadvantage</u>

- Causal relationships — these can't be assumed from a correlation. Results may be caused by a third, unknown variable.

Case studies

Case studies are detailed descriptions of one person. They allow researchers to analyse unusual cases in lots of detail — e.g. the study of Genie (page 51).

<u>Advantage</u>

- Rich data — researchers have the opportunity to study rare phenomena in a lot of detail.

<u>Disadvantage</u>

- Generalisation — only using a single case makes generalising the results extremely difficult.

Interviews

Clinical interviews are used loads in developmental psychology. They're semi-structured, meaning that the researcher asks some specific questions, but also lets the participant ramble on about stuff. Participants could be children, or their carers, teachers or parents. Face-to-face interviews can include **open-ended** (non-specific) or **fixed** (specific) questions.

Figure 3: Clinical interviews with parents, teachers and other carers can tell researchers a lot about child development.

> **Examples**
>
> Fixed questions:
> "Do you get on well with your mother?"
> "Does that make you feel anxious?"
>
> Open-ended questions:
> "Describe the relationship that you have with your mother."
> "How does that make you feel?"

<u>Advantage</u>

- Rich data — especially from open-ended questions.

<u>Disadvantage</u>

- Participants — children can have implicit knowledge but be unable to verbalise it, so their skills can be underestimated.

Tip: Fixed questions are also known as **closed** questions.

Longitudinal and cross-sectional experimental design

Two main kinds of experimental design are used to work out how behaviour changes with age — longitudinal and cross-sectional. These are used alongside the research method.

Longitudinal design

A longitudinal design tests the same people repeatedly as they get older and wrinklier. This means you can plot the group average as a function of age. It also allows you to look at the development of individuals within the group. Researchers can then look at whether the data shows a gradual change, or a more sudden shift that suggests stage-like development. Longitudinal designs can be retrospective. This involves looking back over a period of time — e.g. looking at a child's medical history.

Tip: It's easy to remember the differences between cross-sectional and longitudinal studies — _long_itudinal studies are the ones that take a _long_ time.

Advantage

- You get detailed data about the same people, and individual differences are taken into account.

Disadvantage

- Studying the development of the same people can take years, so it's time-consuming and costly.

> **Example**
>
> If you wanted to look at how vocabulary increases with age, you could measure the vocabulary of particular children repeatedly, over a period of several years.

Cross-sectional design

A cross-sectional design tests different people of different ages.

Advantage

- They provide a quick estimate of developmental changes, and are much less time-consuming than a longitudinal design.

Disadvantage

- They don't take individual differences into account. Different people are measured at each age, so you can't be sure they all developed in the same way.

> **Example**
>
> To look at how vocabulary increases with age, you could measure the vocabulary of children in different year groups. Their performance is then averaged over different individuals at each age.

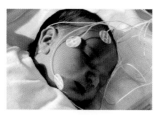

Figure 4: Researchers need to think carefully about the ethics of their work — especially when they're studying young children.

Tip: There's more about ethics in general on pages 81-83.

Ethics in psychological research
Child research

Psychologists have to be extra careful when they're conducting research with children. Under-16s might not understand the implications of participating in a study, so researchers have to get **informed consent** from their parents or guardians. It's important that researchers get the power balance right because children generally view adults as more powerful than them. Extra care has to be taken to inform children of their rights — e.g. the right to withdraw. Researchers need to make sure that a study won't cause the participants physical or psychological harm. They have to use the least stressful procedure possible, and abandon the study if the child seems distressed.

Animal studies

Animal studies have provided valuable information for developmental research. But there's debate about whether they're ethical or not.

Advantage

- Some research designs couldn't have been conducted on humans ethically — e.g. Harlow's study of attachment, where young monkeys were separated from their mothers (see pages 38-39).

Disadvantages

- Some see it as unethical to inflict suffering on animals, especially when they can't give consent.

- Animals and humans are different, so you can't generalise results from one species to the other.

Figure 5: *Using animals for scientific testing is a controversial issue.*

Worked Exam-style Question

1 Explain the advantages and disadvantages of naturalistic observation as opposed to controlled observation. *(4 marks)*

Unlike controlled observations, which often take place in a laboratory, naturalistic observations provide ecological validity. The subject is more likely to behave naturally in a familiar, real-life situation than in a novel laboratory environment.

 On the downside though, naturalistic observations offer much less control of extraneous variables, which can be considered during controlled observations. This means that researchers can't be entirely sure what causes the behaviours that they observe during naturalistic observations.

Exam Tip
There are four marks available — so if you only write about the advantages and don't mention any disadvantages, you're not going to get more than two marks.

Summary Questions

Q1 List four research methods used to study developmental psychology.

Q2 Give one advantage and one disadvantage of correlational studies.

Q3 Give an example of a fixed question.

Q4 A psychologist is looking at the effect of age on memory. He studies three groups of participants. Each group has children of a certain age. Is this a longitudinal or a cross-sectional study?

Q5 Give one advantage and one disadvantage of carrying out studies using animals.

Learning Objective:

- Know about explanations of attachment, including learning theory and Bowlby's theory.

2. Explanations of Attachment

Here are a few pages — just for you — full of everything you need to know about attachment...

What is attachment?

Attachment is a close emotional relationship between infants and their caregivers. 'Attached' infants will show a desire to be close to their primary caregiver (usually their biological mother). They'll show distress when they're separated, and pleasure when they're reunited.

Learning theory and conditioning

Learning theory links attachment to pleasure. This is also known as **behaviourist theory**, and focuses on the baby wanting its needs fulfilled. Conditioning is given as an explanation for how attachments form.

Tip: Behaviourist theory says that all our behaviour develops through learning by conditioning.

Classical conditioning

This is about learning associations between different things in our environment. Getting food naturally gives the baby pleasure. The baby's desire for food is fulfilled whenever its mother is around to feed it. So an association is formed between mother and food. So, whenever its mother is around, the baby will feel pleasure — i.e. 'attachment'.

Tip: Classical and operant conditioning are quite easy to mix up, so it's worth learning the difference between them.

Operant conditioning

Dollard and Miller (1950) claimed that babies feel discomfort when they're hungry and so have a desire to get food to remove the discomfort. They find that if they cry, their mother will come and feed them — so the discomfort is removed (this is 'negative reinforcement'). An easy life. The mother is therefore associated with food and the baby will want to be close to her. This produces 'attachment behaviour' (distress when separated from the mother, etc.).

Tip: Negative reinforcement is where the removal of something bad makes a behaviour more likely to be repeated.

Attachment and comfort

Just because babies spend most of their time either eating or sleeping, it doesn't mean they automatically attach to the person who feeds them.

Figure 1: *One of Harlow's baby monkeys reaching over from the cloth surrogate to feed from the wire surrogate.*

Key study of contact comfort — Harlow (1959)	
Method:	Harlow aimed to find out whether baby monkeys would prefer a source of food or a source of comfort and protection as an attachment figure. In laboratory experiments rhesus monkeys were raised in isolation. They had two 'surrogate' mothers. One was made of wire mesh and contained a feeding bottle, the other was made of cloth but didn't contain a feeding bottle.
Results:	The monkeys spent most of their time clinging to the cloth surrogate and only used the wire surrogate to feed. The cloth surrogate seemed to give them comfort in new situations. When the monkeys grew up they showed signs of social and emotional disturbance. The females were bad mothers who were often violent towards their offspring.
Conclusion:	Infant monkeys formed more of an attachment with a figure that provided comfort and protection. Growing up in isolation affected their development.

Evaluation: This was a laboratory experiment, so there was strict control of the variables. This means that it's unlikely the results were affected by an unknown variable. However, it can be argued that you can't generalise the results of this study to human beings, because humans and monkeys are qualitatively different.

There were also ethical problems with this study — the monkeys were put in a stressful situation, and later they showed signs of being psychologically damaged by the experiment. Monkeys are social animals, so it was unfair to keep them in isolation.

The fact that they were in isolation also means that the study lacked ecological validity — the monkeys weren't in their natural environment, so the results can't be reliably applied to real life. Laboratory experiments can usually be replicated, but ethical guidelines now in place mean that you couldn't repeat this study today to see whether you'd get the same results.

Many studies have looked at attachment in human babies as opposed to other animals. Good quality interaction with the baby seems more important than just who feeds it — the baby will attach to whoever is the most sensitive and loving. This was also seen in Schaffer and Emerson's (1964) study (see below).

Additional study of contact comfort — Schaffer and Emerson (1964)

Schaffer and Emerson (1964) studied 60 babies during the first 18 months of their lives, to see how quickly and strongly they formed attachments. They found that many babies didn't have a strong attachment to their mother, even though she fed them. Babies formed the strongest attachments to the people that played and interacted with them more. This supported the findings of Harlow's study, 'Love in Infant Monkeys'.

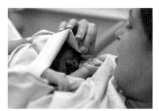

Figure 2: Infants form stronger attachments to whoever is the most sensitive and loving, rather than just whoever feeds them.

The ethological approach

Ethology is the study of animals in their natural environment. Konrad Lorenz (1935) found that geese automatically 'attach' to the first moving thing they see after hatching, and follow it everywhere (I bet this gets quite annoying). This is called **imprinting**. Normally the geese would imprint onto their mother, but Lorenz managed to get them to attach to him because he was the first thing they saw.

Imprinting seems to occur during a '**critical period**' — in this case, the first few hours after hatching. It's a fast, automatic process. It's unlikely to occur in humans. Our attachments take a longer time to develop and we don't automatically attach to particular things — quality care seems more important in human attachment formation.

Tip: Imprinting is just a particular type of attachment.

Key study of imprinting — Lorenz (1935)

Lorenz (1935) randomly divided a clutch of greylag goose eggs into two groups. He left one group with the mother and incubated the other eggs. When the eggs from the incubator hatched, the first (moving) thing they saw was Lorenz.

Figure 3: *Young birds will imprint on the first moving thing they see — in this case it was Konrad Lorenz.*

Lorenz observed that the goslings from the incubator eggs followed him around in exactly the same way that the goslings from the other eggs would follow their mother.

He put both sets of goslings together and observed that when they were released, the two groups quickly re-formed as the goslings went off in search of their respective 'mothers'. Both sets of goslings had imprinted on the first moving object that they had seen.

After further experiments, Lorenz determined that imprinting was most likely between 13 and 16 hours after hatching. He also noted that outside of a critical period (in the first 32 hours after hatching), it was too late for the young birds ever to imprint.

Bowlby's evolutionary theory of attachment

Bowlby (1951) argued that something like imprinting occurs in humans. He developed several main claims:

- We have evolved a biological need to attach to our main caregiver — usually our biological mother. Having one special attachment is called **monotropy**. Forming this attachment has survival value as staying close to the mother ensures food and protection.

- A strong attachment provides a 'safe base', giving us confidence to explore our environment.

- It also gives us a 'template' for all future relationships — we learn to trust and care for others.

- The first 3 years of life are the critical period for this attachment to develop — otherwise it might never do so.

- If the attachment doesn't develop (e.g. because of separation or death), or if it's broken, it might seriously damage the child's social and emotional development (see pages 46-49).

Comments on Bowlby's theory:

- There is some evidence for his claims. Harlow's study supports the idea that we have evolved a need to attach. It also suggests that social and emotional development might be damaged if an attachment isn't formed. See pages 46-48 for more studies that support Bowlby's theory.

- Schaffer and Emerson (1964) provided evidence against Bowlby's claims about monotropy. They found that many children form multiple attachments, and may not attach to their mother.

- Harlow's study of monkeys raised in isolation also goes against the idea of monotropy. Other monkeys who didn't have a mother, but who grew up together, didn't show signs of social and emotional disturbance in later life. They didn't have a primary caregiver, but seemed to attach to each other instead.

- There is mixed evidence for claims of a critical period for attachments to develop (pages 51-53).

- The effect of attachment not developing, or being broken, may not be as bad as Bowlby claimed (pages 48-49).

Tip: The evolutionary approach suggests that particular behaviours exist because they are needed for survival and, therefore, to ensure future reproduction.

Exam Tip
These comments on Bowlby's theory will come in handy if you're ever asked to evaluate his ideas.

Worked Exam-style Questions

1   Outline and explain how learning theory can be used to
    explain attachment.   *(6 marks)*

*Learning theory states that attachments can be explained by two types of
learning; classical conditioning and operant conditioning.*

  *Classical conditioning is learning by association. For example, when
a newborn child is fed by its primary caregiver it learns to associate
proximity to the caregiver with the positive feelings of being fed. This
association between the caregiver and food will bring about attachment
due to the feeling of pleasure caused by the caregiver's presence.*

  *With operant conditioning, a child can learn attachment behaviours,
such as crying, when it's away from its primary caregiver. For example,
initially a child may cry because it feels discomfort, e.g. hunger. Its
caregiver comes to comfort and feed it, and the child learns to associate
its own behaviour (crying) with the positive feelings of being fed and
comforted. This removal of discomfort is negative reinforcement. This
leads to an attachment forming between the child and its caregiver,
whereby being separated appears to distress the child.*

Exam Tip
The question hasn't
specified operant or
classical conditioning,
but make sure you talk
about both of them in
your answer.

Exam Tip
It's no good just writing
down everything
you know about
conditioning. You need
to keep it relevant to the
context of the question,
i.e. attachment.

2   Outline and evaluate Bowlby's theory of attachment.
                                                    (8 marks)

*Bowlby argues that attachment to one caregiver (monotropy) offers
an obvious survival advantage. This is because close proximity to the
caregiver means a child is more likely to be fed and protected from danger.
Bowlby says that attachment provides a 'template' on which to build
future relationships and a 'safe base' from which we are able to explore
our surroundings with confidence. Bowlby's theory states that there is
a critical period (between birth and age 3) for attachment to occur. If
attachments are prevented from developing, or are broken, it may cause
problems with a child's psychological development.*

  *Harlow's (1959) study found that monkeys without a caregiver
showed signs of social and emotional disturbance. This provided evidence
to support Bowlby's theory that it is evolutionarily advantageous to attach,
and that preventing attachments from forming can be psychologically
damaging. However, Harlow also found evidence that contradicted
Bowlby's idea of monotropy. He observed that monkeys raised together,
but without parents, were able to develop normally as they had seemingly
attached to each other. They had just replaced one attachment figure
with another. Schaffer and Emerson (1964) also found evidence against
monotropy as they observed children attach to numerous individuals and
not always to their mothers. They often attached to those who interacted
with them most, showing attachment is not solely for food and protection.*

Exam Tip
When the question
asks you to 'outline' the
theory, it just wants you
to describe the key ideas
of Bowlby's theory.

Exam Tip
The question asks you
to evaluate Bowlby's
theory too, so you may
want to refer to evidence
that both supports it and
contradicts it.

Summary Questions

Q1 What is attachment?

Q2 Briefly describe the method and results of Harlow's (1959) study of
    contact comfort.

Q3 Describe what is meant by imprinting.

- Know about different types of attachment: secure attachment, insecure-avoidant and insecure-resistant.
- Know about the use of the 'strange situation' in attachment research.
- Understand cultural variations in attachment.

3. Types of Attachment

There are two main types of attachment that you need to know about — secure and insecure attachments.

Secure and insecure attachments

Secure attachments

In a secure attachment, there's a strong bond between the child and its caregiver. If they're separated, the infant becomes distressed. However, when they're reunited, the child is easily comforted by the caregiver. The majority of attachments are of this type. Secure attachments are associated with a healthy cognitive, social and emotional development.

Insecure attachments

Attachments can also be insecure. Here, the bond between child and caregiver is weaker. Ainsworth et al (1978) came up with two types of insecure attachment:

Insecure-avoidant

If they're separated from their caregiver, the child doesn't become particularly distressed, and can usually be comforted by a stranger. This type of insecure attachment is shown by children who generally avoid social interaction and intimacy with others.

Insecure-resistant

The child is often uneasy around their caregiver, but becomes upset if they're separated. Comfort can't be given by strangers, and it's also often resisted from the caregiver. Children who show this style of attachment both accept and reject social interaction and intimacy.

The 'strange situation'

Ainsworth came up with the concept of the '**strange situation**'. She used it to assess how children react under conditions of stress (by separation from the caregiver and the presence of a stranger) and also to new situations.

Tip: The 'strange situation' is a classic experiment, so make sure you've got your head around the procedure involved. To help you remember the order of the scenarios you could use one of the mnemonic techniques you learnt about in Unit 1: Section 1.

Key study of attachment — the 'strange situation', Ainsworth et al (1978)

Method: In a controlled observation, 12-18 month old infants were observed whilst eight different scenarios occurred. They were as follows:

1. The mother and infant entered the experimental room.
2. The infant was allowed to explore and play with the toys, while the mother sat on a chair.
3. A stranger entered the room and talked to the mother. The stranger then tried to play with the infant.
4. The mother exited the experimental room, leaving the infant alone with the stranger. The stranger continued to play with the infant or offered it comfort.
5. The mother returned to the experimental room and comforted the infant, while the stranger left.
6. The mother exited the experimental room for a second time, leaving the infant alone.

---

7. The stranger returned to the experimental room and comforted and played with the infant.

8. The mother returned to the experimental room for a second time, greeted the infant and offered comfort. The stranger left the room

Throughout the experiment, the infant's reactions were constantly observed, to see how it reacted to its mother leaving and re-entering the experimental room, and to being left alone with the stranger.

Results: About 15% of infants were 'insecure-avoidant' (type A) — they ignored their mother and didn't mind if she left. A stranger could comfort them. About 70% were 'securely attached' (type B) — content with their mother, upset when she left, happy when she returned and avoided strangers. About 15% were 'insecure-resistant' (type C) — uneasy around their mother and upset if she left. They resisted strangers and were also hard to comfort when their mother returned.

Conclusion: Infants showing different reactions to their carers have different types of attachment.

Evaluation: The research method used allowed control of the variables, making the results reliable. However, the laboratory-type situation made the study artificial, reducing the ecological validity. The parents may have changed their behaviour, as they knew that they were being observed. This could have had an effect on the children's behaviour. Also, the new situation in the experiment may have had an effect on the children's behaviour — the study might not accurately represent their behaviour in real life. Another problem is that the mother may not have been the child's main attachment figure.

Figure 1: *Ainsworth's 'strange situation' experiments showed that about 70% of infants were 'securely attached' to their mothers.*

Tip: Ecological validity is a problem with all laboratory studies. For more on laboratory studies see page 61.

Studies in different cultures

Ainsworth et al's (1978) findings have been shown many times in the USA, but when their results were published, it wasn't known whether they could be applied to other cultures. Cross-cultural studies have since taken place:

Key cross-cultural study of attachment — Van Ijzendoorn and Kroonenberg (1988)

Method: Van Ijzendoorn and Kroonenberg carried out a meta-analysis of 32 studies of the 'strange situation' in different countries (e.g. Japan, Britain, Sweden, etc.). They were analysed to find any overall patterns.

Results: The percentages of children classified as secure or insecure were very similar across the countries tested. Secure attachments were the most common type of attachment in the countries studied. Some differences were found in the distribution of insecure attachments. In Western cultures, it was seen that the dominant type of insecure attachment was avoidant. However, in non-Western cultures, the dominant type was resistant.

Tip: No matter how strong the data from an investigation seems it's only relevant to the specific situation that was tested. Studies need to be repeated with different participants before any more general conclusions can be drawn.

Tip: A meta-analysis is a study which combines the results of several studies all addressing a related topic.

Conclusion: There are cross-cultural similarities in raising children, producing common reactions to the 'strange situation'.

Evaluation: Children are brought up in different ways in different cultures. This might result in different types of attachment in different cultures. Because of this, the 'strange situation' might not be a suitable method for studying cross-cultural attachment. Using a different type of study may have revealed different patterns or types of attachment in different cultures. Also, the study assumes that different countries are the same thing as different cultures. One problem with the research method is that meta-analyses can hide individual results that show an unusual trend.

Figure 2: *Some studies show significant differences between cultures. Takahashi (1990) found that Japanese infants were more distressed by being left alone than American infants.*

Tip: The evaluation points from Ainsworth's original study can be used for these cross-cultural studies too — they use the same method.

Additional cross-cultural study of attachment — Takahashi (1990)

Method: 60 one-year-olds from middle class, Japanese families were observed in the 'strange situation'.

Results: No infants were classed as insecure-avoidant. 32% were identified as being insecure-resistant and the remaining 68% were securely attached to their mothers. All of the Japanese infants were very distressed by being left on their own.

Conclusion: There are cross-cultural differences in raising children, producing different reactions to the 'strange situation'.

Evaluation: The study raised ethical issues, due to the infants becoming so distressed by being left on their own. As the study only focused on a sample of middle-class Japanese infants, it may not reflect attachment trends in Japanese infants as a whole.

Learning from 'strange situation' research

Numerous studies have made use of the 'strange situation' and there have been many important findings.

- Some cultural differences are found. Grossman et al (1985) claimed that more 'avoidant' infants may be found in Germany because of the value Germans put on independence — so 'avoidance' is seen as a good thing.

- The causes of different attachment types are debatable. The causes may be the sensitivity of their carers and/or their inborn temperament.

- The 'strange situation' experiment doesn't show a characteristic of the child. The experiment only shows the child's relationship with a specific person, so they might react differently with different carers, or later in life.

- Attachment type may influence later behaviours. Securely attached children may be more confident in school and form strong, trusting adult relationships. 'Avoidant' children may have behaviour problems in school and find it hard to form close, trusting adult relationships. 'Resistant' children may be insecure and attention-seeking in school and, as adults, their strong feelings of dependency may be stressful for partners.

Worked Exam-style Questions

1 Outline the procedure that you would use to carry out a 'strange situation' experiment. *(8 marks)* ■

I would begin by bringing a mother and her infant into the experimental room. Then the infant would be allowed to explore the room and play with toys, while the mother would sit on a chair. A stranger would then be introduced to the room, who would talk to the mother and try to play with the infant. The mother would then exit the experimental room, leaving the infant alone with the stranger. The stranger would continue to play with the infant or offer it comfort.

I would then re-introduce the mother to the experimental room and get her to comfort the infant, while the stranger leaves. Then the mother would exit the experimental room for a second time, leaving the infant alone. I would re-introduce the stranger to the experimental room and get them to comfort and play with the infant. Finally, the mother would return to the experimental room for a second time, and greet and comfort the infant, while the stranger leaves the room.

During this process I would observe and record the reactions of the infant, in order to see how it reacted to its mother leaving and re-entering the experimental room, and to being left alone with a stranger.

Exam Tip
There are eight steps in the 'strange situation' procedure and eight marks available, so make sure you don't miss any of them out.

---

2 Describe cultural variations in attachments. *(6 marks)*

Ainsworth et al (1978) carried out 'strange situation' research with mothers and infants in the USA. Takahashi (1990) used the same method in Japan. Takahashi's research showed a similar proportion of securely attached infants but a much higher proportion of insecure-resistant infants. The Japanese research identified no insecure-avoidant infants, whereas Ainsworth's research had found 15% of infants to be insecure-avoidant. ■ *The differences between the findings of these two researchers support the idea that there may be cultural or regional differences between the formations of attachments in infants.*

Van Ijzendoorn and Kroonenberg (1988) carried out a meta-analysis of 32 'strange situation' studies from different countries (e.g. Japan, Britain, Sweden, etc.). Although they found that there were some differences in the distribution of insecure attachments, their data showed that the ■ *percentages of children classified as secure or insecure were very similar across the countries tested. This suggests that, although there might be slight cultural differences, attachment formation is essentially very similar in different countries.*

Exam Tip
Including facts and figures from studies in your answers is good exam technique. Knowing your studies is really important.

Exam Tip
You don't have to say that a particular study either supports or contradicts an idea. The study might have findings that help both sides of the argument.

Summary Questions

Q1 What are the characteristics of:
   a) secure attachments?
   b) insecure-avoidant attachments?
   c) insecure-resistant attachments?

Q2 Why is the 'strange situation' good for studying attachment?

Learning Objective:

▪ Know about the effects of disruption and institutional care on attachment.

4. Disruption of Attachment

Attachment can be disrupted by separation or deprivation...

Separation and deprivation

Separation

Separation is where a child is away from a caregiver they're attached to (such as their mother). The term's used when it's for a relatively short time, just hours or days — not a longer or permanent separation.

Deprivation

Deprivation describes the loss of something that is wanted or needed. So, 'maternal deprivation' is the loss of the mother (or other attachment figure). A longer-term or even permanent loss is implied.

Separation

Separation can have major effects on young children. According to several studies, infants or children who have been separated from their carer may react through the following stages.

The stages are referred to as the 'PDD model' — Protest, Despair, Detachment:

Protest

During the first few hours, the child will protest a lot at being separated from its mother (or other attachment figure), by crying, panicking, calling for its mother, etc.

Despair

After a day or two, the child will start to lose interest in its surroundings, becoming more and more withdrawn, with occasional crying. They may also eat and sleep less.

Detachment

After a few days, the child will start to become more alert and interested again in its surroundings. It will cry less and may seem to have 'recovered' from its bad reaction to the separation. However, its previous attachment with its carer may now be permanently damaged — the trust and security may be lost.

Support for the PDD model

Real World Connection

Research like this has had a massive effect on how children are treated when they're in hospital. E.g. parents are now allowed to stay with their children, whereas in the 1950s, they were often restricted, sometimes only being able to visit for an hour on Saturdays and Sundays.

Figure 1: *Separation is not only a stressful experience for young children — it can be psychologically damaging too.*

Key study of the PDD model — Robertson and Robertson (1968)	
Method:	In a naturalistic observation, several children who experienced short separations from their carers were observed and filmed. For example, a boy called John aged around 18 months stayed in a residential nursery for nine days while his mother had another baby.
Results:	John showed the signs of passing through 'protest' for the first day or two. Then he showed despair — he tried to get attention from the nurses but they were busy with other children so he 'gave up' trying. Then he showed detachment — he was more active and content. However, when his mother came to collect him, he was reluctant to be affectionate.

Conclusion: The short-term separation had very bad effects on John, including possible permanent damage to his attachment with his mother.

Evaluation: John's reaction might not have been due to separation — it could have been down to his new environment or the fact that he was getting much less attention than he was used to. There will have been little control of variables, making the results less reliable, and it would be difficult to replicate each individual situation. However, as the study took place in a natural setting, the results will have ecological validity.

Comments on the PDD Model

Findings from research on separation have several implications:

- Findings suggest that separating a child from its carers should be avoided whenever possible. This has important implications for child care practice, e.g. children should be allowed to visit, or remain with, their mothers during a stay in hospital. Sounds fair enough to me.

- Studies have shown that children who receive foster care do better than those placed in an institutionalised setting. It would seem that children manage to cope with the separation as long as they still receive one-on-one emotional support, even though it's not from their primary caregiver.

- Many factors influence how a child reacts to a separation. These include age (older children will cope better), the quality of the care received during the separation, the individual temperament of the child, and how often it has experienced separations. So, separations do not necessarily produce the PDD effects. They may even be good for the child (see pages 56-58).

Figure 1: *Deprivation from a child's main carer can have damaging effects on its development.*

Longer-term maternal deprivation

Even if short-term separation may not necessarily be bad for a child, John Bowlby (1953) argued that long-term deprivation from an attachment figure could be harmful. He produced his maternal deprivation hypothesis:

- Deprivation from the main carer during the critical period (the first 3-5 years), will have harmful effects on a child's emotional, social, intellectual and even physical development. Not so good.

- Long-term effects of deprivation may include separation anxiety (the fear of another separation from the carer). This may lead to problem behaviour, e.g. being very clingy, and avoiding going to school. Future relationships may be affected by this emotional insecurity. Bowlby's research showed evidence for this.

Tip: Bowlby's theories are quite similar to Freud's ideas. They both say that childhood events are key to our development and can influence our behaviour in the future. You'll get a chance to read more about Freud on pages 186-189.

Key study of deprivation — Bowlby (1944)

Method: Case studies were completed on the backgrounds of 44 adolescents who had been referred to the clinic where Bowlby worked because they'd been stealing. There was a control group of 44 'emotionally disturbed' adolescents who didn't steal.

Results: 17 of the thieves had experienced frequent separations from their mothers before the age of two, compared with 2 in the control group. 14 of the thieves were diagnosed as 'affectionless psychopaths' (they didn't care about how their actions affected others). 12 of these 14 had experienced separation from their mothers.

Conclusion: Depriving the child of its main carer early in life can have very harmful long-term consequences.

Evaluation: The results indicate a link between deprivation and criminal behaviour. However, it can't be said that one causes the other. There may be other factors that caused the criminal behaviour. Although case studies provide a lot of detailed information, the study relied on retrospective data, which may be unreliable.

Tip: Retrospective studies involve looking back to the past to recall events and behaviour that have already happened.

Long-term effects of separation

Bowlby's study of the 44 Juvenile Thieves, and others on institutionalisation and hospitalisation, suggested that long-term effects of separation included:

- **Affectionless psychopathy** (as seen in the 44 Juvenile Thieves study).
- **Anaclitic depression** — involving appetite loss, sleeplessness and impaired social and intellectual development.
- **Deprivation dwarfism** — infants are physically underdeveloped due to emotional deprivation.

Strengths and weaknesses of Bowlby's maternal deprivation hypothesis

Strengths

Other evidence supports Bowlby's claims. Goldfarb (1943) found that orphanage children who were socially and maternally deprived were later less intellectually and socially developed.

Weaknesses

The evidence can be criticised: Bowlby linked the thieves' behaviour to maternal deprivation, but other things were not considered, e.g. whether the poverty they grew up in led them to steal. The children in Goldfarb's study may have been most harmed by the social deprivation in the orphanage rather than the maternal deprivation.

Tip: Some of Bowlby's critics argue that although developmental problems and maternal deprivation are correlated with one another, neither one causes the other. See pages 94-96 for more on correlation and cause.

Reversing the effects of deprivation

Even when deprivation has harmful effects, these may be reversed with appropriate, good quality care in some cases.

Key study of reversing the effects of deprivation — Skeels and Dye (1939)

Method: Skeels and Dye aimed to find out whether the IQ scores of children who had been socially deprived (in an orphanage) during their first two years of life could be improved by moving them to an institution that provided better stimulation. The IQs of 13 children were measured before they were transferred to a school where they got one-to-one care. Two years later, their IQs were measured again.

Results: The IQs of the children increased from an average of 64 to 92 over the 2 year period. In contrast, it was found that the IQs of a control group of 12 children who remained in the orphanage fell from 92 to 60.5 over the same period.

Conclusion: Children who have been socially deprived (in an orphanage) during their first two years of life can quickly improve their IQ scores if they are transferred to a school where they get one-to-one care. The effects of social deprivation can be reversed with appropriate, good quality care.

Evaluation: The longitudinal experimental design of this study produced detailed quantitative data. Having a control group showed that the differences in IQ over the two years were a result of the change in care, not just a result of getting older, or any other factor. However, these results only apply to children who have been socially deprived in an orphanage, and can't be generalised to all socially deprived children. Using such a small sample size means the results also can't be generalised to a wider population.

Tip: In this study, 'normal' children were classified as those who had completed mental ability tests and gained an average result.

Tip: For a reminder about longitudinal experimental design, flick back to page 36.

Additional studies of reversing the effects of deprivation

Despite Bowlby's claims that deprivation is irreversible, several studies have shown this might not be as clear cut. Rutter et al (1998) recorded what happened to a group of Romanian orphans who came over to the UK before they were 2 years old. By the time they were 4 they appeared to have no negative effects of the deprivation they had experienced.

Tizard and Hodges (1978) carried out a natural experiment with a matched pairs design. Participants were children who had been taken into care before they were 4. These were matched with a control group of children who had grown up in a stable home. Some of the children from the care group were then adopted, whilst others remained in care. The results of the study showed that those in the experimental group who had been adopted had managed to form attachments with their adopted parents, showing that the results of deprivation had been reversed.

Spitz and Wolf (1946) carried out a study of 100 children who had become depressed after being separated from their mothers during a stay in hospital. It was found that they would only make a full recovery if their stay was less than 3 months long. However, it must be noted that this study was carried out in the 1940s, when the hospital care offered to children was fairly poor in comparison to that found today.

Goldfarb (1947) studied two groups of children. One group had spent the first few months of their life in an orphanage before being fostered. The other group had spent three years in an orphanage and were then fostered. Both groups were tested frequently up to the age of 12 on various social skills such as making friends and keeping to rules, as well as IQ. Goldfarb found that the children who had spent three years at the orphanage performed poorly on IQ tests, were socially underdeveloped, and were more likely to be aggressive.

Tip: Find out more about natural experiments on page 62 and matched pairs designs on page 70.

Exam Tip
There are a lot of studies listed here. Don't worry — just learn as many as you can. It's useful to have a few examples of studies up your sleeve to support the points you make in the exams.

Tip: These studies show quite a mixed bag of results. This is often the case — some studies will support a theory whilst others will contradict it.

Exam Tip
You could also write about deprivation here instead.

1   Outline **one** way attachment might be disrupted.   *(2 marks)*

■ *Attachment can be disrupted by separation. This is where a child is away from a caregiver they're attached to (such as their mother). Separation episodes last a relatively short time, just hours or days.*

Exam Tip
Outline and evaluate questions are a good chance to show the examiner you know your facts, but also that you can use wider reading to pull in all the information about studies to support your argument.

2   Outline and evaluate research into the effects of
■   disruption on attachment.   *(12 marks)*

Bowlby suggested that disruption had long-term impacts on attachment. According to Bowlby's maternal deprivation hypothesis, deprivation from the main carer during the first 3-5 years (the critical period) of a child's development will have damaging impacts on the child. In the long term, deprivation may lead to separation anxiety, whereby the child is fearful of further separations from their main carer.

Bowlby's theory was based on his 1944 study of 44 juvenile thieves. He did case studies on the backgrounds of 44 adolescents who had been stealing, and noticed a correlation between deprivation as an infant and criminal behaviour later in life. From this, and other studies, he concluded that separation can lead to affectionless psychopathy, anaclitic depression and deprivation dwarfism.

Exam Tip
Make sure you know your studies. This question isn't tricky if you know a few, but you'd find it pretty hard if you hadn't learnt any.

Other studies have provided evidence that supports Bowlby's theory, e.g. Goldfarb (1943) showed that children suffered social and intellectual ■ *development problems when they were maternally deprived by growing up in an orphanage environment. However, other studies have shown that the effects of deprivation can be reversible, contradicting Bowlby's ideas. For example, Rutter studied a group of Romanian orphans brought to England before the age of 2 years. At 4, they showed no negative effects of their deprivation.*

Bowlby's study relied on retrospective data, which may be unreliable. Also, critics have pointed out that Bowlby linked the thieves' behaviour to maternal deprivation, without considering other factors that might have ■ *caused them to steal. This objection is also relevant for other evidence that is used to support Bowlby's theory, e.g. the social deprivation in the orphanage might have caused the developmental problems highlighted in Goldfarb's study, rather than maternal deprivation.*

Exam Tip
This question gives you quite a lot of freedom. For instance, you could have focused on research into the PDD model, or discussed research looking at reversing the effects of deprivation. Pick whichever you are most confident with — just make sure it answers the question.

Summary Questions

Q1   What is deprivation?

Q2   Name the three stages of the PDD model.

Q3   What did Robertson and Robertson (1968) conclude after studying the effect of separation on John?

Q4   Give two long-term effects of separation that were suggested by Bowlby's (1944) study of the 44 Juvenile Thieves.

Q5   What did Skeels and Dye's (1939) study suggest was needed to reverse the effects of deprivation?

5. Failure to Form Attachments — Privation

Learning Objective:
- Know about failure to form attachments (privation) and institutional care.

When children don't form attachments with their caregivers, for whatever reason, it can lead to problems with their social and emotional development.

What is privation?

Privation means never forming a bond with a caregiver. It is different to deprivation, which is the loss of an attachment figure, with whom a bond has already been formed.

Rutter (1981) claimed that the effects of maternal privation are more likely to be serious than the effects of maternal deprivation. Evidence for this comes from case studies of children who have suffered difficult conditions or cruel treatment. Some nasty stuff coming up...

Tip: It's easy to get privation confused with deprivation (see page 46) — so make sure you know the difference between them.

Case studies of privation

Key studies of privation

Curtiss (1977) — the case of Genie

This reported the case of a girl who suffered extreme cruelty from her parents, and never formed any attachments. Her father kept her strapped to a high chair with a potty in the seat for most of her childhood. She was beaten if she made any sounds, and didn't have the chance to play with toys or with other children. She was finally discovered when she was 13 years old. She was physically underdeveloped and could only speak with animal-like sounds. After a lot of help she learned some language, but her social and intellectual skills never fully developed.

Koluchova (1976) — the case of the Czech twin boys

This is the case of twin boys whose mother died soon after they were born. Their father remarried and their stepmother treated them very cruelly. They were often kept locked in a cellar, beaten, and had no toys. They were found when they were seven with rickets (a bone development disease caused by a lack of vitamin D), and very little social or intellectual development. They were later adopted and made lots of progress. By adulthood they had above average intelligence and had normal social relationships.

Skuse (1984) — the case of Louise and Mary

Louise and Mary were found by Social Services when they were aged 3½ and 2½ respectively. They had been raised in a small room, tied to a bed with dog leads. Their mother suffered from severe learning difficulties and would cover them with a blanket when they were noisy. They hadn't learnt any language and didn't play. Both girls underwent speech therapy, but Mary never developed language skills and was eventually transferred to a care centre for autistic children. Louise was able to pick up language skills and started school aged five.

© BETTMANN/CORBIS

Figure 1: *Genie suffered long-term effects of privation. Although she eventually picked up some language and social skills, they never developed fully.*

Differences between cases

Differences between the cases might explain why the Czech twins recovered better than Genie. We should consider...

- The length of privation and how old the children were when they were discovered — the Czech twins were much younger than Genie, so still had time to develop once they were in a better environment.

- Their experiences during the isolation — the twins were kept together, so they may have attached to each other.

- The quality of care they received after the isolation — the twins were adopted, but Genie was passed between psychologists and eventually put in an institution.

- Individual differences, including ability to recover.

The evidence suggests that recovery from privation is possible. However, because of the lack of information about what had happened to the children, we can't know for sure exactly what they experienced, e.g. whether they had ever had even a brief attachment. So we can't ever be sure why the twins recovered more than Genie.

Limitations of this evidence

- The children didn't just suffer maternal privation — they also had very little social and intellectual stimulation, and were generally treated horribly. So all of these factors have to be taken into account when we're looking at their development.

- There are problems with generalising the findings because they only focus on individual cases (see page 35, and also have a look at page 64 for more general stuff on case studies).

- The case studies show mixed results for how much children can recover from privation early in life. The Czech twins recovered well, but Genie didn't.

- More controlled, scientific evidence is needed, but it would be ethically wrong to actually put children in situations of privation to see what might happen. Some studies of children raised in institutions have provided evidence of the effects of privation, although we still can't be precisely sure of the reasons behind these effects.

Early institutional care

Studies of children raised in institutions (e.g. orphanages) may provide more accurate records of what the children experienced, seeing as they can be properly scientifically observed over a long period of time.

Key study of children raised in institutions — Hodges and Tizard (1989)

Method:	This was a longitudinal (long-term) study of 65 children who had been placed in a residential nursery before they were four months old. They hadn't had the opportunity to form close attachments with any of their caregivers. By the age of four, some of the children had returned to their birth mothers, some had been adopted, and some stayed in the nursery.

Tip: Case studies give us loads of really detailed information. But as the circumstances around each of them are different, such as the age of participants, their social background or even their gender, it's difficult to apply the findings to other situations. Generalisation is impossible in such unique situations.

Tip: These studies show a correlation between privation and serious developmental problems. Remember though that this alone isn't enough to prove a causal link between the two. Other factors in these children's lives might have caused their social and intellectual problems in later life.

Results: At 16 years old, the adopted group had strong family relationships, although compared to a control group of children from a 'normal' home environment, they had weaker peer relationships. Those who stayed in the nursery or who returned to their mothers showed poorer relationships with family and peers than those who were adopted.

Conclusion: Children can recover from early maternal privation if they are in a good quality, loving environment, although their social development may not be as good as children who have never suffered privation.

Evaluation: This was a natural experiment, so it had high ecological validity. However, the sample was quite small and more than 20 of the children couldn't be found at the end of the study, so it's hard to generalise the results. The results are supported by other studies (see below).

Tip: Don't forget how the scientific process works. Studies that agree with each other provide more support for ideas and theories, making them more likely to be accepted. They're also seen as being more reliable if different studies produce the same findings. Take a look back at the How Science Works section on page 6.

Additional study of children raised in institutions — Rutter et al (1998)

Rutter et al (1998) studied 111 Romanian orphans adopted by British families before they were two years old. Their development was compared to a control group of British adopted children. They were initially below normal development, but by four years of age their development had caught up. This supports Hodges and Tizard's findings that children can recover from privation if they have good quality care.

Variation in the effects of privation

Privation of attachments early in life will damage a child's development, although how much it's damaged depends on several factors, such as:

- Age
- Quality of care during and after privation
- Social experiences later in life.

Example

Studies have shown that age can affect how much a child's development is damaged by privation and institutionalisation. For example, it was found that if orphans in Romania were adopted within six months, their development would suffer less damage than those who were institutionalised for longer.

Figure 2: *Studies of privation have shown links to poor social relationships and involvement in crime.*

Long-term effects of privation

Children can recover to some extent, but some of the effects of privation might be permanent:

Reactive attachment disorder

Parker and Forrest (1993) outlined this rare but serious condition, which occurs in children who have been permanently damaged by early experiences such as privation of attachment.

Symptoms include:

- an inability to give or receive affection
- poor social relationships
- dishonesty
- involvement in crime.

Disinhibited attachment disorder

Children with disinhibited attachment disorder have no preference for an attachment figure. They have often had several broken attachments or have been cared for by a number of different caregivers, and have never bonded properly with any of them. As a result, they often lack the typical wariness that normal children display of strangers and will often approach near-strangers for affection or attention.

Symptoms include:

- attention seeking
- inappropriate familiarity with strangers.

The cycle of privation

Some studies suggest that children who experience privation go on to have difficulties caring for their own children.

┌─ **Example** ─────────────────────────────────

Quinton et al (1985) compared 50 women who had experienced institutional care as children, with 50 women who hadn't. They found that the women who had been raised in institutions were more likely to have parenting difficulties later in life.

└──

This suggests that there is a cycle of privation — children who have experienced privation later go on to become less caring parents. Therefore their children are deprived of a strong maternal attachment and may then be less caring to their children, and so on.

Tip: Both reactive attachment disorder and disinhibited attachment disorder are included in the DSM-IV (see pages 171-172 for more on the DSM-IV).

Tip: If you understand the cycle of privation, it's a lot easier to remember:

less caring parents

The Cycle of Privation

privation in children

It makes sense really, that less caring parents will raise children who are poor parents themselves.

Exam Tip
Part (b) of this question's only worth 6 marks, so you don't have to write everything you know about the study you choose. Pick out the key bits of information.

Worked Exam-style Questions

1 (a) What is meant by the term 'privation'?   *(1 mark)*

1 (b) Outline and evaluate **one** study into the effects of privation.
                                                          (6 marks)

■

(a) Privation is when a child never forms an attachment with a caregiver.

(b) Curtiss (1977) reported the case of Genie, who was abused by her parents and experienced privation, never forming any attachments. Genie had been kept strapped to a high chair with a potty for most of her childhood and beaten if she made any noise. She was forbidden to play with any toys and was kept isolated. Genie was found when she was 13 years of age. She was physically underdeveloped and only able to speak using animal-like sounds. Following extensive therapy, Genie eventually learned some language skills, but her social and intellectual development were permanently affected by her childhood experiences.

This study seems to provide evidence of the damaging effects of privation and the social and intellectual problems it can cause. However, it's not clear whether the privation that Genie experienced was the cause of her developmental problems. The abuse that she received and her deprivation of social and intellectual stimulation might also have been responsible for the problems with her development.

The findings of this study cannot be generalised as it's a very rare and unusual case.

---

2   Describe the limitations of the evidence for the effects of privation.
                                                                          (6 marks)

The evidence for the effects of privation has several limitations. Children who suffer maternal privation also tend to have poor social and intellectual stimulation. These factors, rather than maternal privation, might actually be responsible for the problems with development that are attributed to privation.

Evidence for the effects of privation also tends to be based on ■ individual cases, so might not apply to wider samples of people. Case studies can also show conflicting results, e.g. Koluchova's (1976) study of the Czech twins showed that they were able to recover almost fully from privation, whereas Genie (Curtiss (1977)) never recovered from her experiences, despite making some progress.

More scientific evidence is needed to make firmer conclusions, but more case studies of extreme neglect are the only real way to study the effects of privation, as deliberately putting children in situations of privation would be ethically and morally wrong.

Exam Tip
The question doesn't ask you to evaluate the evidence — just to explain the limitations — so there's no point writing about the strengths of these studies. It won't get you any extra marks.

Summary Questions

Q1 Curtiss's (1977) case study of Genie illustrated extreme privation. Describe one other case of privation.

Q2 Outline a study that investigates the effects of institutional care.

Q3 Name one factor which might affect the extent of damage caused by privation early in life.

Q4 a) An inability to give or receive affection, poor social relationships, dishonesty and involvement in crime are all potential symptoms of which disorder resulting from privation?

      b) Give one other possible disorder resulting from privation.

Q5 What evidence is there for the existence of a cycle of privation?

Learning Objectives:

- Know about the impact of different forms of day care on children's social development, including effects on aggression and peer relations.
- Understand how research into attachment and day care has influenced child care practices.

Tip: There are many different types of day care available, e.g. playgroups, nurseries, nannies, babysitters...

Figure 1: *Day care can have significant effects on the social development of a child.*

6. The Effects of Day Care on Child Development

Being abandoned by your mum and dad and left with a bunch of strange, snotty children can be a traumatic experience, but it's not all bad — child care has its benefits too.

Day care and social development

It may be necessary for children to form a strong attachment with their main carer before they can learn social skills and have relationships with others (see pages 46-48). Here are some studies that explore the impact of day care on attachment, peer relations and aggression.

Key study of peer relationships and attachment — Clarke-Stewart et al (1994)

Method:	This study was made up of a series of separate observations, to examine the effects of day care.
	One observation looked at the peer relationships of 150 children aged 2-3 years, who came from different social backgrounds. In another observation, the strength of attachment in a group of 18-month-old children was studied. These children had at least 30 hours of day care per week. The 'strange situation' was used (see pages 42-43). The results were compared with those of children who had 'low intensity' day care (less than 10 hours per week).
Results:	The 2-3 year olds who had experienced day care were good at coping with social situations and negotiating with each other. In the 'strange situation' experiment, the 18-month-olds who had high intensity day care were just as distressed when separated from their mothers as those who had low intensity day care.
Conclusion:	Day care can have a positive effect on the development of peer relationships in 2-3 year olds. Attachment in 18-month-olds is not affected by temporary separation.
Evaluation:	The observations were controlled, so the study could easily be replicated. However, because the situation was artificial, the study lacks ecological validity. Also, the results can't be generalised to other children.

Key study of peer interaction and aggression — Shea (1981)

Method:	Infants aged between 3 and 4 were videotaped in the playground during their first 10 weeks at nursery school. Their behaviour was assessed in terms of rough-and-tumble play, aggression, frequency of peer interaction, distance from the teacher and distance from the nearest child.
Results:	Over the 10 weeks the children's peer interaction increased and their distance from the teacher increased. There was a decrease in aggression and an increase in rough-and-tumble

play. The increase in sociability was more evident in children who attended day care 5 days a week than in those who went 2 days a week.

Conclusion: Day care causes children to become more sociable and less aggressive.

Evaluation: This was a naturalistic observation, meaning that the study had high ecological validity because none of the behaviour was manipulated. However, it means that the results could have been affected by extraneous variables. The behaviour was open to interpretation, so the findings could be biased — e.g. it could be difficult to differentiate between 'aggression' and 'rough-and-tumble play'.

Figure 2: *Day care can cause a child to become less aggressive.*

Key study of attachment and day care — Belsky and Rovine (1988)

Method: Infants were placed in the 'strange situation' to assess how secure their attachments with their mothers were. One group had experienced no day care and one had experienced at least 20 hours of day care per week before their first birthday.

Results: The infants who had received day care were more likely to have an insecure attachment type. They were either 'insecure-avoidant' (type A) — ignored their mother and didn't mind if she left, or 'insecure-resistant' (type C) — uneasy around their mother and upset if she left. Those who hadn't had day care were more likely to be securely attached (type B).

Conclusion: Day care has a negative effect on an infant's social development.

Evaluation: The 'strange situation' is a controlled observation, so there was good control of the variables. However, this meant that the study lacked ecological validity, because it created an artificial situation. DiLalla (1998) also found negative effects on children's peer relationships — the more day care children had, the less prosocially they behaved, i.e. the less they helped, shared, etc.

Tip: Remember, Ainsworth designed the 'strange situation' — if you need a reminder of the method, look back at pages 42-43.

Research into day care and development

All these different studies and still nobody can decide whether day care is good or bad for children. They might as well not have bothered... But they did, which means more for you to learn. Hurrah. Here are some of the reasons why the findings vary so much:

- The studies focus on slightly different things (e.g. quality of care, age of child), and use different samples.

- There are methodological problems with the studies that might lead to inconsistent results. E.g. Clarke-Stewart has admitted that the 'strange situation' isn't a good way of assessing attachment in infants who have day care (despite using it in her study). They're used to temporary separation, so might respond like they don't care and be wrongly classed as 'insecure'.

- All of these studies rely on correlations, so it's not possible to establish cause and effect.
- The studies don't take individual differences like temperament into account.

Real World Connection
Research into day care has helped put child care schemes in place. E.g. in 2001 the government implemented the 'Sure Start' initiative, targeting young children in over 500 local programmes. The aim of the programme is to improve early education and child care, to offer children the best possible start in life.

Impacts on day care practices

Research into child development and day care has influenced decisions about what might be best for children in day care. Scarr (1998) identified several factors that make for good day care:

- Good staff training
- Adequate space
- Appropriate toys and activities
- A good ratio of staff to children
- Minimising staff turnover so that children can form stable attachments with carers.

Key studies of pre-school care

Sylva et al (2003)

Sylva et al (2003) carried out a study called The Effective Provision of Pre-school Education (EPPE) project. The aim of the EPPE project was to discover what factors were necessary for effective pre-schooling. It was a longitudinal study that looked at 3000 children between the ages of three and seven from a variety of backgrounds who attended one of six types of pre-school:

- playgroups
- nursery schools
- nursery classes
- free day nurseries (run by local authorities or volunteers)
- private day nurseries
- integrated centres (which combine care with learning).

At age seven, the children were compared to a control group of children who hadn't been to day care. Sylva et al were interested in the effects that day care had had on the children's development.

The EPPE project found that the children who attended pre-school had better cognitive development than the children who didn't attend pre-school. They also displayed better social development.
The project suggested that high quality pre-school care could reduce the risk of antisocial behaviour too. The type of pre-school that children attended also affected their development — integrated centres encouraged both social and intellectual development.

Vandell et al (1998)

Vandell et al (1988) found that children who had good quality day care were more likely to have friendly interactions with others compared to those receiving lower quality day care.

Figure 3: *High quality day care can have beneficial effects on a child's development.*

Scarr (1998), Vandell et al's (1988) and Sylva et al's (2003) studies show that high quality day care can have a positive effect on social development.

Worked Exam-style Questions

1   Outline and evaluate one study into the effects of
    day care on social development.   *(6 marks)* ■

Shea (1981) carried out a study to explore the effects of day care on peer interaction and aggression. Infants aged between 3 and 4 were videotaped in the playground during their first 10 weeks at nursery school. To study peer interaction, their behaviour was assessed in terms of frequency of peer interaction, distance from the teacher and distance from the nearest child.

The study found that over the 10 weeks the children's peer interaction increased and their distance from the teacher increased. The increase in sociability was more evident in children who attended day care 5 days a week than in those who went 2 days a week. It was concluded that day care causes children to become more sociable.

This was a naturalistic observation, meaning that the study had high ecological validity because none of the behaviour was manipulated. However, it means that the results could have been affected by extraneous variables. Also, the behaviour was open to the interpretation of the observers, so the findings could be biased.

Exam Tip
Always look at the number of marks available. Then re-read your answer and ask yourself if you've written enough to get the marks. On the other hand, watch out for writing too much — you won't get extra marks and it wastes valuable time.

Exam Tip
There's more than one study that you could use to answer this question, so don't worry if you would have come up with a different one.

Exam Tip
Make sure you don't skip over the evaluation otherwise you won't be able to get full marks. Choose a study that you know enough about.

Summary Questions

Q1 Name three different types of day care.

Q2 a) What did Clarke-Stewart et al (1994) discover when the 'strange situation' was carried out to compare children who had high intensity day care and those who had low intensity day care?

    b) Give one limitation of this research.

Q3 Evaluate the research by Belsky and Rovine (1988).

Q4 What did the EPPE project involve?

Q5 Give three factors that make for good day care.

Exam-style Questions

1   The developmental approach often involves observational techniques.

1 (a)   Give **one** advantage of observational techniques.

(1 mark)

1 (b)   Give **one** disadvantage of observational techniques.

(1 mark)

2   Sandra wants to look at how IQ changes with age. She uses a longitudinal design
     to test the same individuals repeatedly over a period of time. She then plots the
     group average as a function of age.
     Give **one** limitation of Sandra's experiment.

(1 mark)

3   Carole is six years old. She cried a lot when she was younger.
     She is now securely attached to her mother.
     How might learning theory explain this?

(5 marks)

4 (a)   Jane's attachment has been described as insecure-avoidant, whereas Antonio's
         has been described as insecure-resistant. How might their behaviour differ?

(4 marks)

  (b)   What is the term used to describe what happens when someone has
         failed to form an attachment?

(1 mark)

5   Outline and evaluate **one** study of attachment that uses the 'strange situation'.

(8 marks)

6   Outline and evaluate **one** study of institutional care.

(6 marks)

7 (a)   What has research shown us about the effect of day care on aggression?

(3 marks)

  (b)   Discuss how research into day care has influenced child care practice.

(6 marks)

1. Research Methods

If a psychologist has a theory, they're going to need to test it out.
This section is all about how they would go about doing this...

Laboratory experiments

An experiment is a way of conducting research in a controlled and scientific way. The aim is to control all relevant **variables** except for one key variable, which is altered to see what the effect is. The variable that you alter is called the **independent variable** (IV) (see page 67).

> **Example**
>
> In a study investigating the effects of alcohol on reaction time, the IV is the amount of alcohol the participants consume. This is the variable that you would alter. You would control all other variables, e.g. how you measure reaction time, the participants used, distractions in the experimental setting, etc. to ensure that these factors don't affect the results — this way you know that any change in reaction time is due to the effects of alcohol.

Laboratory experiments are conducted in an artificial setting, e.g. Milgram's study (see pages 155-156).

Advantages

- Control — the effects of confounding variables (those that have an effect in addition to the variable of interest — see page 67) are minimised.

- Replication — strict controls mean you can run the study again to check the findings.

- Causal relationships — ideally it's possible to establish whether one variable actually causes change in another.

Disadvantages

- Artificial — experiments might not measure real-life behaviour (i.e. they may lack ecological validity).

- Demand characteristics — participants may respond according to what they think is being investigated, which can bias the results.

- Ethics — deception is often used, making informed consent difficult.

Field experiments

In **field experiments** behaviour is measured outside the laboratory in a natural environment like a school, the street or on a train. A key variable is still altered so that its effect can be measured.

> **Examples**
>
> Piliavin et al (1969) conducted a field experiment to investigate bystander intervention. They staged the collapse of a person on a New York subway (a natural setting) and then observed the reactions of the people in the carriage. They wanted to investigate whether the type of victim (a drunk, or a person with a cane) influenced whether or not people helped. This was the key variable — the type of victim was altered and its effect measured.

Learning Objectives:

Know about the following research methods, including an understanding of their advantages and weaknesses:

- Experimental method, including laboratory, field and natural experiments

- Studies using a correlational analysis

- Observational techniques

- Self-report techniques including questionnaire and interview

- Case studies

Figure 1: *Laboratory experiments allow research to be conducted in a controlled and scientific way.*

Figure 2: *Field experiments take place outside the laboratory, in natural settings.*

- Causal relationships — you can still establish causal relationships by manipulating the key variable and measuring its effect, although it's very difficult to do in a field experiment.

- Ecological validity — field experiments are less artificial than those done in a laboratory, so they relate to real life better.

- Avoids demand characteristics (participants trying to guess what the researcher expects from them and performing differently because of it) — these can be avoided if participants don't know they're in a study.

Tip: For more on demand characteristics see page 79.

Disadvantages

- Less control — confounding variables may be more likely in a natural environment.

- Ethics — participants who didn't agree to take part might experience distress and often can't be debriefed. Observation must respect privacy.

Natural experiments

Natural experiments measure but don't control variables. A natural experiment is a study that measures variables that aren't directly manipulated by the experimenter.

> **Examples**
> - Comparing behaviour in a single-sex school and a mixed school.
> - Looking at whether being an only child has an effect on social relationships — researchers can't control whether the child has any brothers or sisters, but they can measure the effects.

Advantage

- Ethical — it's possible to study variables that it would be unethical to manipulate, e.g. you can compare a community that has TV with a community that doesn't to see which is more aggressive.

Tip: Ethics are really important in psychology — see pages 81-83.

Disadvantages

- Participant allocation — you can't randomly allocate participants to each condition, and so confounding variables (e.g. what area the participants live in) may affect results. Let's face it — you've got no control over the variables so it's ridiculously hard to say what's caused by what.

- Rare events — some groups of interest are hard to find, e.g. a community that doesn't have TV.

- Ethics — deception is often used, making informed consent difficult. Also, confidentiality may be compromised if the sample is identifiable.

Naturalistic observation

Naturalistic observation involves observing subjects in their natural environment. Researchers take great care not to interfere in any way with the subjects they're studying.

> **Examples**
> - Observing children in a playground to see if they behave aggressively.
> - Observing whether men or women are more likely to hold the door open for others in a restaurant.

Figure 3: Observing children playing to see if they display aggressive behaviour is an example of naturalistic observation.

Researchers just observe and record behaviour — they have no control over any variables.

Advantages

- Ecological validity — behaviour is natural and there are no demand characteristics, as the participant is unaware of being observed.

- Theory development — can be a useful way of developing ideas about behaviour that could be tested in more controlled conditions later.

Disadvantages

- Extraneous variables — can't control variables that may affect behaviour.

- Observer bias — observers' expectations may affect what they focus on and record. This means the reliability of the results may be a problem — another observer may have come up with very different results.

- Ethics — you should only conduct observations where people might expect to be observed by strangers. This limits the situations where you can do a naturalistic observation. Debriefing is difficult. Observation must respect privacy. Getting informed consent can be tricky.

Tip: If you need a reminder of what any of these terms mean, don't forget about the glossary — see pages 222-230.

Correlational research

Correlational research looks for relationships between variables. **Correlation** means that two variables rise and fall together, or that one rises as the other falls — but not always that one variable causes a change in the other.

> **Examples**
>
> As age increases so might intelligence, but ageing doesn't cause intelligence. Another example is that as the temperature increases, more people get eaten by bears. This doesn't mean that sunny weather makes bears want to eat people — people are more likely to go walking when it's sunny, so are at greater risk of being eaten by bears.

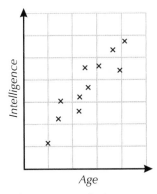

Figure 4: *Graph showing a positive correlation between age and intelligence.*

Advantages

- Causal relationships — these can be ruled out if no correlation exists.

- Ethics — can study variables that would be unethical to manipulate, e.g. is there a relationship between the number of cigarettes smoked and incidences of ill health?

Disadvantages

- Causal relationships — these cannot be assumed from a correlation, which may be caused by a third, unknown variable.

- Ethics — misinterpretation can be an issue. Sometimes the media (and researchers) infer causality from a correlation.

Tip: See pages 94-96 for more on correlations.

Questionnaires

Questionnaires can be written, face-to-face, on the phone, or via the internet.

Advantage

- Practical — can collect a large amount of information quickly and relatively cheaply.

Disadvantages

- Bad questions — leading questions (questions that suggest a desired answer) or unclear questions can be a problem.

- Biased samples — some people are more likely to respond to a questionnaire, which might make a sample unrepresentative.

- Self report — people sometimes want to present themselves in a good light (social desirability bias — see page 79). What they say and what they actually think could be different, making any results unreliable.

Figure 5: *The internet has made it easy for psychologists to collect large amounts of information quickly and cheaply.*

- Ethics — confidentiality can be a problem, especially around sensitive issues.

Interviews

Interviews are more like a conversation than a face-to-face questionnaire. **Structured interviews** follow a fixed set of questions that are the same for all participants. **Unstructured interviews** may have a set of discussion topics, but are less constrained about how the conversation goes.

Advantages

- Rich data — can get detailed information, as there are fewer constraints than with a questionnaire. Unstructured interviews provide richer information than structured interviews.

- Pilot study — interviews are a useful way to get information before a study.

Disadvantages

- Self report — can be unreliable and affected by social desirability bias (see questionnaires).

- Impractical — conducting interviews can be time-consuming and requires skilled researchers.

- Ethics — confidentiality can be a problem, especially around sensitive issues.

Case studies

Case studies are intensive descriptions of a single individual or case. They allow researchers to analyse unusual cases in a lot of detail.

Examples

- Milner et al's (1957) study of HM (see pages 10-11).
- Gardner and Gardner (1969) (see page 11).
- The case of Genie (see page 51) by Curtiss (1977).

Advantages

- Rich data — researchers have the opportunity to study rare phenomena in a lot of detail.

- Unique cases — can challenge existing ideas and theories, and suggest ideas for future research.

Disadvantages

- Difficult to establish causal relationships — the researcher has very little control over variables.

- Lack of generalisation — only using a single case makes generalising the results extremely difficult.

- Ethics — informed consent can be difficult to obtain if the subject has a rare disorder.

Worked Exam-style Questions

1 Outline and evaluate the use of interviews as a psychological research method. *(6 marks)*

Interviews are like a conversation and can be structured or unstructured. Structured interviews follow a fixed set of questions that are the same for

Figure 6: *Interviews can be structured or unstructured depending on the type of information the researcher wants to collect.*

Tip: Case studies are often carried out on people in unusual circumstances. Although interesting, the findings of case studies can rarely be generalised to the population as a whole.

all participants. Unstructured interviews may have a set of discussion topics, but are less constrained about how the conversation goes.

Using interviews in psychological research is advantageous as it allows researchers to gather detailed information. Unstructured interviews provide particularly rich information. Conducting interviews as part of a pilot study is also a useful way to get information before a study.

Interviews have their disadvantages. They rely on self reporting, which means that they can be unreliable and affected by social desirability bias — people sometimes want to present themselves in a good light. Another problem is that conducting interviews is sometimes impractical — they can be time-consuming and require skilled researchers. Using interviews can also have ethical issues — confidentiality can be a problem, especially around sensitive issues.

Exam Tip
When you use psychological terms like 'social desirability bias' it's often a good idea to explain what they mean. This way you are showing that you have a good knowledge of key psychological terms.

---

2   A psychologist investigates aggression in sports spectators by observing the behaviour of people watching a rugby match in a pub.

(a) What type of research method is being used here? *(1 mark)*

(b) Evaluate the use of this type of research method.   *(6 marks)*

(a) Naturalistic observation.

(b) Naturalistic observations have high ecological validity — behaviour is natural and there are no demand characteristics, as the participants are unaware of being observed. Naturalistic observations are also a useful way of developing ideas about behaviour that could be tested in more controlled conditions later.

Naturalistic observations also have disadvantages. Researchers have no control over extraneous variables that may affect behaviour. For instance, in the example of the rugby match, any aggressive behaviour displayed may be as a result of factors other than watching sport, for example, drinking alcohol.

Researchers also have to be aware of observer bias. This is where the observers' expectations may affect what they focus on and record. This means the reliability of the results may be a problem — another observer may have come up with very different results.

Ethics are also an issue. Observations should only be conducted where people might expect to be observed by strangers — observations must respect privacy. This limits the situations where you can do a naturalistic observation. Debriefing participants is also difficult, and getting informed consent can be tricky.

Exam Tip
If you can give an example to help explain a point you are making, then go for it — it'll let the examiner know that you really know what you are talking about.

Summary Questions

Q1 Describe one disadvantage of using a laboratory experiment in psychological research.

Q2 Give one advantage of using field experiments in research.

Q3 a) Give one advantage of using a naturalistic observation in research.

   b) Give one ethical problem with using naturalistic observations in research.

Q4 Give an example of a study which used a case study.

Understand the
following features of
investigation design:

- Aims
- Hypotheses, including
directional and
non-directional
- Operationalisation of
variables, including
independent and
dependent variables

2. Aims and Hypotheses

*Aims and hypotheses are statements about a piece of research — they show
what a researcher is trying to find out...*

Research aims

An aim is a statement of a study's purpose. Research should state its aim
beforehand so that it's clear what the study intends to investigate.

--- Examples ---

Asch's aim (see pages 142-143) might have been: 'To study majority
influence in an unambiguous task'. The aim of the study by Loftus and
Palmer (see pages 23-24) may have been: 'To investigate the effects that
leading questions have on the ability to accurately recall events.'

Hypotheses

Hypotheses are theories tested by research. Although the aim states the
purpose of a study, it isn't usually precise enough to test. What is needed
are clear statements of what's actually being tested — the hypotheses.

1. Research hypothesis

The research hypothesis is proposed at the beginning of a piece of research
and is often generated from a theory.

--- Example ---

Bowlby's research hypothesis was that maternal deprivation causes
delinquency. (See pages 47-48 for the details of Bowlby's study.)

2. Null hypothesis

The null hypothesis is what you're going to assume is true during the study.
Any data you collect will either back this assumption up, or it won't. If the
data doesn't support your null hypothesis, you reject it and go with your
alternative hypothesis instead. Very often, the null hypothesis is a prediction
that there will be no relationship between key variables in a study — and any
correlation is due to chance.

--- Example ---

There is no difference in exam grades between students who use a revision
guide and students who don't.

Tip: It's quite usual to
have something you
don't actually believe
as your null hypothesis.
You assume it's true for
the duration of the study
— but if your results
lead you to reject this
null hypothesis, you've
got evidence that it
wasn't true after all.

3. Experimental hypothesis (or alternative hypothesis)

If the data forces you to reject your null hypothesis, then you accept your
experimental (alternative) hypothesis instead. If your null hypothesis was that
two variables aren't linked, then your alternative hypothesis would be that
they are linked.

--- Example ---

There is a difference in exam grades between students who use a revision
guide and students who don't.

Tip: An experimental
hypothesis is only used
in experiments. It's
usually the same as the
research hypothesis.

Or you can be more specific, and be a bit more precise about how they are
linked, using directional hypotheses.

4. Directional hypothesis

A hypothesis might predict a difference between the exam results obtained
by two groups of students — a group that uses a revision guide and another
group that doesn't. If the hypothesis states which group will do better, it is
making a directional prediction.

> **Example**
> Students who use a revision guide will get higher exam grades than students who don't.

Directional hypotheses are often used when previous research findings suggest which way the results will go.

5. Non-directional hypothesis

A non-directional hypothesis would predict a difference, but wouldn't say which group would do better.

> **Example**
> There will be a difference in exam grades between students who use a revision guide and students who don't — this is a non-directional hypothesis, since you're not saying which group will do better.

Non-directional hypotheses can be used when there is little previous research in the area under investigation, or when previous research findings are mixed and inconclusive.

Variables

A **variable** is a quantity whose value can change — for example, the time taken to do a task, anxiety levels, or exam results. There are various different kinds of variable.

The independent variable

An **independent variable** (IV) is a variable directly manipulated by the researcher.

> **Example**
> In the example above about students, exams and revision guides, there are two variables. One is 'whether or not a revision guide is used' (so this variable has only two possible values: yes or no).
> The other is the 'exam grade' (and this could have lots of possible values: e.g. A, B, C, D, E, N, U). In this case, the independent variable is 'whether or not a revision guide is used' — since this is directly under the control of the researcher.

The dependent variable

The **dependent variable** (DV) is the variable that you think is affected by changes in the independent variable. (So the DV is dependent on the IV.)

> **Example**
> In the exam grades example, the dependent variable is the 'exam grade'. The exam grade is dependent on whether a revision guide was used (or at least, that's what's being investigated).

Ideally in a study the only thing that would influence the DV (the thing you're measuring) would be the IV (the thing you're manipulating). Usually though, there are other things that will have an effect. An **extraneous variable** is any variable (other than the IV) that could affect what you're trying to measure. If these things are actually influencing the DV then they're called **confounding variables**.

> **Examples**
> In the exam grades example, confounding variables could be things like how much they've listened in class, problems at home, etc.

Tip: Directional and non-directional hypotheses could predict a correlation between two variables too. The directional hypothesis would predict the type of correlation.

Tip: So, you need a research hypothesis (or an experimental hypothesis) and a null hypothesis. The experimental hypothesis is either directional or non-directional.

Tip: The IV in a naturalistic observation is a bit of an exception to the rule — the researcher has no control over it. In the study by Shea (1981) (pages 56-57), the IV was the amount of time the children had spent in day care. Although the researchers were unable to manipulate this variable, it was the factor that was believed to affect the child's behaviour (the DV).

Figure 1: *Confounding variables influence the DV.*

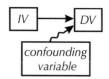

Figure 2: *The DV is dependent on the IV. However, confounding variables can also have an impact on the DV.*

Example

In the study by Loftus and Palmer (1974 — see pages 23-24), the IV was the wording of the leading question, while the DV was the estimate of speed given. Confounding variables in this study could include things like demand characteristics — if the participants had guessed what the study was trying to measure, it might have affected their estimates of speed.

Operationalisation

Variables must be **operationalised**. This means describing the process by which the variable is measured. Some things are easy to operationalise (e.g. height might be operationalised as 'the distance in centimetres from the bottom of an object to the top'). Other things are difficult to operationalise (e.g. a mother's love for her newborn baby). Operationalisation allows others to see exactly how you're going to define and measure your variables.

Worked Exam-style Questions

1   Kate is conducting a study to see if students prefer Australian daytime soaps to British daytime soaps. She thinks students will prefer the Australian soaps.

(a) What is the dependent variable in Kate's study?   *(1 mark)*

(b) Write a directional hypothesis for Kate's study.   *(1 mark)*

(c) Write a non-directional hypothesis for Kate's study.   *(1 mark)*

(a)   The type of daytime soap (Australian or British).

(b)   Students will prefer Australian daytime soaps to British daytime soaps.

(c)   There will be a difference between students' preferences for Australian and British daytime soaps.

Summary Questions

Q1 What is a research aim?

Q2 What is a hypothesis?

Q3 What is an independent variable?

Q4 "The IV is dependent on the DV." Is this true or false?

Q5 A psychologist is conducting a study to test the effects of stress on a person's heart rate. Before the study, participants were asked if they were taking any heart medication. In relation to variables, why is it important that the participants were not on heart medication?

Q6 Why is operationalisation important in psychological research?

3. Research Design

Once you've got your hypothesis sorted, you've got to decide how to test it...

Making the hypothesis testable

The research design must make the hypothesis testable.

> **Example**
>
> Research example — does the presence of an audience help or hinder people doing the 'wiggly wire' task (moving a loop along a wire without touching it and setting off the buzzer)? Based on previous research, we expect people to do this better without anyone watching them.

The IV (the variable being manipulated) is the presence or absence of an audience. The DV (the variable being measured) is 'how well' the participants do on the task — but it must be testable. You need a precisely defined (or operationalised) DV, which should be quantitative wherever possible. An operationalised DV for this experiment might be 'the time taken to move the loop from one end of the wire to the other without setting off the buzzer'.

Types of experimental design

1. Independent groups design

An **independent groups** design means there are different participants in each group.

> **Example**
>
> In the 'wiggly wire' task example, one group does the task with an audience and another group does it alone.

This avoids the problem that if all the participants did the test in both conditions, any improvement in performance might be due to them having two goes at the task (which would be a confounding variable).

Advantage
- No order effects — no one gets better through practice (learning effect) or gets worse through being bored or tired (fatigue effect).

Disadvantages
- Participant variables — differences between the people in each group might affect the results (e.g. the 'without audience' group may just have people who are better at the task — so we can't safely compare groups).
- Number of participants — twice as many participants are needed to get the same amount of data, compared to having everyone do both conditions.

2. Repeated measures design

A **repeated measures** design is where participants take part in all conditions.

> **Example**
>
> All participants do the task with an audience and then without.

You can compare the performances in each condition, knowing the differences weren't due to participant variables.

Advantages
- No participant variables — the same people do the test in both conditions, so any differences between individuals shouldn't affect the results.

Figure 1: *The 'wiggly wire'.*

Tip: Make sure you know the advantages and disadvantages that go with each type of experimental design. An exam question might ask you to evaluate the experimental design of a psychological study.

- Number of participants — fewer participants are needed to get the same amount of data.

Disadvantage

- Order effects — if all participants did the 'with audience' condition first, any improvements in the second condition could be due to practice, not the audience's absence. (But see counterbalancing below.)

3. Matched pairs design

A **matched pairs** design means there are different participants in each condition, but they're matched on important variables (like age, sex and personality). Some studies use control groups. These groups have not experienced any of the manipulations of the IV that an experimental group might have. This allows the researcher to make a direct comparison between them.

> **Example**
>
> In the 'wiggly wire' task example, the group that didn't have an audience would be the control group.

Advantages

- No order effects — there are different people in each condition.
- Reduced participant variables — important differences are minimised through matching.

Disadvantages

- Number of participants — need twice as many people compared to repeated measures.
- Practicalities — time-consuming and difficult to find participants who match.

Pilot studies

No piece of research is perfect. To help foresee any problems, a small-scale **pilot study** can be run first. This should establish whether the design works, whether participants understand the wording in instructions, or whether something important has been missed out. Problems can be tackled before running the main study, which could save wasting a lot of time and money.

Controlling variables

Variables can be 'controlled' so their unwanted effects are minimised.

Counterbalancing

Counterbalancing (mixing up the order of the tasks) can solve **order effects** in repeated measures designs.

> **Example**
>
> In our 'wiggly wire' task example, half the participants do the task with an audience first and then without. The others do the conditions the other way round. Any order effects would then be equal across conditions.

Random allocation

Random allocation (e.g. by drawing names out of a hat) means everyone has an equal chance of doing either condition. An independent measures study with, for example, more men in one group than the other could have a confounding variable. Any difference in performance may be due to sex rather than the real IV. Random allocation should ensure groups are not biased on key variables because they are determined by chance.

Research design	Participants
independent groups	different
repeated measures	same
matched pairs	different but matched

Figure 2: *Summary of the three research designs.*

Tip: Pilot studies are a bit like a practice run — they help you spot any issues before doing the real thing.

Tip: For a reminder on confounding variables see page 67.

Extraneous variables

Extraneous variables can be controlled by:

┌─ **Examples** ─────────────────────────────
- keeping them constant for all participants (e.g. everyone does the wiggly wire task in the same place so distractions are similar)
- eliminating them altogether (e.g. everyone does the wiggly wire task somewhere with no noise distractions).

Standardised instructions

Standardised instructions should ensure the experimenters act in a similar way with all participants. Everything should be as similar as possible for all the participants, including each participant's experience in such studies.

Reliability and validity

Reliability

If a test is consistent within itself, it has **internal reliability**. The split-half technique assesses this. A questionnaire is randomly split in two — if all participants score similarly on both halves, the questions measure the same thing. If the measure is stable over time or between people, then it has **external reliability**. This can be assessed by measuring test-retest reliability (does the same person always score similarly on the test?) or inter-rater reliability (do different assessors agree, i.e. do they both give the same score?).

Validity

If an experiment shows that the results were caused by the manipulation of the variables, rather than the effect of something else, then it has **internal validity**. If the findings can be generalised beyond the experimental setting (e.g. to different groups of people or different settings), then the experiment has **external validity**.

Research design and ethics

Research should be designed with ethical issues in mind. Ethical guidelines assist researchers who have ethical dilemmas, and should ensure that research is acceptable and participants are protected.

Tip: For more on extraneous variables see page 67.

Tip: All conditions need to be standardised in a study. For example, as well as the instructions, the experimental environment should be kept the same to ensure that each person has the same overall experience.

Tip: Reliability and validity are really important in psychology. They're not the same thing, so make sure you know which is which. Reliability is about consistency — it's whether you're always testing the same thing every time.
Validity is a measure of whether a study tests what it's actually supposed to be testing.

Tip: Ethical guidelines are discussed more fully on pages 81-83.

Worked Exam-style Question

1   A study investigating the effect of distractions on memory uses the same group of participants in all of its conditions.

    (a) (i)   What type of experimental design was used in this investigation? *(1 mark)*

        (ii)   Evaluate this type of experimental design. *(4 marks)*

    (b) The study is repeated, this time using a matched pairs design. Outline and evaluate this type of experimental design. *(6 marks)*

(a) (i) repeated measures

(ii) Using a repeated measures design is beneficial as you can compare the performances in each condition, knowing the differences weren't due to participant variables. In a repeated measures design,

Exam Tip
If you don't know the differences between the different types of experimental design then this question will be pretty tricky.
See pages 69-70 if you are struggling.

the same people are used in all conditions, so any differences between individuals shouldn't affect the results. If you use different participants in each experimental condition, differences between the people in each group might affect the results.

Using repeated measures also means that fewer participants are needed to get the same amount of data. This makes conducting the study cheaper and easier as you have to recruit fewer participants.

However, using repeated measures has its drawbacks. Order effects can be a big problem. If all participants did the same condition first, any improvements in the following conditions could be due to practice, not as a result of the independent variable — the learning effect. Similarly participants may get worse through being bored or tired — this is known as the fatigue effect.

(b) A matched pairs design means there are different participants in each condition, but they're matched on important variables (like age, sex and personality). Some studies also use control groups. These groups have not experienced any of the manipulations of the independent variable that an experimental group might have. This allows the researcher to make a direct comparison between them.

An advantage of using this design is that there are no order effects. Because there are different people in each condition, they will not experience the learning effect or the fatigue effect. Also, using matched pairs minimises the effects of participant variables, by matching important variables.

A disadvantage of this design is that twice as many participants are required as in a repeated measures design. It is often time-consuming and difficult to find participants who match on the key variables.

Exam Tip
If you are using a psychological term, show the examiner that you know what it means.

Exam Tip
Start off by defining what happens in a matched pairs experiment, before you go into the evaluation. Keep your answers clear and ordered.

Exam Tip
Remember, evaluate means weigh up the positives and negatives.

Summary Questions

Q1 Give one advantage of an independent groups design.

Q2 What are participant variables?

Q3 What is the purpose of a pilot study?

Q4 Participants' names are drawn out of a hat. What is the term for this way of choosing experimental groups?

Q5 Outline the split-half technique.

Q6 What is test-retest reliability?

4. Observations, Questionnaires and Interviews

Learning Objectives:

Understand the following features of investigation design:

- Design of naturalistic observations, including the development and use of behavioural categories

- Design of questionnaires and interviews

There's more to observations than just watching people. And more to questionnaires and interviews than just asking a few random questions...

Participant and non-participant observation

1. Participant observation

Participant observation is when the researcher participates in the activity under study, e.g. posing as a gang member in order to study gang culture.

Advantage

- The researcher develops a relationship with the group under study, so they can gain a greater understanding of the group's behaviour.

Disadvantages

- The researcher loses objectivity by becoming part of the group.

- The participants may act differently if they know a researcher is amongst them.

2. Non-participant observation

Non-participant observation is when the researcher observes the activity without getting involved in it, for example, observing a group of children during class in order to study their social interactions.

Advantage

- The researcher can remain objective throughout the study.

Disadvantage

- The researcher loses a sense of the group dynamics by staying separate from the group.

Sometimes researchers undertake **structured observations**. This is where the behaviour categories that are going to be used are defined in advance.

Advantage

- You can gather relevant data because you know what you're looking for.

Disadvantage

- Interesting behaviours could go unrecorded because they haven't been pre-defined as important.

Tip: Participant and non-participant observations can either be overt (the researcher's presence is obvious to the participants), or covert (their presence is unknown to the participants).

Figure 1: In non-participant observation researchers observe activity without getting involved.

Collecting observation data

There are various ways of organising structured observations to make sure no behaviours are missed. You need to make lots of design decisions for a naturalistic observation.

1. Recording Data

If you want qualitative data you could just make written notes. But video or audio recording means that you have a more accurate permanent record.

2. Categorising behaviour

You must define the behaviours you aim to observe. For example, if you were going to observe children in a school playground to see how many behave aggressively, you'd have to decide what counts as aggression. This involves giving an operationalised definition (i.e. some specific, observable behaviours). For example, you might say that 'aggression is any physical act made with the intention to harm another person — such as punching,

Figure 2: Making notes provides qualitative data.

Figure 3: Aggression needs to be given an operationalised definition if it is to be accurately recorded.

kicking, etc.' But you have to be careful not to miss out anything important otherwise your definition may not be valid, e.g. aggression can also be verbal.

3. Rating behaviour

The behaviours that you're interested in may be things that are a matter of degree, so you might need to use a rating scale to classify behaviour. You could put each participant's behaviour into one of several categories, e.g. not aggressive, mildly aggressive or very aggressive. Or you could use a coding system where each participant is given a number (e.g. between 1 and 10) to represent how aggressive they are, where a higher score indicates more aggression. However, you still have to define what kinds of behaviour are included for each number on the scale (e.g. 5 = pushing and 10 = kicking or punching more than once) — see Figure 4. Behaviour rated in this way provides quantitative data (data in the form of numbers).

Code	Behaviour description
1	shouting
2	stamping feet
3	grabbing others' objects
4	breaking others' objects
5	pushing
6	hair pulling
7	scratching others
8	kicking
9	punching
10	kicking or punching more than once

Figure 4: Child aggression coding system.

4. Sampling behaviour

You have to decide how often and for how long you're going to observe the participants.

Event sampling — this is when you only record particular events that you're interested in (e.g. aggression shown by the children) and ignore other behaviours.

Advantage

Researchers know exactly what behaviours they're looking for.

Disadvantage

Potentially interesting behaviours could be ignored.

Time-interval sampling — if the behaviours occur over a long time period you might choose to observe for only set time intervals e.g. the first 10 minutes of every hour. The time intervals could be chosen randomly.

Advantage

Very convenient for the researchers to carry out.

Disadvantage

If interesting behaviours occur outside the time sample they won't be recorded.

Tip: A pilot study can help you make decisions about how often and for how long you're going to observe the participants.

Figure 5: Observers should compare their data to ensure inter-observer reliability.

5. Inter-Observer reliability

Even after you've defined the behaviours you're interested in, you have to make sure that the observers are actually putting each participant in the right category or giving the right rating. This might involve comparing the data from two or more observers to make sure they're giving the same scores (i.e. that they are 'reliable').

Code	Behaviour description	Child A	Child B	Child C	Child D
1	shouting				
2	stamping feet				
3	grabbing others' objects				
4	breaking others' objects				
5	pushing				
6	hair pulling				
7	scratching others				
8	kicking				
9	punching				
10	kicking or punching more than once				

Figure 6: *Data collection grid for use during a naturalistic observation of child aggression.*

Questionnaire design

There are various things you need to consider when designing a questionnaire for a survey.

1. Type of data

Whether you want qualitative data and/or quantitative data will affect whether you ask open and/or closed questions.

- **Open questions** are questions where the participant can reply in any way, and in as much detail as they want.

Examples
'What kinds of music do you like?'
'What do you like to do on a weekend?'

- This gives detailed, qualitative information, although it may be hard to analyse, as the participants could give very different answers.

- **Closed questions** limit the answers that can be given.

Examples
'Which do you like: Pop, Rock or neither?'
'What do you prefer to eat at the cinema: popcorn, chocolate, or nachos?'
'Which is your favourite hot drink: tea, coffee or hot chocolate?

- They give quantitative data that is relatively easy to analyse — e.g. you can say exactly how many people liked each type of music. However, less detail is obtained about each participant.

2. Ambiguity

You have to avoid questions and answer options which are not clearly defined.

Examples
'Do you listen to music frequently?' What is meant here by 'frequently' — once a day, once a week?
'Do you drink enough water per day?' How much is 'enough'? Different people may consider different amounts to be 'enough'. An actual volume of water needs to be defined.

Tip: Whether observers are giving the same scores is a measure of inter-rater reliability (see page 71). Again, using a pilot study can ensure that all of the observers are clear on what each behaviour is, before the actual study takes place.

Tip: Don't get qualitative and quantitative confused. Think 'quality' for qualitative data — you get lots of quality detailed information. Think 'quantity' (i.e. numbers) for quantitative data — you get data that is easier to analyse. (See pages 85-87 for more on types of data.)

Figure 7: *Closed questions can use things like rating scales — these limit the answers that can be given but are easy to analyse.*

3. Double-barrelled questions

Best not to use these, since a person may wish to answer differently to each part.

> **Examples**
>
> 'Do you agree that modern music is not as good as the music of the 1960s and that there should be more guitar-based music in the charts?'
> 'Do you agree that wild animals don't belong in zoos and that it is cruel to have a rabbit as a pet?'

4. Leading questions

These are questions that lead the participant towards a particular answer.

> **Examples**
>
> 'How old was the boy in the distance?'
> They might have seen an older person, but by saying 'boy' you're leading them to describe the person as young. You're also leading them to think that the person was male, but they might not have been sure.
>
> It's really important to avoid leading questions in eyewitness testimony. A study by Loftus and Zanni (1975) found participants were more likely to report having seen a non-existent broken headlight when asked the leading question "Did you see **the** broken headlight?" compared to those asked "Did you see **a** broken headlight?" (For more details see page 24.)

Figure 8: *Loftus and Zanni's (1975) study famously displayed the effects of leading questions.*

Tip: Writing questionnaires is harder than you'd think. You have to word questions really carefully to make sure they are not ambiguous, unclear, misleading or difficult to understand.

5. Complexity

Whenever possible clear language should be used, avoiding jargon. However, if specialist terms are included, they should be clearly defined.

> **Examples**
>
> The question 'Do you prefer music written in unusual time signatures?' probably isn't ideal for most people. Equally, if you asked a person 'Have you ever experienced an acute myocardial infarction?' they'd be unlikely to know what you're asking if they've never had a heart attack.

Interviews

All of the above goes for interviews as well, but you also have to consider the following:

* How structured the interview will be. Interviews can be very unstructured with few set questions, and new questions being asked depending on the participant's previous answers. This gives detailed qualitative data, which may be difficult to analyse. Alternatively, they may be more structured, with set questions and closed answers, giving less detail but being easier to analyse.

* Using a question checklist — if the interview is structured, a checklist ensures that no questions are left out and questions aren't asked twice.

* The behaviour or appearance of the interviewer — this could influence how the participants react.

Figure 9: *The behaviour or appearance of the interviewer could influence how the participant answers.*

Worked Exam-style Questions

1   Tom is researching how sixth form chemistry students interact with each other during practical sessions. Unknown to the students, Tom observes and records their behaviour. He is looking for certain behaviours and records them as he sees them being displayed.

(a) Tom is using non-participant observation.
    State one advantage and one disadvantage of this
    type of observation design.   *(2 marks)*

(b) Tom is using a structured observation.
    State one advantage and one disadvantage of this.
                                                    (2 marks)

(c) Tom's friend, Henry, helps Tom by observing the students
    as well. After the observation they compare their results. ■
    Why do they do this?   *(2 marks)*

(d) Tom wants to write a questionnaire to assess the students'
    own views about their relationships with fellow students.
    He decides to use open questions in his questionnaire.
    What are open questions and what is their main advantage?
                                                    (2 marks)

Exam Tip
All of these questions want you to apply your knowledge to the scenario you have been given — this is why it's really important not to write everything you know about a topic. You have to pick out the important bits that apply to the question.

(a) An advantage of non-participant observation is that the researcher can remain objective throughout the study. They don't become part of the group, which could cause them to lose objectivity.

A disadvantage of this method is that the researcher loses a sense of the group dynamics by staying separate from the group. Often if the researcher develops a relationship with the group under study, they can gain a greater understanding of the group's behaviour.

(b) An advantage of using a structured observation is that it's easier to gather relevant data because you already know what you're looking for. ■

A disadvantage is that potentially interesting behaviours could go unrecorded because they haven't been pre-defined as important.

(c) They are checking to ensure that they have good inter-observer reliability. Even though they have defined the behaviours they're interested in, they have to make sure that they are both actually putting each participant in the right category or giving the right rating. This ensures that their data is reliable.

(d) Open questions are questions where the participant can reply in any way, and in as much detail as they want. The main advantage of open questions is that they provide detailed, qualitative information.

Exam Tip
Read the question carefully — only give what it is asking for — in this case one advantage and one disadvantage.

Summary Questions

Q1 a) What is time-interval sampling?
    b) Give one advantage of time-interval sampling.
    c) Give one disadvantage of time-interval sampling.

Q2 Give one advantage of using closed questions.

Q3 What is a leading question?

Q4 Give one problem with using unstructured interviews.

Q5 Why might interviewers use a question checklist?

5. Selecting and Using Participants

Participants are pretty important to psychology — without them you couldn't do many studies. In fact, picking participants is a bit of a science in itself...

Selecting a sample of participants

- The part of a **population** that you're interested in studying is called the **target group** — e.g. all the people in a particular city, or all people of a certain age or background.
- Usually you can't include everyone in the target group in a study, so you choose a certain **sample** of participants.
- This sample should be representative, i.e. it should reflect the variety of characteristics that are found in the target group.
- A sample that is unrepresentative is **biased**.

There are various methods of selecting a sample:

Random sampling

This is when every member of the target group has an equal chance of being selected for the sample.

> **Examples**
>
> This could be done by giving everyone in the target group a number and then getting a computer to randomly pick numbers to select the participants. Participants' names could also be drawn out of a hat — a more old fashioned, but equally random method.

<u>Advantage</u>

Random sampling is 'fair'. Everyone has an equal chance of being selected and the sample is likely to be representative.

<u>Disadvantages</u>

This method doesn't guarantee a representative sample — there's still a chance that some subgroups in the target group may not be selected (e.g. people from a minority cultural group). Also, if the target group is large it may not be practical (or possible) to give everyone a number that might be picked. So in practice, completely random samples are rarely used.

Opportunity sampling

This is when the researcher samples whoever is available and willing to be studied.

> **Example**
>
> Since many researchers work in universities, they often use opportunity samples made up of students.

<u>Advantage</u>

This is a quick and practical way of getting a sample.

<u>Disadvantage</u>

The sample is unlikely to be representative of a target group or population as a whole. This means that we can't confidently generalise the findings of the research. However, because it's quick and easy, opportunity sampling is often used.

Tip: If you wanted to know about AS level psychology students' views on exams, you could interview all AS level psychology students. However this would take forever and be difficult to do. Instead you'd choose a sample of participants representative of all AS level psychology students.

Tip: No method can guarantee a completely representative sample, but you need to have confidence that your sample is (quite) representative if you want to generalise your results to the entire target group.

Figure 1: *Students are often the participants in psychology studies.*

Volunteer sampling

This is when people actively volunteer to be in a study.

Example

People volunteer by responding to a request for participants advertised by the researcher, e.g. in a newspaper, on a notice board or in the post.

The researcher may then select only those who are suitable for the study.

<u>Advantage</u>

If an advert is placed prominently (e.g. in a national newspaper) a large number of people may respond, giving more participants to study. This may allow more in-depth analysis and more accurate statistical results.

<u>Disadvantages</u>

Even though a large number of people may respond, these will only include people who actually saw the advertisement — no one else would have a chance of being selected. Also, people who volunteer may be more cooperative than others. For these reasons the sample is unlikely to be representative of the target population.

Figure 2: *In volunteer sampling researchers advertise for participants.*

Tip: This method was used by Milgram — see pages 155-156). He put an advert in a newspaper.

Participant behaviour

Participants sometimes act differently when they're being observed. Human participants will usually be aware that they are being studied. This may mean they don't show their true response, and so their data may not be valid or reliable. Some of these effects are explained below:

The Hawthorne effect

If people are interested in something and in the attention they are getting (e.g. from researchers), then they show a more positive response, try harder at tasks, and so on. This means their results for tests are often artificially high (because they're trying harder than normal), which could make a researcher's conclusions inaccurate. The opposite effect may occur if the participants are uninterested in the task.

Demand characteristics

This is when participants form an idea about the purpose of a study. If they think they know what kind of response the researcher is expecting from them, they may show that response to 'please' the researcher (or they may deliberately do the opposite). Either way, the conclusions drawn from the study would be inaccurate.

Social desirability bias

People usually try to show themselves in the best possible light. So in a survey, they may not be completely truthful, but give answers that are more socially acceptable instead (e.g. people may say they give more money to charity than they really do). This would make the results less accurate.

Tip: If you know your teacher is watching you, then you're more likely to behave... probably. You change your behaviour because you're being observed. This sort of thing can also happen between participants and researchers in psychology studies.

Investigator Effects

The researchers can also affect the outcomes in undesirable ways. The reliability and validity of results may also be influenced by the researcher, since he or she has expectations about what will happen. This can produce the following effects:

Researcher (or experimenter) bias

The researchers' expectations can influence how they design their study and how they behave towards the participants, which may then produce demand characteristics. Also, their expectations may influence how they take

Tip: For a reminder on reliability and validity see page 71.

measurements and analyse their data, resulting in errors that can lead, for example, to accepting a hypothesis that was actually false.

Interviewer effects

The interviewer's expectations may lead them to ask only questions about what they are interested in, or to ask leading questions. Or, they may focus on the aspects of the participant's answers which fit their expectations. Also, the participant may react to the behaviour or appearance of an interviewer and then not answer truthfully.

Worked Exam-style Questions

1   (a)   Outline **one** sampling technique that researchers may use when recruiting participants.   *(2 marks)*

    (b)   Describe **one** advantage and **one** disadvantage of the sampling technique that you outlined in part (a). *(4 marks)*

(a)   Volunteer sampling is one sampling strategy researchers may use to recruit participants. It is where people actively volunteer to be in a study by responding to a request for participants advertised by the researcher, e.g. in a newspaper, on a notice board or in the post. The researcher may then select only those participants who are suitable for the study.

(b)   An advantage of volunteer sampling is that if an advert is placed prominently (e.g. in a national newspaper) a large number of people may respond, giving more participants to study. This may allow more in-depth analysis and more accurate statistical results.

A disadvantage of volunteer sampling is that people who volunteer may be more cooperative than others. For this reason the sample is unlikely to be representative of the target population.

2   Describe how investigator effects might affect the outcome of a study.   *(6 marks)*

The reliability and validity of results may be influenced by the researcher's behaviour, since he or she has expectations about what will happen. This can produce two effects, which can have an impact on the outcome of the study.

The first is researcher (or experimenter) bias — the researcher's expectations can influence how they design their study and how they behave towards the participants, which may then produce demand characteristics. Also, their expectations may influence how they take measurements and analyse their data, resulting in errors that can lead, for example, to accepting a hypothesis that was actually false.

The second is interviewer effects. The interviewer's expectations may lead them to ask only questions about what they are interested in, or to ask leading questions. They may also focus on the aspects of the participant's answers which fit their expectations. Also, the participant may react to the behaviour or appearance of an interviewer and then not answer truthfully.

Summary Questions

Q1   Give an example of how you would select a random sample.

Q2   Give an advantage of opportunity sampling.

Q3   Explain the Hawthorne effect.

6. Ethical Issues in Psychological Research

Ethical issues are all to do with the treatment of participants when they take part in psychological studies. Ethical guidelines aim to protect participants.

The British Psychological Society (BPS)

The British Psychological Society (BPS) has developed ethical guidelines to help psychologists resolve ethical issues in research and protect participants. They include advice on deception, consent and psychological harm.

Deception

Deception means misleading or withholding information from participants.

> **Example**
>
> Asch (see pages 142-143) deceived participants about his study's purpose and about the confederates who pretended to be real participants. Asch argued that without deception the aim of this study could not be achieved.

If deception has to be used, participants should be told of the true nature of the research as soon as possible, during the debriefing.

<u>BPS Guidelines for Deception</u>

- Deception should be avoided wherever possible and only be used when it's scientifically justified — when the study would be meaningless otherwise.

- Deception shouldn't be used if it's likely that the participant will be unhappy when they discover the study's true nature.

Informed Consent

Informed consent should be given where possible. Giving consent means agreeing to participate in a study. When a participant is told the research aim and procedure and then agrees to it, this is informed consent. They are fully informed before their decision to participate. If deception is used, participants can't give informed consent until they've been debriefed.

> **Example**
>
> Asch's participants did not give informed consent when they agreed to take part. They were deceived about aspects of the study and didn't have enough information for an informed decision.

<u>BPS Guidelines for Informed Consent</u>

- Participants should be given all the information they need to decide whether to participate in research and shouldn't be coerced or pressured.

- Some people may not be able to give real informed consent — for example children. In these cases informed consent should be obtained from parents or guardians.

Psychological Harm

Psychological harm means any negative emotion (e.g. stress, distress, embarrassment).

> **Example**
>
> Asch's participants may have experienced stress and were possibly embarrassed about being 'tricked' into conforming.

Learning Objectives:
- Be aware of the British Psychological Society (BPS) Code of Ethics.
- Understand ethical issues and ways in which psychologists deal with them.

Tip: Ethical guidelines are put in place to ensure participants are treated correctly when taking part in psychological studies. Imagine if you'd been a participant in the studies you've read about so far. Would you have been happy with your treatment during the studies? How would you have felt? Would the studies have had any long term effects on you?

Tip: Debriefing is informing the participants about the nature of the study. It takes place after the study and is an opportunity for the researchers to explain the purpose of the study and to ensure there are no unforeseen effects on the participants.

Figure 1: *Children are unable to give real informed consent.*

- Researchers have a responsibility to protect participants from physical and psychological harm during the study. Any risk of harm should be no greater than what the participant might experience in their normal life.

'Necessary' deception and consent

Deception

Tip: See page 79 for more on participant behaviour and its implications on psychological research.

Sometimes it's difficult to conduct meaningful research without a bit of deception. If participants know exactly what's being studied then their behaviour might change, and the data you get would be useless. Psychologists don't usually tell participants every last detail, but they do try to minimise deception. That way participants aren't likely to be upset when they find out the true nature of the study.

> **Example**
>
> Milgram's experiment (pages 155-156) is an example of a study that would probably not be considered ethical today. He deceived participants about the true purpose of the study and many of them showed signs of stress when taking part.

Consent

Gaining consent is central to conducting research ethically. But telling participants they're being observed could change the way they behave.

> **Example**
>
> Milgram's participants couldn't give informed consent until after they were debriefed. If they'd known about the nature of the study, it wouldn't have worked.

Confidentiality

Tip: Confidentiality is a really important ethical consideration. If you had been a participant in studies such as those by Milgram and Zimbardo would you want people to know what you did? (see pages 155-156 and 145-146 for more details).

Confidentiality means keeping information private.

- Participants should feel safe that any sensitive information, results or behaviour revealed through research won't be discussed with others.
- Information obtained during a study should remain confidential unless the participant agrees it can be shared with others.
- The study's report shouldn't reveal information or data identifiable to an individual. You shouldn't be able to tell who took part or what their individual data was — these should remain anonymous.

Animal rights

Research with non-human animals has caused heated debate.

- In support, people argue that animal research has provided valuable information for psychological and medical research.
- Some research designs couldn't have been conducted on humans.

> **Example**
>
> Harlow's study on attachment, where young monkeys were separated from their mothers and reared alone (pages 38-39).

- Some disagree with the idea of conducting research with non-human animals. They may argue that it's ethically wrong to inflict harm and suffering on animals, and obviously animals can't give consent to take part.

- Some argue that it's cruel to experiment on animals that have a similar intelligence to humans, because they might suffer the same problems we would. It'd be OK to experiment on animals that are far less developed than us, but there is no point because they'll be too different from us to give results that apply to humans.

Problems with ethical guidelines

There may be researchers who don't follow the guidelines properly. Naughty. If a psychologist conducts research in an unacceptable way, they can't be banned from research (unlike a doctor who can be 'struck off' for misconduct). But they'd probably be kicked out of their university and the BPS. Even when guidelines are followed, it can be difficult to assess things like psychological harm, or to fully justify the use of deception. Deciding whether the ends (benefits from the study) justify the means (how it was done and at what cost) is not straightforward either. This creates another dilemma for psychologists.

Figure 2: *Conducting research on non-human animals has caused a lot of controversy over the years.*

Worked Exam-style Question

1   Milgram et al (1963) investigated obedience to authority. Participants were assigned the role of 'teacher' and witnessed a 'learner' getting strapped into a chair and connected up to a shock generator (the learner was in fact a confederate of the study and did not receive any electric shocks).
  The participant taught the 'learner' pairs of words over an intercom. They had to administer electric shocks of increasing strength for any incorrect answers. As the shocks increased, the learner screamed, and after shocks of 330 V they made no further noise. During the experiment many participants displayed obvious signs of stress, such as sweating, groaning and trembling. Following the experiment the participants were debriefed.

(a) Use the above information to outline the ethical problems associated with this study.   *(6 marks)*

(b) Participants were debriefed after the experiment. Explain why debriefing in this experiment was important.
                                                              (4 marks)

(a) There were many ethical issues associated with this study. Firstly, participants were deceived — they were misled and believed that they were administering electrical shocks to a person and causing them harm when actually they were not.

Also, participants could not give informed consent. They were deceived about aspects of the study and so didn't have enough information for an informed decision — if they had known the true nature of the study it wouldn't have worked.

Finally, many of the participants appeared to suffer from psychological harm during the experiments. They displayed obvious signs of stress, such as sweating, groaning and trembling.

(b) Debriefing was necessary in Milgram's study for a number of reasons. Deception was used during the study. When deception is used,

Exam Tip
Even if you know about this study in great detail, the question just wants you to write about the ethical problems to do with the information given to you in the question.

Exam Tip
Don't just write 'debriefing was necessary as deception was used.' To get all of the available marks you need to explain why participants who have been deceived need to be debriefed.

participants should be told of the true nature of the research as soon as possible after the study.

Debriefing is also an opportunity for the researchers to ensure there are no unforeseen effects on the participants. As participants were seen to experience signs of stress during the study, it was particularly important that the researchers fully debriefed the participants once the experiment was completed.

Summary Questions

Q1 Give a group of people that are unable to give informed consent.

Q2 a) What is confidentiality?

b) Give three reasons why confidentiality is important when conducting psychological research.

Q3 a) Give one argument for using non-human animals in research.

b) Give one argument against using non-human animals in research.

7. Data Analysis

Learning Objective:
- Know about processes involved in content analysis.

Analysing data is where the fun really begins...

Observations

Data from observations should be analysed carefully. If you've got **quantitative data** (i.e. numbers), you can use statistics to show, for example, the most common behaviours. (Quantitative data can be obtained by categorising and rating behaviour — see page 73-74.) **Qualitative data** might consist of a video or audio recording, or written notes on what the observers witnessed. Analysis of qualitative data is less straightforward, but it can still be done. Whatever kind of data you've got, there are some important issues to bear in mind:

- There must be adequate data sampling to ensure that a representative sample of participants' behaviour has been seen.
- Language must be used accurately — the words used to describe behaviour should be accurate and appropriate (and must have valid operationalised definitions).

> **Example**
>
> For example, it might not be appropriate to describe a child's behaviour as 'aggressive' if he or she is play-fighting.

- Researcher bias must be avoided — e.g. it's not okay to make notes only on events that support the researcher's theories, or to have a biased interpretation of what is observed.

Tip: Having a valid operationalised definition allows others to see exactly how you're going to define and measure the behaviour you are observing.
See page 68 for more about operationalised variables.

Interviews

The same goes for data obtained from interviews. When **closed questions** are used as part of an interview's structure, quantitative data can be produced (e.g. the number of participants who replied 'Yes' to a particular question). Statistics can then be used to further analyse the data. When **open questions** are used, more detailed, qualitative data is obtained. Again, whatever you've got, there are certain things you'll need to remember:

- Context — the situation in which a participant said something, and the way they were behaving at the time, may be important. It may help the researcher understand why something was said, and give clues about the honesty of a statement.
- The researcher should clearly distinguish what was said by the participant from how they interpreted it.
- Selection of data — a lot of qualitative data may be produced by an interview, which may be difficult for the researcher to summarise in a report. The researcher must avoid bias in selecting what to include (e.g. only including statements that support their ideas). The interviewees may be consulted when deciding what to include and how to present it.
- The interviewer should be aware of how their feelings about the interviewee could lead to biased interpretations of what they say, or how it is later reported.

Tip: See pages 89-92 for how to statistically analyse data.

Questionnaires

The same also goes for data from questionnaire surveys. Like observations and interviews, surveys can give you both quantitative and qualitative data,

Figure 1: Interviews can produce lots of qualitative data — this can be difficult to summarise objectively.

and so most of the points above are relevant to surveys as well. Again, it's especially important to distinguish the interpretations of the researcher from the statements of the participant, and to be unbiased in selecting what to include in any report on the research. However, the analysis of written answers may be especially difficult because the participant is not present to clarify any ambiguities, plus you don't know the context for their answers (e.g. what mood they were in, and so on).

Qualitative data

Qualitative data is sometimes seen as 'of limited use' because it's difficult to analyse. This is why it's often converted into quantitative data using **content analysis**.

Content analysis

- A representative sample of qualitative data is first collected — e.g. from an interview, printed material (newspapers, etc.) or other media (such as TV programmes).

- Coding units are identified to analyse the data. A coding unit could be, for example, an act of violence, or the use of gender stereotypes (though both of these must be given valid operationalised definitions first — e.g. a definition of an 'act of violence').

- The qualitative data is then analysed to see how often each coding unit occurs (or how much is said about it, etc.).

- A statistical analysis can then be carried out (see pages 89-92).

Figure 2: Qualitative data can be converted into quantitative data using content analysis.

Tip: Gender stereotypes are attitudes and beliefs based on the traditional stereotypical views that are held about each gender.
For instance, women were traditionally seen as the 'home-maker' and therefore have nurturing traits, such as being loving, caring and sensitive.

― Example ―――――

Content analysis could be used to identify the use of gender stereotypes in 'personal ads'.

- Firstly a representative sample of qualitative data is collected — in this example the following 'personal ads' were taken out of a newspaper:

Advert 1:
Sincere, genuine male, 26, seeking attractive, blonde women with good sense of humour. Good looking, likes cheesy music and shark diving.

Advert 2:
Muscular, athletic male, 25, enjoys running, canoeing and football. Seeks sporty female for outdoor pursuits.

Advert 3:
Confident, good looking, muscular male, 32, high earner, fast car. Seeking older woman for long term relationship. Good sense of humour required.

- Coding units are then decided upon — in this case it's gender stereotypical words used to describe males:

Gender stereotypical word
good looking
muscular
athletic
high earner
genuine

Figure 3: Content analysis can be used in many situations — for example qualitative 'personal ads' can be quantified to investigate gender stereotyping.

- The qualitative data is then analysed to see how often each coding unit occurs in each personal ad:

Gender stereotypical word	Advert 1	Advert 2	Advert 3
good looking	✓		✓
muscular		✓	✓
athletic		✓	
high earner			✓
genuine	✓		
Total:	2	2	3

- A statistical analysis can then be carried out.

Tip: Carrying out a statistical analysis allows you to draw conclusions from your results.

Advantages of quantifying data
- It becomes easier to see patterns in the data, and easier to summarise and present it (see pages 100-101).
- Statistical analysis can be carried out.

Disadvantages of quantifying data
- Care is needed to avoid bias in defining coding units, or deciding which behaviours fit particular units.
- Qualitative data has more detail (context, etc.), which is lost when it's converted into numbers.

Because of the detail (and hence the insight) that qualitative data can give, some researchers prefer to avoid 'reducing' it to numbers. Instead they analyse the data into categories or 'typologies' (e.g. sarcastic remarks, statements about feelings, etc.), quotations, summaries, and so on. Hypotheses may be developed during this analysis, rather than being stated previously, so that they are 'grounded in the data'.

Worked Exam-style Questions

1   Jenny is an AS level psychology student. She has conducted an interview using open questions as part of her coursework. She has obtained a lot of qualitative data which she now needs to analyse.

Explain what things Jenny should consider when analysing her data.
(6 marks)

There are a lot of things Jenny needs to consider when analysing her data. She needs to think about the context — the situation in which a participant said something, and the way they were behaving at the time. This is important as it may help Jenny to understand why something was said, and give clues about the honesty of a statement. Jenny also needs to be careful to clearly distinguish what was said by the participant from how she interpreted it — these could be two different things.

Jenny needs to be careful when selecting her data — she has a lot of qualitative data so it may be difficult to summarise it all in a report. Jenny must avoid bias in selecting what to include (e.g. she must not only include statements which support her ideas). She could consult her interviewees when deciding what to include and how to present it.

Exam Tip
Don't just list the things that Jenny should consider — explain why they are important.

Jenny should also be aware of how her feelings about the interviewee could lead to biased interpretations of what they say, or how it is later reported — she needs to remain objective.

---

2 (a) Outline the process involved in content analysis. *(4 marks)*

(b) Give **two** advantages and **two** disadvantages of quantifying data. *(4 marks)*

(a) Content analysis involves converting qualitative data into quantitative data so it can be statistically analysed. Firstly a representative sample of qualitative data is collected, e.g. from an interview, printed material (newspapers, etc.) or other media (such as TV programmes).

Coding units are then identified to analyse the data. These must also be given valid operationalised definitions. A coding unit could be, for example, an act of violence. An operationalised definition would then be a definition of an 'act of violence'.

The qualitative data is then analysed to see how often each coding unit occurs (or how much is said about it, etc.). A statistical analysis can then be carried out.

(b) The advantages of quantifying data are that it becomes easier to see patterns in the data. This makes it easier to summarise and present. It also allows statistical analysis to be carried out, which allows you to see if your results are significant.

Disadvantages are that care must be taken to avoid bias in defining coding units, or when deciding which behaviours fit particular units. Qualitative data also has more detail (context, etc.) than quantitative data, which is lost when it's converted into numbers. This could mean that valuable data is discarded and important information could be overlooked.

Exam Tip
Make sure you've got qualitative and quantitative data sorted in your head. It's really easy to write one when you mean the other. Always read your answers through if you have time at the end of the exam — it'll help you spot any silly mistakes you might have made.

Summary Questions

Q1 A researcher has made a video recording of adults participating in a memory task. What type of data has the researcher collected?

Q2 A researcher observes children playing with a toy in order to study their sharing behaviours. He makes written notes on the behaviours he observes, but only records events that support his theory. What is wrong with this?

Q3 What sort of data is produced when conducting a questionnaire consisting only of closed questions?

8. Descriptive Statistics

Descriptive statistics sound scary and look like maths but actually they're not too bad. They're basically just a way of saying what you see in your data...

Learning Objectives:
Know about the following features of data analysis, presentation and interpretation:

- Analysis and interpretation of quantitative data
- Measures of central tendency including median, mean, mode.
- Measures of dispersion including ranges and standard deviation

What are descriptive statistics?

Descriptive statistics simply describe the patterns found in a set of data. Descriptive statistics uses the fancy term 'central tendency' to describe an average.

┌─ **Examples** ─────────────────────
  The central tendency (average) for the height of a group of 18-year-olds might be about 1.70 metres. The central tendency for coffee consumption in first year university students might be 3 cups per day.

Measures of dispersion describe how spread out the data is.

┌─ **Examples** ─────────────────────
  The difference in height between the shortest 18-year-old and the tallest might be 35 cm. The difference in coffee consumption in first year university students might be 0 cups per day as the minimum and 10 cups per day as the maximum.

Measures of central tendency

There are three measures of central tendency (aka average) you need to know:

The mean

The mean is the 'normal average'. You calculate the mean by adding all of the scores in a data set and then dividing by the number of scores.

$$\text{Mean} = \overline{X} = \frac{\sum X}{N},$$ where $\sum X$ is the sum of all the scores (and there are N of them).

┌─ **Examples** ─────────────────────
  If you've got scores of 2, 5, 6, 7 and 10,
  then $\sum X = 30$ (since all the scores add up to 30),
  and $N = 5$ (since there are 5 of them)...

  ...so the mean is $\overline{X} = \dfrac{30}{5} = \mathbf{6}$.

  Or if you've got scores of 34, 45, 2, 37, 11, 53 and 19,
  then $\sum X = 201$ (since all the scores add up to 201),
  and $N = 7$ (since there are 7 of them)...

  ...so the mean is $\overline{X} = \dfrac{201}{7} = \mathbf{28.71}$.

Figure 1: The central tendency for coffee consumption in students is probably quite high.

Tip: Σ (pronounced 'sigma') just means you add things up.

Tip: Remember to change N to the amount of values in the data set.

Advantages

- It uses all the scores in a data set.
- It's used in further calculations (e.g. standard deviation — see pages 91-92), and so it's handy to work it out.

Disadvantages

- It can be skewed (distorted) by extremely high or low scores. This can make it unrepresentative of most of the scores, and so it may be misleading. For example, the scores 10, 40, 25, 20 and 650 have a mean of 149, which is not representative of the central tendency of the data set. In these cases, it's best to not use the mean.

Tip: Using the median would be a better measure of central tendency here.

- It can sometimes give an unrealistically precise value (e.g. the average home has 2.4 children — but what does 0.4 of a child mean...?)

The median
The median is the middle score when the data is put in order.

> **Examples**
>
> The median of the scores 4, 5, 10, 12 and 14 is **10**.
> In this example there is one score in the middle.
>
> The median of the scores 2, 6, 27, 45, 52, 63 is **36**.
> In this example there are two middle scores (27 and 45). In this case you add these two scores together and then divide by 2 to get the median.
> e.g. 27 + 45 = 72, 72 ÷ 2 = 36

Advantages

- It's relatively quick and easy to calculate.
- It's not affected by extremely high or low scores, so it can be used on 'skewed' sets of data to give a 'representative' average score.

Disadvantages

- Not all the scores are used to work out the median.
- It has little further use in data analysis.

Tip: Remember if data is 'skewed' it means it's distorted and not representative of the scores in the data set.

The mode
The mode is the score that occurs most often.

> **Examples**
>
> The mode (or the modal score) of 2, 5, 2, 9, 6, 11 and 2 is **2**.
>
> If there are two scores which are most common then the data set is 'bimodal'. If there are three or more scores which are most common then the data set is 'multimodal'.
>
> For example, 12, 24, 6, 32, 18, 12, 32, 15, and 10 is a bimodal data set. The modes are **12** and **32**.
>
> For example, 2, 4, 6, 2, 6, 6, 7, 2, 5, 9, 1, 7 and 7 is a multimodal data set. The modes are **2**, **6** and **7**.

Tip: Just think: <u>med</u>ian = <u>med</u>ium (like middle) and <u>mo</u>de = <u>mo</u>st.

Advantages

- It shows the most common or 'important' score.
- It's always a result from the actual data set, so it can be a more useful or realistic statistic, e.g. the modal average family has 2 children, not 2.4.

Disadvantages

- It's not very useful if there are several modal values, or if the modal value is only slightly more common than other scores.
- It has little further use in data analysis.

Tip: The median and the mode are not the most useful measures of central tendency, although they both have their advantages. The mean is probably the most useful — it's often used in further calculations such as standard deviation, which are commonly used when analysing data from psychological experiments.

Measures of dispersion
Measures of dispersion tell you how spread out the data is.

Range
The range is the highest score minus the lowest score.

> **Example**
>
> The range of the scores 6, 10, 35 and 50, is 50 − 6 = **44**
>
> Note that (highest − lowest) +1 can also be used, so the range would then be 45.

Advantage

▪ It's quick and easy to calculate.

Disadvantage

▪ It completely ignores the central values of a data set, so it can be misleading if there are very high or low scores.

The **interquartile range (IQR)** can be calculated to help avoid this problem.

Quartiles divide the data into four equal groups. The median of the lower half of the data is called the lower quartile (or Q1). The median of the upper half is called the upper quartile (or Q3). Q2 is the median of all the data.

1. First put the data in ascending order.
2. Work out which position the quartiles come in the list of numbers using the following formulas:
   Q1 position number = (N + 1)/4
   Q2 position number = 2(N + 1)/4
   Q3 position number = 3(N + 1)/4

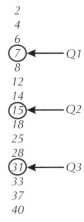

2
4
6
7 ← Q1
8
12
14
15 ← Q2
18
25
28
31 ← Q3
33
37
40

Figure 2: *Example of a data set showing the median, lower quartile and upper quartile.*

--- Example ---

3, 4, 5, 5, 6, 7, 9, 11, 12.

There are 9 values, so N = 9.
        Q1 position no. = (9 + 1)/4 = 2.5
        Q2 position no. = 2(9 + 1)/4 = 5
        Q3 position no. = 3(9 + 1)/4 = 7.5

So in the list of numbers:

3	4	5	5	6	7	9	11	12

Q_1 Q_2 Q_3
(4 + 5)/2 = **4.5**   (9 + 11)/2 = **10** = **6**

Tip: If you get position numbers that are 'half values', like in this example, find the halfway point of the two numbers either side of this position. This is just like finding the median (see page 90).

Standard deviation

The standard deviation measures how much scores deviate from the mean. It looks at the 'spread' of data. Unlike the range, the standard deviation uses all the values in a data set to give a measure of spread.

--- Example ---

Working out the standard deviation of the height of a group of 18-year-olds, would tell us how spread out the heights are, in relation to the mean height of the group.

Tip: X represents a score in the data set. $\bar{X}$ stands for the mean.

It's calculated by $s = \sqrt{\dfrac{\sum (X - \bar{X})^2}{N}}$, where s = standard deviation

The smaller the standard deviation is, the narrower the data range, and the closer the data values are to the mean.

--- Examples ---

Example 1: Scores = 5, 9, 10, 11 and 15. The mean = 10.

So the standard deviation is:

$$s = \sqrt{\frac{(5-10)^2 + (9-10)^2 + (10-10)^2 + (11-10)^2 + (15-10)^2}{5}} = \textbf{3.22} \text{ (to 3 s.f.)}$$

Figure 3: *The standard deviation measures the 'spread' of data — for example the 'spread' of heights across this group of 18-year-olds.*

Example 2: Scores = 12, 33, 18, 27, 14 and 16. The mean = 20.

So the standard deviation is:

$$s = \sqrt{\frac{(12-20)^2 + (33-20)^2 + (18-20)^2 + (27-20)^2 + (14-20)^2 + (16-20)^2}{6}} = 7.51 \text{ (to 3 s.f.)}$$

Advantage

- All scores in the set are taken into account, so it's more accurate than the range. It can also be used in further analysis.

Disadvantage

- It's not as quick or easy to calculate as the range.

Worked Exam-style Questions

1   Joanne conducted an experiment to test the capacity of short term memory. She gave her participants a list of letters and asked them to repeat the letters back to her in the same order. The participants were given a score resulting from the maximum number of letters they remembered correctly.
    Joanne's results are shown in the table below:

Participant	Score
1	8
2	7
3	9
4	7
5	7
6	4

(a) Calculate the mean of Joanne's data.   (1 mark)

(b) Calculate the median for Joanne's data.   (1 mark)

(c) Calculate the mode for Joanne's data.   (1 mark)

(d) What is the range of Joanne's data?   (1 mark)

(a) $mean = \bar{X} = \dfrac{\sum X}{N}$

$\sum X = 8 + 7 + 9 + 7 + 7 + 4 = 42, \quad N = 6$

$\bar{X} = \dfrac{42}{6} = 7$

(b) 4, 7, 7, 7, 8, 9
    $7 + 7 = 14, \ 14 \div 2 = 7$
    Median = 7

(c) 4, 7, 7, 7, 8, 9
    Mode = 7

(d) Range = 9 − 4 = 5

2   Zainab measured people's heart rates after a staged car crash in
    order to study the body's initial reaction to stress.
    Her results are shown in the table below:

Participant	Heart rate (bpm)
A	115
B	94
C	119
D	97
E	117
F	150
G	101
H	111

Calculate the standard deviation of Zainab's results.
Give your answer to 3 significant figures.   *(5 marks)*

$$s = \sqrt{\frac{\sum (X - \bar{X})^2}{N}}, \text{ where } s = \text{standard deviation} \ \blacksquare$$

$$mean = \bar{X} = \frac{\sum X}{N}$$

$$\sum X = 115 + 94 + 119 + 97 + 117 + 150 + 101 + 111 = 904 \ \blacksquare$$

$$N = 8$$

$$\bar{X} = \frac{904}{8} = 113$$

$$s = \sqrt{\frac{\begin{array}{c}(115-113)^2 + (94-113)^2 + (119-113)^2 + (97-113)^2 \\ + (117-113)^2 + (150-113)^2 + (101-113)^2 + (111-113)^2\end{array}}{8}} = 16.5 \ (to \ 3 \ s.f.) \ \blacksquare$$

Exam Tip
Make sure you write out
the equation. It'll make
sure you don't forget to
do anything important in
your calculation.

Exam Tip
The first thing you have
to do is work out the
mean for the data set.

Exam Tip
Finally stick all your
values into the standard
deviation equation.

Summary Questions

Q1 Mean and mode are two ways of measuring central tendency.
    What is the other measure of central tendency?

Q2 Give one disadvantage of using the mean as a measure of
    central tendency.

Q3 What is the mode?

Q4 What do measures of dispersion tell you?

Q5 Steve is investigating the audience effect. He times how long it takes
    for people to complete a mental arithmetic test in the presence of an
    audience. His results are shown below:

Participant	A	B	C	D	E	F	G	H	I	J	K
Time (minutes)	3	4	5	11	9	12	7	6	5	7	9

Calculate the interquartile range for Steve's data.

9. Correlations

Learning Objectives:

Know about the following features of data analysis, presentation and interpretation:

- Analysis and interpretation of correlational data
- Positive and negative correlations and the interpretation of correlation coefficients

There's a bit more maths here so brace yourself...

Correlation between variables

Correlation is a measure of the relationship between two variables.

> **Examples**
>
> Correlation can tell you how closely exam grades are related to the amount of revision that someone's done, or how the number of fillings a person has relates to how many sweets they eat.

In a correlational study, data is collected for some kind of correlational analysis.

The correlation coefficient

The **correlation coefficient** is a number between –1 and +1. To find the correlation between two variables, you first have to collect some data. For example, you could ask every student in a class how many hours of study they did each week, and note their average test result.

Student	Hours of study	Average test score — %
A	4	58
B	1	23
C	7	67
D	15	89
E	2	34
F	11	78
G	8	60
H	18	98
I	12	86
J	5	45

Figure 1: You can use the correlation coefficient to see if there's a relationship between the hours spent studying per week and a person's test scores.

You can then work out a correlation coefficient (e.g. Spearman's rho — see page 96). This is a number between –1 and +1, and shows:

- How closely the variables are linked. This is shown by the size of the number — if it's close to +1 or –1, then they are very closely related, while a smaller number means the relationship is less strong (or maybe not there at all if it's close to 0).

- The type of correlation — a positive correlation coefficient (i.e. between 0 and +1) means that the variables rise and fall together, while a negative correlation coefficient (i.e. between –1 and 0) means that as one variable rises, the other falls.

Tip: If you work out a correlation coefficient and get a value that doesn't fall between +1 or –1 then you know that you've gone wrong somewhere.

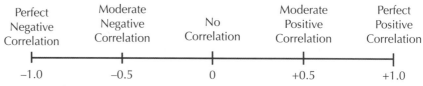

Perfect Negative Correlation	Moderate Negative Correlation	No Correlation	Moderate Positive Correlation	Perfect Positive Correlation
–1.0	–0.5	0	+0.5	+1.0

Figure 2: Scale showing correlation coefficients and their meanings.

The correlation coefficient for the data above is around 0.97. This means that there is a strong positive correlation coefficient — as hours of study increase, the average test score increases. As the number is very close to +1 it shows that there is a very close relationship between the two variables.

Scattergrams

Correlation is easy to see on scattergrams.

Tip: For more information on scattergrams see page 101.

1. Positive correlation

This means that as one variable rises, so does the other (and likewise, if one falls, so does the other.)

Example

Hours of study and average test score — the correlation coefficient is roughly 0.75 (close to +1).

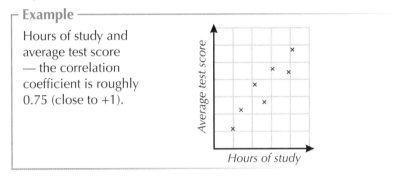

Tip: You can draw a line of best fit on your scattergram to show the general pattern of the data and to highlight the correlation shown. You can do it by eye — just remember that it needs to pass as close to as many points as possible, and you should end up with roughly the same number of points on each side of the line — see Figure 3 for an example.

2. Negative correlation

This means that as one variable rises, the other one falls (and vice versa).

Example

Hours of TV watched each week and average test score — the correlation coefficient is roughly −0.75 (close to −1).

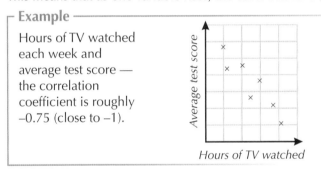

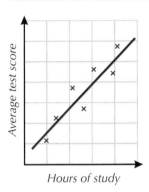

Figure 3: *Scattergram with line of best fit.*

3. No correlation

If the correlation coefficient is 0 (or close to 0), the variables aren't linked.

Example

A student's height and their average test score — the correlation coefficient is roughly 0.01 (close to 0).

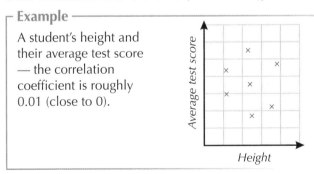

Tip: It's easy to tell if there's no correlation when looking at a scattergram — there's no pattern at all to the plotted points.

Advantages of correlational research

- Because correlational research doesn't involve controlling any variables, you can do it when (for practical or ethical reasons) you couldn't do a controlled experiment. For example, an experiment into the effects of smoking on humans probably wouldn't be done for ethical reasons, but a correlation between smoking and cancer could be established from hospital records.

- Correlational analysis can give ideas for future research (e.g. biological research on the effects of smoking).
- Correlation can even be used to test for reliability and validity (e.g. by testing the results of the same test taken twice by the same people — a good reliable test will show a high correlation).

Limitations of correlational research

- Correlational analysis can't establish 'cause and effect' relationships — it can only show that there's a statistical link between the variables. Variables can be closely correlated without changes in one causing changes in the other — a third variable could be involved. Only a controlled experiment can show cause and effect relationships.
- Care must be taken when interpreting correlation coefficients — high correlation coefficients could be down to chance. To decide whether a correlation is significant, you have to use a proper significance test.

***Figure 4:** A positive correlation between the number of storks in a town and the number of births doesn't necessarily mean that storks cause women to get pregnant. Perhaps a third variable is at work.*

> ### Examples
>
> The number of births in a town was found to be positively correlated to the number of storks that nested in that town — but that didn't mean that more storks caused the increase. (It was because more people in the town led to more births, and also to more houses with chimneys to nest on.)
>
> A study found that the level of stress experienced at work was positively correlated to the risk of suffering from a heart attack. There may be a statistical link between work related stress levels and heart attacks but we can't conclude that stress causes heart attacks. A third variable may also be at work, for instance all the people in the study may have a poor diet, be obese and smoke — all factors known to increase the risk of heart attacks.

Spearman's rho correlation coefficient

To work out (and then test the significance of) **Spearman's rho correlation coefficient**, you need values for two different variables (e.g. hours of revision and average test scores for 10 students).

- The values for each variable are placed into rank order (each variable is ranked separately). The lowest value for each variable gets rank 1 (and in the above example, the biggest value will get rank 10).
- The difference (d) in ranks for each student's variables is calculated. (So a particular student may have done the most revision, but got the 3rd best results, in which case the difference in ranks will be d = 3 − 1 = 2.)
- The value of d for each student is squared, then the results are added together (to get $\sum d^2$).
- Then the special Spearman's correlation coefficient calculation is done, which is:

$$r_s = 1 - \frac{6 \times \sum d^2}{N \times (N^2 - 1)}$$, where N is the number of students, or whatever.

- To find out whether the result is significant (and so whether the variables are linked), you compare the outcome of the calculation with a critical value that you look up in a statistics table.

Tip: If you have two values the same they share a rank — add the two ranks together and divide by 2.
For example, if you had two identical values at rank 3 and 4 then you would do 3 + 4 = 7, then 7 ÷ 2 = 3.5.
They would both get the rank 3.5.

Tip: r_s is just a shortened way of saying Spearman's rho correlation coefficient, (which is a bit of a mouthful).

Example

The hours of study and average test scores for the class are shown in the table below. The first thing to do is place the variables in rank order:

Student	Hours of study	Rank	Average test score — %	Rank
A	4	3	58	4
B	1	1	23	1
C	7	5	67	6
D	15	9	89	9
E	2	2	34	2
F	11	7	78	7
G	8	6	60	5
H	18	10	98	10
I	12	8	86	8
J	5	4	45	3

Tip: The lowest value for each variable gets rank 1. In this example the biggest value gets rank 10.

- Then work out the difference (d) in ranks for each student's variables.

  Student A — Hours of study rank = 3   Average test score rank = 4
  d = 4 – 3 = 1

  Student B — Hours of study rank = 1   Average test score rank = 1
  d = 1 – 1 = 0

  Student C — Hours of study rank = 5   Average test score rank = 6
  d = 6 – 5 = 1

  etc.

Tip: You just find the difference between the two numbers, so always subtract the lowest from the highest, e.g. for student A you get d = 1, not d = -1.

- Once you have done this for all your data the value of d for each student is squared, then the results are added together (to get $\sum d^2$):

Student	Hours of study	Rank	Average test score — %	Rank	d	d^2
A	4	3	58	4	1	1
B	1	1	23	1	0	0
C	7	5	67	6	1	1
D	15	9	89	9	0	0
E	2	2	34	2	0	0
F	11	7	78	7	0	0
G	8	6	60	5	1	1
H	18	10	98	10	0	0
I	12	8	86	8	0	0
J	5	4	45	3	1	1
					$\sum d^2$	4

Tip: It's handy to add rows for d and d^2 to your table — it will help you avoid silly mistakes when calculating d and will make sure you don't forget to square your d values.

- The Spearman's correlation coefficient calculation can now be done:

$$r_s = 1 - \frac{6 \times \sum d^2}{N \times (N^2 - 1)}, \quad N = 10$$

Tip: N is the number of students in the sample.

Tip: Significance is really important in psychology. It's all to do with the likelihood that the results aren't just down to chance, and whether or not you should accept or reject the null hypothesis. However, you don't need to worry about it until A2, so for now, just get your head around correlation.

$$r_s = 1 - \frac{6 \times 4}{10 \times (10^2 - 1)}$$

$= \mathbf{0.976}$ (3 s.f.)

- The result is very close to +1. This shows that there is a strong positive correlation between hours spent studying and average test score. You could also compare the result of the calculation with a critical value from a statistics table to see if the result is significant.

Worked Exam-style Questions

1 Charlotte is studying the effect of heart rate on people's reaction times. Participants completed a simple reaction test with very loud music playing. Their heart rate and reaction times are shown below:

Participant	Heart rate (bpm)	Reaction time (s)
A	128	2.6
B	132	1.2
C	76	0.4
D	136	2.1
E	69	0.5
F	72	0.6
G	69	0.7
H	68	0.8
I	71	0.9
J	84	1.3

(a) Calculate Spearman's rho correlation coefficient for this data. Give your answer to 3 significant figures. *(8 marks)*

(b) Use your answer to part (a) to comment on the relationship between heart rate and reaction time. *(3 marks)*

Tip: Drawing out the table in the exam will probably make the question easier to answer, and stop you making mistakes. It also allows the examiner to see your working.

(a)

Participant	*Heart rate (bpm)*	*Rank*	*Reaction time (s)*	*Rank*	*d*	*d²*
A	*128*	*8*	*2.6*	*10*	*2*	*4*
B	*132*	*9*	*1.2*	*7*	*2*	*4*
C	*76*	*6*	*0.4*	*1*	*5*	*25*
D	*136*	*10*	*2.1*	*9*	*1*	*1*
E	*69*	*2.5*	*0.5*	*2*	*0.5*	*0.25*
F	*72*	*5*	*0.6*	*3*	*2*	*4*
G	*69*	*2.5*	*0.7*	*4*	*1.5*	*2.25*
H	*68*	*1*	*0.8*	*5*	*4*	*16*
I	*71*	*4*	*0.9*	*6*	*2*	*4*
J	*84*	*7*	*1.3*	*8*	*1*	*1*

Exam Tip
Remember that if two scores are the same then they share a rank. In this case they score 2nd and 3rd for heart rate, so they both rank 2.5.

$$\sum d^2 = 61.5$$

$$r_s = 1 - \frac{6 \times \sum d^2}{N \times (N^2 - 1)}, \ N = 10 \ \blacksquare$$

$$r_s = 1 - \frac{6 \times 61.5}{10 \times (10^2 - 1)}$$

$= 0.627$ to 3 s.f.

(b) There is a positive correlation between heart rate and reaction time as the correlation coefficient has a positive value. This means that as heart rate increases, reaction time also increases. The value of 0.628 is between 0.5 and 1.0, so the relationship is fairly strong.

Exam Tip
It's helpful to write out the equation in full — it shows the examiner your working and you're less likely to make mistakes than if you just put the numbers into your calculator.

---

2   José is conducting an investigation to look at the effects of alcohol consumption on aggression levels. After statistical analysis of the results, a correlation coefficient of 0.98 is produced between the amount of alcohol consumed and acts of aggression displayed.

   (a) Using the correlation coefficient, comment on the relationship between alcohol consumption and aggression.

(3 marks)

   (b) José concludes that alcohol causes aggression. Explain why many psychologists would disagree with José's conclusion.

(4 marks)

Exam Tip
There are 3 marks, so comment on whether the correlation coefficient is positive or negative, what this means, and how strong the relationship is.

(a) A correlation coefficient value of 0.98 shows a positive correlation between alcohol and aggression as the value is a positive number. So, as alcohol consumption increases, so does aggression level. 0.98 is very close to 1.0, therefore the relationship between the two variables is very strong.

(b) José can't conclude that alcohol definitely causes aggression. Just because there is a strong positive correlation between the two variables does not mean that one variable causes another. Correlational analysis cannot establish 'cause and effect' — it can only show that there's a statistical link between the variables. Variables can be closely correlated without changes in one causing changes in the other — a third variable could be involved. In addition, high correlation coefficients could just be down to chance.

Exam Tip
Start off by saying whether you agree with José, and then go on to say why — this is where the marks come from.

Summary Questions

Q1 a) Troy works out a correlation coefficient and gets a value of 2.56. How can you tell his value is wrong?

   b) Troy does the calculation again and gets a correlation coefficient of −0.5. How would you describe this correlation?

Q2 Clark gets a correlation coefficient of 0. How would you describe this correlation?

Q3 Give one advantage of correlational research.

Q4 How can you check to see if your correlation coefficient is significant?

10. Summarising the Data

Once you've collected your data presenting it as a graph or table can help you to visualise trends and make comparisons...

Presenting data

Data can be presented in various ways. Qualitative data from observations, interviews, surveys, etc. (see pages 85-87) can be presented in a report as a 'verbal summary'. The report would contain summaries of what was seen or said, possibly using categories to group data together. Also quotations from participants can be used, and any research hypotheses that developed during the study or data analysis may be discussed. When quantitative data is collected (or produced from qualitative data, e.g. by a content analysis), it can be summarised and presented in various ways.

Tip: Have a look at pages 86-87 for more on content analysis. It's a way of turning qualitative data into quantitative data.

Tables

Tables are a good way to summarise quantitative data. They can be used to clearly present the data and show any patterns in the scores. Tables of 'raw data' show the scores before any analysis has been done on them. Other tables may show descriptive statistics such as the mean, range and standard deviation (see pages 89-92).

Type of ice cream	Quality (score out of 10)		
	Tastiness	Thickness	Throwability
Chocolate	9	7	6
Toffee	8	6	7
Strawberry	8	5	4
Earwax	2	9	8

Figure 1: *Table to show the qualities of different types of ice cream.*

Bar Charts

Bar charts (bar graphs) are usually used to present 'non-continuous data' (like when a variable falls into categories rather than being measured on a numbered scale). The bar chart below shows the mean number of words recalled by different groups in a memory experiment. Note that the columns in bar charts don't touch each other. Also, it's preferable to always show the full vertical scale, or clearly indicate when it isn't all shown (otherwise it can be misleading — see Figure 3).

Bar chart showing customer service satisfaction.

Figure 3: *Not showing a full vertical scale can be misleading. Customer service may look good in this graph, but in fact the rating scale went up to 100 — not such great service now.*

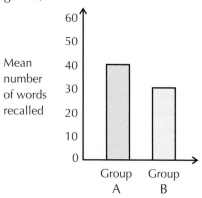

Figure 2: *Bar chart showing the mean number of words recalled by two groups in a memory experiment.*

Histograms

Histograms are for when you have continuous data — they show data measured on a 'continuous' scale of measurement. The histogram below shows the time different participants took to complete a task. Each column shows a class interval (here, each class interval is 10 seconds), and the columns touch each other. It's the height of the column that shows the number of values in that interval. (All intervals are shown, even if there are no scores within them.)

Tip: At first glance a bar chart and a histogram might look like the same thing. The big clue is if there are gaps between the bars — if there are, it's a bar chart. If not, it's a histogram.

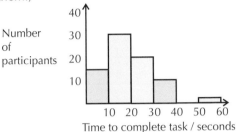

Figure 4: Histogram showing the time participants took to complete a task.

Tip: Continuous data includes things like, height, temperature and time — it's things that fall on a scale. Non-continuous data includes things like exam grades, types of ice cream and names of football teams — things that fall into distinct categories.

Frequency polygons

Frequency polygons are good for showing more than one set of data. They are similar to histograms, but use lines to show where the top of each column would reach. It can be useful to combine two or more frequency polygons on the same set of axes — then it's easy to make comparisons between groups.

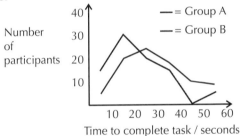

Figure 5: Frequency polygon showing the time participants in two groups took to complete a task.

Scattergrams

Scattergrams are a good way of visualising relationships between variables — correlation is really easy to spot on scattergrams. On a scattergram the data points are just plotted — they're never joined together. However, if there's a relationship between variables, you can draw a line of best fit to show the trend. This is a line that fits the general pattern of the data and that passes as close to as many of the points as possible. You should end up with roughly the same number of points plotted on each side of your line.

Tip: Scattergrams can also be called scatter graphs or scatter diagrams — they're all the same thing.

Tip: For more on scattergrams and correlations see pages 94-96.

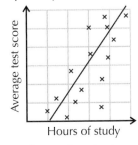

Figure 6: Scattergram showing hours of study plotted against average test scores.

Worked Exam-style Question

1 Yvonne is investigating the relationship between the time spent playing violent video games and aggression levels in children. Her results are shown in the table below.

Participant	Hours per week spent playing violent video games	Aggression rating
A	5	7
B	4	5
C	2	4
D	8	6
E	9	10
F	1	2
G	7	8
H	2	1
I	6	5
J	10	9

(a) Draw a scattergram of the results. *(3 marks)*

(b) Draw a line of best fit on your graph *(1 mark)*

(a) & (b)

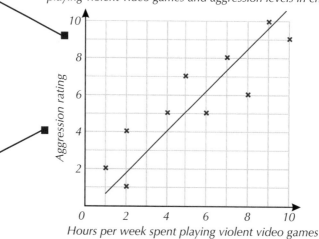

Scattergram to show the relationship between time spent playing violent video games and aggression levels in children.

Exam Tip
Drawing a scattergram is worth 3 marks in this question. You get 1 mark for the title, 1 mark for labelling the axes, and 1 mark for accurately plotting the points on the graph. So, plot your points carefully, and don't forget to label the axes and give your graph a title — it's an easy way to lose marks if you don't.

Exam Tip
Remember, a line of best fit follows the general pattern of the data. It should pass as close to as many points as possible, and should have roughly the same number of points either side of the line.

Summary Questions

Q1 How might qualitative data from an interview be presented?

Q2 What is raw data?

Q3 Why is it important to try and show the full vertical scale in a bar chart?

Q4 What kind of data is shown on histograms — continuous or non-continuous?

Q5 What is the difference between a frequency polygon and a histogram?

Section Summary

- Research methods in psychology include, laboratory experiments, field experiments, natural experiments, observations, correlations, questionnaires, interviews and case studies.

- An aim is a statement of a study's purpose, while a hypothesis is a clear statement of what's being tested. There are different kinds of hypotheses, and they can be directional or non-directional.

- The independent variable (IV) is a variable directly manipulated by the researcher, and the dependent variable (DV) is the variable that you think is affected by changes in the IV.

- Extraneous variables are any variables that could affect what you're trying to measure. If these variables are actually influencing the DV then they're called confounding variables.

- Variables need to be operationalised — this means describing how the variable will be measured.

- There are three types of experimental design — independent groups, repeated measures and matched pairs.

- Pilot studies help foresee any problems before running the main study.

- Variables need to be controlled to minimise any unwanted effects.

- Reliability and validity are really important things in psychological research.

- In participant observations the researcher participates in the activity under study, while in non-participant observations the researcher observes the activity without getting involved in it.

- When designing a naturalistic observation it must be decided how data is going to be recorded, categorised and rated. How often and for how long participants are going to be observed must also be considered. Inter-observer reliability is another important factor — it ensures that observers agree on what behaviours are being displayed and what scores to give, etc.

- Questionnaires and interviews can consist of open questions or closed questions. Open questions produce qualitative data, while closed questions produce quantitative data. The use of complex language, double-barrelled, leading or ambiguous questions should be avoided.

- A sample for a study should be representative of the target group. Random sampling, opportunity sampling and volunteer sampling are ways of selecting people to participate in a study.

- Participants sometimes act differently when they're being observed so their data may not be valid or reliable. Researcher behaviour can also influence the outcome of a study.

- Ethics must be considered when designing an experiment.

- The British Psychological Society has developed ethical guidelines to help psychologists resolve ethical issues such as deception, informed consent, psychological harm, confidentiality and animal rights.

- Observations, questionnaires and interviews can produces lots of qualitative data. This can be converted into quantitative data using content analysis — this data can then be statistically analysed.

- Descriptive statistics describe patterns found in a set of data. Measures of central tendency (averages) include mean, mode and median, while measures of dispersion (the spread of data) include range, the interquartile range and standard deviation.

- Correlation is a measure of the relationship between two variables. Spearman's rho correlation coefficient is a calculation which produces a value between -1 and $+1$. If the value is between 0 and $+1$, the correlation is positive — as one variable increases so does the other. If the value is between -1 and 0, the correlation is negative — as one variable increases the other decreases. The size of the number represents the strength of the relationship between the variables.

- Qualitative data can be presented as a 'verbal summary'. Quantitative data can be presented as a table, bar chart, histogram, frequency polygon or scattergram.

Exam-style Questions

1   A psychologist conducts a study investigating the effectiveness of a new type of anti-anxiety drug. The drug is believed to decrease the body's response to stressful situations. Participants complete a health questionnaire and have their heart rate taken. They are then allocated to either the study group or a control group. The study group are given the anti-anxiety drug, but the control group are given a placebo. Both groups are told that it reduces heart rate when the body responds to a stressful situation.

Participants are then taken to a waiting room where a staged stress-inducing event takes place. A man enters and begins shouting at the participants, before being removed by a security guard. Immediately afterwards the participants have their heart rates taken again. The results are shown in the table below:

Condition	Participant	Heart rate before stress-inducing event (bpm)	Heart rate after stress-inducing event (bpm)
Study group	A	67	89
	B	85	110
	C	76	92
	D	101	115
	E	92	134
	Mean heart rate	84.2	108
Control group	A	66	159
	B	87	117
	C	88	180
	D	98	99
	E	84	163
	Mean heart rate		

1 (a) (i)   The psychologist puts up posters around a university asking for volunteers to participate in a study looking at the effects of a new drug on heart rate. What sampling technique is being used in this study?

(1 mark)

(a) (ii)   Give **one** advantage and **one** disadvantage of this sampling technique.

(2 marks)

1 (b)   The participants in each condition are matched on variables like age, sex, body weight, lifestyle choices, etc. What experimental design is used in this study?

(1 mark)

1 (c)   Calculate the mean heart rate of the control group before and after the stress-inducing event.

(2 marks)

Exam-style Questions

1 (d)   Outline the ethical issues in this study.

(6 marks)

2   A psychologist is investigating the effects of day care on social development.
She watches videotapes of children playing in the playground during their first
3 months of day care and makes written notes of various behaviours she observes.

2 (a)   What type of research method is this?

(1 mark)

2 (b)   The psychologist thinks that the longer the children spend in day care, the less time
they will spend playing alone. Her results are shown in the table below:

Child	Hours per week spent in day care	Average time spent playing alone (minutes per hour)
A	30	12
B	10	25
C	5	50
D	15	41
E	32	7
F	5	48
G	35	10
H	7	60
I	12	38
J	2	52

2 (b) (i)   Write a non-directional hypothesis for this study.

(1 mark)

(b) (ii)   Write a directional hypothesis for this study.

(1 mark)

2 (c)   The correlation coefficient for the data is –0.855.
Comment on the relationship between time spent in day care and
time spent playing alone.

(3 marks)

2 (d)   The psychologist conducted her study in one day care centre.
Explain whether the sample used in this study is representative of
the target population.

(2 marks)

Learning Objective:
- Know about the research methods associated with biological psychology.

1. The Biological Approach

The biological approach is all about, well, biology really. Biological psychologists try to explain behaviour in relation to what's going on in the body.

Assumptions of the biological approach

The biological approach has three key assumptions:

- Human behaviour can be explained by looking at biological stuff such as hormones, genetics, evolution and the nervous system.
- In theory, if we can explain all behaviour using biological causes, unwanted behaviour could be modified or removed using biological treatments such as medication for mental illness.
- Experimental research conducted using animals can inform us about human behaviour and biological influences, because we share a lot of biological similarities.

Research methods in biological research

Here are some of the research methods used in biological research that you should know about:

Experiments (also see pages 61-62)

Experiments try to establish cause and effect by comparing groups and analysing any differences between them. For example, Krantz et al (1991) conducted a laboratory experiment into the impact of stress on the heart (page 115). Experiments are useful in this area because they can investigate possible biological causes of behaviour. However, other variables have to be very tightly controlled, as they can affect the results of a study.

Correlations (also see page 63, and pages 94-96)

Correlations describe the relationship between two variables. For example, Holmes and Rahe (1967) (page 119) found a positive correlation between the amount of stressful life events and ill health experienced. As one variable increases, so does the other. Correlations only show a relationship, not a cause and effect — e.g. we can't say that the stressful life events themselves caused the health problems. They're useful for establishing relationships between variables and often lead to further research.

Case studies (also see page 64)

Case studies are used to investigate things that couldn't be investigated any other way. For example, Milner et al (1957) reported a case study of a man who suffered memory loss after having part of his brain removed to reduce his epilepsy (see pages 10-11). Case studies are useful for investigating a situation in great depth. However, they can't be generalised to other people as they're often unique situations.

Questionnaires and interviews (also see pages 63-64)

Questionnaires and interviews are used to collect information from

Figure 1: *Experiments on animals can tell researchers a lot about biological influences on behaviour.*

Tip: You also need to know about the ethical issues of these research methods — see pages 81-83.

people directly. For example, Holmes and Rahe (1967) used these techniques to get people to rate how stressful individual events were to them (see page 119). They rely on the honesty of the person but can provide very detailed information.

Brain scanning

Brain scanning is used to investigate possible abnormalities. There are various types of brain scanning out there — some just look at the structure and others look at function.

┌─ Examples ──────────────────────────────

Brain scanning techniques include computed tomography (CT), diffuse optical imaging (DOI), positron emission tomography (PET — see below), magnetoencephalography (MEG), event-related optical signalling (EROS) and magnetic resonance imaging (MRI — see below).

Magnetic Resonance Imaging (MRI)

MRI scans use magnetic fields to produce a detailed image of the brain that can show up abnormalities such as tumours and structural problems. It can also show brain activity by monitoring blood flow to different areas.

Positron Emission Tomography (PET)

PET scans measure brain activity by using sensors placed on the head to track a radioactive substance that is injected into the person. PET scans can show which areas of the brain are more active when the person performs an activity such as counting. This helps us to understand about function and communication within the brain.

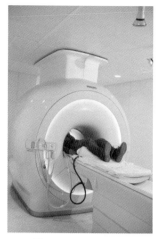

Figure 2: A patient undergoing an MRI scan.

Both techniques are pretty expensive to use during research. However, it's useful to be able to see which parts of the brain are activated during certain activities, as different functions are performed in different parts of the brain. Certain functions are generally localised more in one of the two hemispheres of the brain. This is known as **brain lateralisation**.

┌─ Examples ──────────────────────────────

Left hemisphere functions:

language (e.g. speech, reading, writing)

arithmetic

visually recognising words and letters

logical functioning

Right hemisphere functions:

problem solving

recognising faces

emotion

music

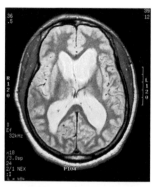

Figure 3: MRI scan of the brain of a patient with Alzheimer's disease.

Strengths and weaknesses of the biological approach

Strengths

- The approach can provide evidence to support or disprove a theory — it's a very scientific approach.

- If a biological cause can be found for mental health problems or for unwanted behaviour such as aggression, then biological treatments can be developed to help individuals.

Weaknesses

- The approach doesn't take into account the influence of people's environment, their family, childhood experiences or their social situation. Other approaches see these as being important factors in

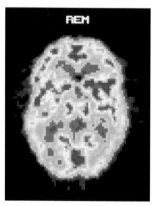

Figure 4: PET scan of the brain showing activity during REM sleep.

explaining behaviour.

- Using a biological explanation for negative behaviour can lead to individuals or groups avoiding taking personal or social responsibility for their behaviour.

Worked Exam-style Questions

1   Case studies are used in the biological approach.

1   (a) Give one advantage and one disadvantage of using case studies in the biological approach.   *(2 marks)*

1   (b) Outline and evaluate one other research technique used in the biological approach.   *(6 marks)*

(a) An advantage of using case studies is that they can be used to investigate things that couldn't be investigated any other way. For example, Milner et al (1957) reported a case study of a man who suffered memory loss after having part of his brain removed to reduce his epilepsy.

A disadvantage of using case studies is that the findings can't be generalised to other people as they're often unique situations.

(b) Brain scanning is another technique used in the biological approach. For example, Magnetic Resonance Imaging (MRI) and Positron Emission Tomography (PET) are two types of brain scanning often used to investigate brain abnormalities in biological psychology.

MRI uses magnetic fields to produce a detailed image of the brain that can show up abnormalities such as tumours and structural problems. It can also show brain activity by monitoring blood flow to different areas.

PET measures brain activity by using sensors placed on the head to track a radioactive substance that is injected into the person. PET scans can show which areas of the brain are more active when the person performs an activity such as counting. This helps us to understand about function and communication within the brain.

One problem is that both techniques are pretty expensive to use during research. However, if a biological cause can be found for mental health problems or for unwanted behaviour such as aggression, then biological treatments can be developed to help individuals.

It's also useful to be able to see which parts of the brain are activated during certain activities, as different functions are performed in different parts of the brain. As it's a very scientific approach, brain scanning can provide evidence to support or disprove a theory.

Exam Tip
You need to give one advantage and one disadvantage for the marks. Giving two advantages and no disadvantages will only get you one mark.

Exam Tip
You don't need to talk about loads of scanning methods — just pick one or two. Start by outlining each technique. Just briefly describe how each one works and what it can show.

Exam Tip
Then go on to evaluate the techniques. This means that you have to give a balanced assessment of any positive and negative points.

Summary Questions

Q1 Give one basic assumption of the biological approach.

Q2 A psychological study finds a positive correlation between having a stressful job and having a heart attack. Can it be concluded that having a stressful job causes heart attacks? Explain your answer.

Q3 Give a disadvantage of using questionnaires and interviews as a research method.

Q4 What is meant by the term 'brain lateralisation'?

2. Stress as a Bodily Response

Before we get going on stress it's probably a good call to cover some biology basics about the nervous and hormonal systems. Just so you know what I'm talking about really...

Learning Objective:
- Know about the body's response to stress, including the pituitary-adrenal system and the sympathomedullary pathway in outline.

The nervous system

The nervous system consists of two key parts, the **central nervous system (CNS)** and the **peripheral nervous system (PNS)**:

1. The CNS

The CNS is made up of the brain and the spinal cord (see Figure 1).

2. The PNS

The PNS is made up of the neurones that connect the CNS to the rest of the body. Within the PNS is the autonomic nervous system (ANS). The ANS is responsible for our unconscious activities, e.g. digestion, breathing, etc.

The ANS has two divisions which have opposite effects on the body. One branch, the sympathetic nervous system, gets the body ready for action. It's the 'fight or flight' system. The other branch, the parasympathetic nervous system, calms the body down. It's the 'rest and digest' system (see Figure 2).

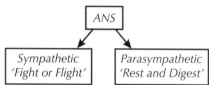

Figure 2: The two branches of the autonomic nervous system.

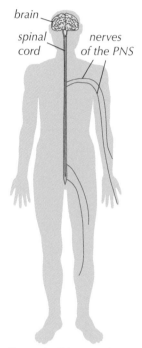

Figure 1: Diagram showing the CNS along with some of the nerves of the PNS.

Neurones

The cells of the nervous system are called neurones (see Figure 3). They transmit information as electrical impulses around the body. Neurones have branched endings called dendrons — these allow them to connect to and communicate with lots of other neurones. The connection between two neurones is called a synapse. It's basically just a very small gap — the nerve impulse is transmitted across it by chemicals called neurotransmitters. When an electrical impulse reaches a synapse it causes neurotransmitter molecules to be released. These molecules diffuse across the synapse and stimulate receptors on the next neurone. This then sets off a new impulse in the next neurone (see Figure 4). This allows the nervous system to transmit information very quickly.

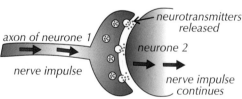

Figure 4: Transmission of an electrical impulse across a synapse.

The hormonal system

Hormones are chemicals which are produced by glands. They're released directly into the bloodstream and travel around the body in the blood. They can only affect cells which have the right receptors for each specific hormone — these are target cells. An organ that contains target cells is called a target organ. Hormones transmit information much more slowly than neurones.

> **Examples**
>
> Examples of hormones include insulin, glucagon, adrenaline, noradrenaline, oestrogen and corticosteroids.

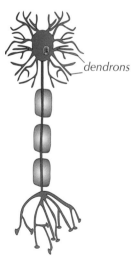

Figure 3: Diagram of a neurone.

Stress

Stress is a word with two meanings.

- It can be the environmental stimulus that triggers a stress response, e.g. a giant cockroach running towards you. In other words, it's the thing that causes you to act stressed.

- But it can also be the response to the stimulus — our reaction, e.g. running for the hills.

Tip: Pressures from the environment can be things like having a lot of work to do, starting a new job, looking after children, revising for exams — anything that puts an additional strain on our lives.

However, psychologists have agreed to explain stress as 'the response that occurs when we think we can't cope with the pressures in our environment'. This is shown in Figure 5 below:

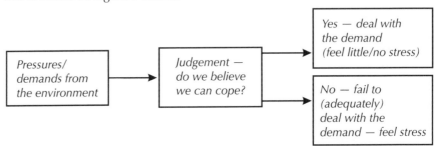

Figure 5: *Diagram showing how stress occurs.*

So, stress is the response that occurs when we think the demands being placed on us are greater than our ability to cope. These are our own judgements — so we could over or underestimate the demands, or our ability to cope. Whether the stress is justified or not doesn't matter — if we think we can't cope, we get stressed. And when we get stressed something physically changes in us.

The hypothalamus

The evaluation of whether something is a stressor occurs in the higher brain centres — the cerebral cortex. When there's a stressor in the environment, these higher areas send a signal to the hypothalamus.

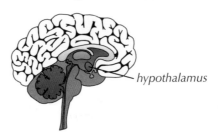

Figure 6: *Location of the hypothalamus in the brain.*

Tip: The sympathomedullary pathway involves both the nervous and the hormonal systems — see page 109.

This tiny part of the brain makes up for its size by having many functions — including controlling the physiological activities involved in stress. In response to the higher areas, the hypothalamus triggers two processes in the body:

1. The activation of the sympathomedullary pathway

Tip: Adrenaline and noradrenaline are types of hormones.

In the initial shock response, the hypothalamus triggers activity in the sympathetic branch of the autonomic nervous system — which is a branch of the peripheral nervous system. The sympathetic branch becomes more active when the body is stressed and using energy. It stimulates the adrenal medulla within the adrenal glands, which releases adrenaline and noradrenaline into the bloodstream. These affect the body in several ways, including:

- Blood pressure and heart rate increase to get blood quickly to areas of the body where it's needed for activity.
- Digestion decreases so that blood can be directed to the brain and muscles.
- Muscles become more tense so that the body is physically responsive.
- Perspiration increases so that the body can cool down and burn more energy.
- Breathing rate increases so that more oxygen can be sent to the muscles.

The result of these changes is that the body is ready to use energy to deal with the stressful situation, e.g. running away from the rhino that's escaped from the zoo.

Tip: This happens pretty quickly, preparing us for 'fight or flight' — an important evolutionary response. It allows us to quickly mobilise our energy stores, making our bodies as responsive as possible to deal with the situation.

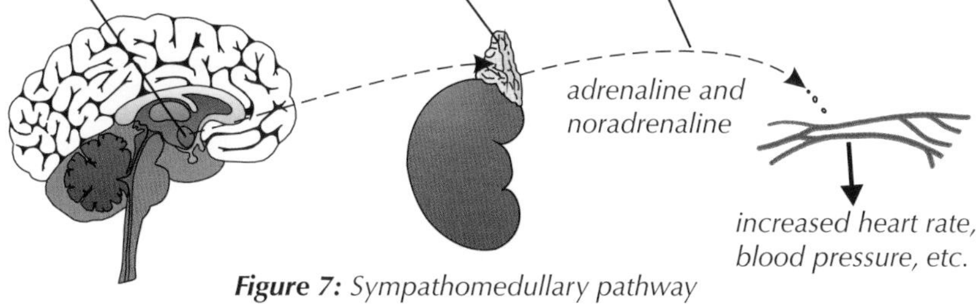

(1) Hypothalamus triggers activity in the sympathetic branch of the ANS.

(2) The ANS stimulates the adrenal medulla.

(3) Stress hormones are released into the bloodstream causing physical effects on the body.

adrenaline and noradrenaline

increased heart rate, blood pressure, etc.

Figure 7: Sympathomedullary pathway

2. The activation of the pituitary-adrenal system

If the stress is long-term, say several hours or more, then the sympathomedullary response will start to use up the body's resources. So, a second system produces a countershock response — which supplies the body with more fuel. It's like putting your body on red alert.

- The hypothalamus also triggers the release of CRH (corticotropin-releasing hormone).
- CRH stimulates the anterior pituitary gland.
- This then releases a hormone called ACTH (adrenocorticotropic hormone).
- ACTH travels through the body and then stimulates the adrenal cortex, which is near the kidneys.
- The adrenal cortex then releases corticosteroids which give us energy by converting fat and protein.
- This energy is needed to replace that used up by the body's initial reaction to the stress, e.g. running away.

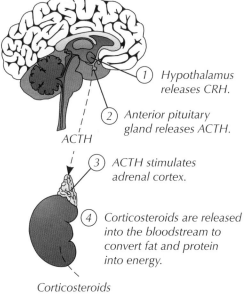

(1) Hypothalamus releases CRH.

(2) Anterior pituitary gland releases ACTH.

ACTH

(3) ACTH stimulates adrenal cortex.

(4) Corticosteroids are released into the bloodstream to convert fat and protein into energy.

Corticosteroids

Figure 8: Pituitary-adrenal system

Tip: If you're finding this difficult to learn, practise scribbling the diagram out and labelling it. Do it over and over again till you get it.

The two stress responses are summarised in Figure 9:

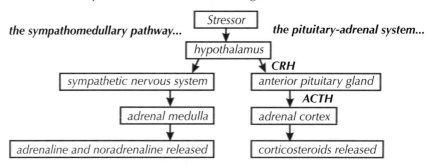

the sympathomedullary pathway...   *the pituitary-adrenal system...*

```
                              Stressor
                                  |
                                  v
                            hypothalamus
                         /                \  CRH
                        v                   v
        sympathetic nervous system    anterior pituitary gland
                        |                   |  ACTH
                        v                   v
                 adrenal medulla       adrenal cortex
                        |                   |
                        v                   v
       adrenaline and noradrenaline    corticosteroids released
              released
```

Figure 9: *The two stress responses.*

The survival value of stress

Changes in the body can be seen as having survival value. During our evolution many threats to us would have been from predators or other physical dangers. So, to successfully respond to them, we would have required energy to fight or run away — the 'fight or flight' response.

However, in modern society stressors are more likely to be psychological than physical and are more long-term.

Examples

Modern society stressors include:
Working at a desk, commuting, noisy neighbours, looking after elderly relatives, getting a flat tyre, deadlines at work, exams, money troubles, the pressures of a big football match and arguing with our partner.

Therefore the physical stress response is not really needed, and in the long term it may actually be harmful to our bodies — pages 114-117 explain how. Some stress can be positive and exhilarating — this is known as eustress, e.g. a parachute jump might lead to this kind of arousal.

Figure 10: *Eustress is stress that is exhilarating.*

Exam Tip
Remember to answer the question that is being asked. Don't just write everything you know about the hypothalamus and the stress response.

Worked Exam-style Questions

1   In stressful situations, Laura finds that she sweats more and that her breathing rate increases. Explain why this happens.   *(6 marks)*

Laura's body is reacting to the stressful situation that she is in. The initial response to stress is via activation of the sympathomedullary pathway. The hypothalamus triggers activity in the sympathetic branch of the autonomic nervous system (a branch of the peripheral nervous system). This stimulates the adrenal medulla within the adrenal glands. The adrenal medulla releases adrenaline and noradrenaline into Laura's bloodstream. These hormones then travel around Laura's body where they act on specific target cells and organs.

Adrenaline and noradrenaline have a number of effects on Laura's body. Laura finds herself sweating. This increase in perspiration is so that her body can cool down and burn more energy. Laura's breathing rate also increases so that more oxygen can be sent to her muscles.

These changes make Laura's body ready to use energy in order to deal with the stressful situation.

2 The pituitary-adrenal system is often activated after a prolonged stressful situation.
Describe what happens when the pituitary-adrenal system is activated. *(6 marks)*

If a stressful situation is prolonged, say several hours or more, then the sympathomedullary response starts to use up the body's energy resources. In this case the pituitary-adrenal system produces a countershock response which acts to supply the body with more fuel.

Here the hypothalamus triggers the release of CRH (corticotropin-releasing hormone). This hormone stimulates the anterior pituitary gland, causing it to release a hormone called ACTH (adrenocorticotropic hormone) into the blood.

ACTH travels through the body in the bloodstream. It stimulates the adrenal cortex, located near the kidneys. The adrenal cortex releases corticosteroids. These hormones cause fat and protein to be converted into energy. This energy is needed to replace that used up by the body's initial reaction to the stress, e.g. running away.

Exam Tip
This question is quite easy if you know your stuff (see pages 111-112). Be careful of rushing your answer in the exam though. Sometimes it helps to scribble down a quick plan — then you can check that you haven't missed out any key information.

Summary Questions

Q1 What is the definition of 'stress'?

Q2 Alex is revising for her exams. She has worked hard all year and has left plenty of time for revision. Even though she is prepared for her exams she feels stressed. Explain why this might be.

Q3 From which area of the brain does the hypothalamus receive information about a stressor?

Q4 Give two physical effects that the activation of the sympathomedullary pathway has on the body.

Q5 In modern day society the physical stress response could be harmful to our bodies. Explain why.

Q6 What is eustress?

3. Stress and Physical Illness

When you're stressed your body reacts physically. These days it's not often that you get chased by a pack of wolves, so this isn't necessarily a good thing...

Hans Selye's three-stage response to stress

In the 1930s, Hans Selye was researching the effects of hormones when he noticed that rats would become ill (e.g. develop stomach ulcers) even when they were given harmless injections (can't have been that harmless). He concluded that the stress of the daily injections caused the illness and suggested that all animals and humans react to stressors through a three-stage physiological response. Selye called this the General Adaptation Syndrome (GAS) (1936) — see Figure 1.

The alarm stage

When we perceive a stressor, our body's first reaction is to increase arousal levels so that we're ready to make any necessary physical response (described on pages 110-112). These mean we're able to run away (the 'fight or flight' response) if we're faced with a big-toothed hairy monster.

The resistance stage

If the stressor remains for a long time, our bodies can adapt to the situation and we seem to be able to cope in a normal way. For example, if we start a high-pressure job we would initially be unable to cope and go into the alarm stage, but after time we would seem to adapt. However, physiologically, arousal levels would still be higher than normal to cope with the situation.

The exhaustion stage

After long-term exposure to a stressor our bodies will eventually be unable to continue to cope with the situation. Alarm signs may return and we may develop illnesses, e.g. ulcers, high blood pressure, depression, etc. Selye called these 'diseases of adaptation'.

The stages Selye identified are supported by a lot of scientific research. However, the GAS theory describes a single type of response and so neglects the fact that the body's reaction to stress does vary, e.g. how much adrenaline is released depends on how the stressor is perceived by the person (how frightening it is, etc.). Also, a certain bacterium has been found to be involved in the formation of ulcers. It could still be the case, though, that stress weakens the immune system making ulcers more likely.

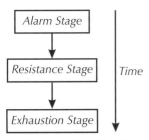

Figure 1: *Hans Selye's General Adaptation Syndrome (GAS).*

Long-term stress and the cardiovascular system

The "cardiovascular system" is just a fancy name for the heart and blood vessels. A long-term stress response may have a direct effect on this system. For instance, increased stress levels can lead to an increase in blood pressure. This is turn can increase the risk of various cardiovascular disorders.

> **Example**
>
> High blood pressure can lead to arteriosclerosis (hardening of the blood vessels) and coronary heart disease (restricted blood flow to the heart — see Figure 2). These disorders may lead to potentially fatal conditions, such as thrombosis (blood clots), heart attacks and strokes (decreased blood flow to the brain, which can cause loss of brain function).

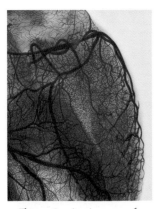

Figure 2: *Angiogram of a patient with coronary heart disease. A blockage in one of the arteries supplying the heart muscle can be seen (top centre). This patient is at risk of suffering from a heart attack.*

Key study of stress and cardiovascular disorders — Krantz et al (1991)

Method: In a laboratory experiment, 39 participants did one of three stress-inducing tasks (a maths test, a Stroop test and public speaking). Their blood pressure and the extent to which the vessels around their heart contracted (low, medium or high myocardial ischaemia) was measured. Participants were instructed not to take any prescribed heart medication prior to the study.

Results: Participants with the greatest myocardial ischaemia showed the highest increases in blood pressure. A small number of participants who showed mild or no myocardial ischaemia only had a very moderate increase in blood pressure.

Conclusion: Stress may have a direct influence on aspects of body functioning, making cardiovascular disorders more likely.

Evaluation: Although the effects were clearly linked to stress, it can't be said that one causes the other. Also, it wasn't shown whether the effects also occur at other times. They might sometimes happen even if the person feels relaxed — and therefore couldn't just be linked to feeling stressed. Not everybody showed the same reaction, which suggests that individual differences between the participants may also have played a role. The ecological validity of the study was reduced because it took place under laboratory conditions that weren't fully representative of real-life stress. However, the findings of the study are supported by Williams (2000) — it was seen that people who got angry easily or reacted more angrily to situations had a higher risk of cardiovascular problems.

Tip: A Stroop test measures reaction time. Participants read two lists of colours aloud. In one list the word being read matches its printed colour, e.g. purple, red, green. In a second list the printed colour does not match the word, e.g. purple, red, green. In general it takes people longer to read the second list and they make more errors.

Tip: Remember, correlations don't necessarily show cause and effect — see page 96.

Additional study of stress and cardiovascular disorders — Russek (1962)

Russek (1962) carried out an experiment to look at the relationship between cardiovascular disorders and occupational stress (having a stressful job). He compared two groups of doctors. One group were considered to have 'low stress' jobs (pathologists and dermatologists) while the other group had 'high stress' jobs (GPs and anaesthetists).

More doctors in the 'high stress' group suffered from heart disease than those in the 'low stress' group. This supports the theory that stress can lead to cardiovascular disorders. However, as with Krantz et al's (1991) study, it can't be said whether having a stressful job itself causes heart disease — there might be other factors (e.g. certain personality types might choose certain types of job). Also the participants were all doctors, so the findings may not be representative of the population.

Tip: GPs have a large workload and a busy schedule, while anaesthetists care for patients under anaesthetic — these are high pressure jobs. In contrast, pathologists often work in laboratories, while dermatologists diagnose and treat patients with skin conditions. These jobs are seen as much less stressful.

Stress and the immune system

The **immune system** is made up of cells (e.g. white blood cells) and chemicals that seek and destroy bacteria and viruses (pathogens). The immune system has a number of defence mechanisms that help the body to fight invading pathogens. For example, phagocytes (a type of white blood cell) engulf and

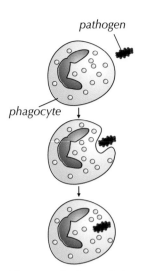

Figure 3: *Pathogen being engulfed by a phagocyte.*

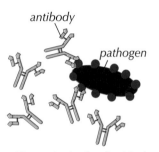

Figure 4: *Antibodies bind to a pathogen, preventing it from binding to a human cell.*

Tip: It's important to be aware of the ethical issues in a study. These are covered in more detail on pages 81-83.

destroy pathogens, as shown in Figure 3.

T-cells are another type of white blood cell. These cells attach to pathogens and kill them. T-cells also produce memory cells. These cells remember the invading pathogen, which means that if the same pathogen invades the body again, the memory cells will recognise it. This allows the immune system to quickly respond to a second infection.

The immune system also consists of B-cells. B-cells produce antibodies — a type of protein that neutralise pathogens in a number of ways. For example, antibodies can destroy pathogens directly, or prevent them from binding to human cells (see Figure 4). B-cells can also produce memory cells.

The immune response also consists of non-specific barriers — those that prevent the pathogens entering in the first place. These include the skin and mucous membranes (such as at the mouth, nostrils, genitals, etc.). Lovely.

When someone experiences long-term stress their immune system can stop functioning properly. Loads of studies have tested whether long-term stress makes us more vulnerable to infection and illness.

Key study of stress and ulcers — Brady et al (1958)

Method:	Monkeys were put in pairs and given electric shocks every 20 seconds for 6 hour sessions. One monkey of each pair (the 'executive') could push a lever to postpone each shock. The other could not delay them.
Results:	The 'executive' monkeys were more likely to develop illness (ulcers) and later die.
Conclusion:	The illness and death was not due to the shocks but due to the stress that the executives felt in trying to avoid them. In the long term, this stress reduced the immune system's ability to fight illness.
Evaluation:	The experiment has ethical issues — the experiment was very cruel and would not be allowed today. Also, we can't generalise results from monkeys to humans. Furthermore, we know that people with little control over their own lives (such as those with low-level jobs and the long-term unemployed), can experience high levels of stress, which this research cannot explain.

Immune system suppression in humans

Research on humans (fortunately not quite as unethical as the monkey study) has also supported the theory that stress can reduce the effectiveness of the immune system. Take the following study, for example:

Key study of stress and the immune response — Kiecolt-Glaser et al (1995)

Method:	In a study with an independent measures design, a punch biopsy was used to create a small wound on the arms of 13 women who cared for relatives with Alzheimer's disease (a very stressful responsibility). A control group of 13 people also took part.
Results:	Wound healing took an average of 9 days longer for the carers than those in the control group.

Conclusion: Long-term stress impairs the effectiveness of the immune system to heal wounds.

Evaluation: Sweeney (1995) also found that people caring for relatives with dementia took longer than a control group to heal their wounds. However, for both studies the two groups may have varied in other ways apart from the stress of being a carer.

The effects on the carers could be due to poor diet, lack of sleep, etc, and not just the stress they experienced. The study only contained a small number of participants — for more reliable results it should be repeated with a larger number.

Tip: Alzheimer's disease is a form of dementia affecting the central nervous system. It occurs in the elderly and causes symptoms such as memory loss, confusion and changes in personality.

Additional study of stress and the immune response — Cohen et al (1993)

Cohen et al (1993) investigated the relationship between stress and immune system function. Participants completed a questionnaire designed to measure their general life stress levels, and were given a 'stress index' score as a result of their answers. Following this, participants were exposed to the common cold virus. Of the 394 initial participants, 82% were infected with the virus. After 1 week the number of participants who had gone on to develop a clinical cold was measured. It was found that participants with a higher stress index score were significantly more likely to develop a clinical cold than those with lower measures of stress.

The results of this study support Kiecolt-Glaser et al's (1995) study and also support the idea that having high levels of general life stress reduces the ability of the immune system to fight off viral infection.

Worked Exam-style Questions

1 Describe and evaluate research into stress-related illness.
(12 marks)

In a laboratory study by Krantz et al (1991) 39 participants did one of three stress-inducing tasks (a maths test, a Stroop test and public speaking). Their blood pressure and the extent to which the vessels around their heart contracted (low, medium or high myocardial ischaemia) was measured. It was found that participants with the greatest myocardial ischaemia showed the highest increases in blood pressure. From the results of the experiment, it was concluded that stress may have a direct influence on the way that the body functions, making cardiovascular disorders more likely.

A problem with the study was that although the effects seem to be linked to stress, it cannot be concluded that one causes the other. In addition, it wasn't shown whether the effects also occur at other times — they might sometimes happen even if the person feels relaxed, and therefore couldn't just be linked to feeling stressed. Not everybody showed the same reaction, which suggests that individual differences between the participants may also have played a role. The ecological validity of the study was also reduced because it took place under laboratory conditions that weren't fully representative of real-life stress.

Exam Tip
For this question you can choose any relevant study to talk about — but pick the one you know most about. You can then use your knowledge of other similar studies to support your answer.

Exam Tip
Once you've summarised the study, don't forget to evaluate it — think of both positive and negative things about it.

However, the findings of the study are supported by a number of other studies. For example, Williams (2000) found that people who got angry easily or reacted more angrily to situations had a higher risk of cardiovascular problems, and Russek (1962) found that individuals with more stressful jobs were more likely to suffer from heart disease than those with less stressful jobs.

2   Many psychologists have found a relationship between stress and immune system activity.

2   (a) Briefly outline this relationship.   *(1 mark)*

2   (b) Outline and evaluate one study providing evidence for this relationship.   *(8 marks)*

(a) Long-term stress can cause the immune system to stop functioning properly, leaving us more vulnerable to illness and infections.

(b) A study by Kiecolt-Glaser et al (1995) provides support for the theory that stress can reduce the effectiveness of the immune system. In this study a punch biopsy was used to create a small wound on the arms of 13 women who cared for relatives with Alzheimer's disease (a very stressful responsibility). A control group of 13 people also took part.

It was found that wound healing took an average of 9 days longer for the carers than those in the control group, suggesting that long-term stress impairs the effectiveness of the immune system to heal wounds. However, the effects on the carers' wound healing rates could be due to a factor other than stress experienced as a result of caring for someone, e.g. poor diet, lack of sleep, etc.

Other studies have found similar results though. Sweeney (1995) found that people caring for relatives with dementia took longer than a control group to heal their wounds. However, for both of these studies, the experimental groups may have varied in other ways apart from the stress of being a carer, e.g. in age, weight, level of physical activity, etc.

The study only contained a small number of participants. To produce more reliable results a larger sample size should have been used.

Exam Tip
A question worth one mark only needs a short answer — be concise and don't waffle on for ages.

Exam Tip
Don't get the terms 'reliability' and 'validity' confused — make sure you know exactly what each one means. Check out page 71 if you're unsure.

Summary Questions

Q1 Describe 'The exhaustion stage' of Hans Selye's General Adaption Syndrome.

Q2 Give one problem with the study by Russek (1962).

Q3 John has been doing a stressful job in a bank for 25 years. His doctor has recently told him that he has high blood pressure. Why should John think about retiring?

Q4 Why would the study by Brady et al (1958) not be allowed today?

Q5 What were the findings of the study by Cohen et al (1993)?

4. Sources of Stress — Life Changes

Sometimes things happen to us that are pretty life changing. And what often comes hand in hand with a big change... you guessed it — stress.

Sources of stress — life changes

Throughout our lives, we all experience major **life events** — like the death of a close relative, getting married or moving house. These events, and the adjustments they cause us to make, can be a major source of stress. When psychologists want to find out what level of stress these events cause, they look at health because it's likely to be linked to stress.

Stress of life changes and illness

Holmes and Rahe (1967) assumed that both positive and negative life events involve change, and that change leads to experiencing stress. To test this assumption, they studied approximately 5000 hospital patients' records and noted any major life events that had occurred before the person became ill. It was found that patients were likely to have experienced life changes prior to becoming ill and that more serious life changes seemed to be more linked to stress and illness.

The Social Readjustment Rating Scale (SRRS)

Holmes and Rahe made a list of 43 common life events and asked loads of people to give each one a score to say how stressful it was. They called the numbers that made up each score the Life Change Units (LCU). The higher this number of LCUs, the more stressful it was. Then they ranked the events from most stressful to least stressful and called it the Social Readjustment Rating Scale (SRRS) — see Figure 1. They found a positive correlation between the likelihood of illness and the score on the SRRS — as one variable increases, so does the other. So, the more stress a person experienced, the more likely they were to suffer illness.

Life Event	Rank	Score (LCU)
Death of a spouse	1	100
Divorce	2	73
Retirement	10	45
Change in school	17	37
Christmas	42	12

Figure 1: *Examples of life events, their rank, and their LCU scores from Holmes and Rahe's SRRS.*

Further correlational research supporting the findings of Holmes and Rahe (1967)

Key study of LCU score and illness — Rahe et al (1970)

Method: In a correlational study, more than 2500 American Navy seamen were given a form of the SRRS to complete just before they set sail on military duty. They had to indicate all of the events that they had experienced over the previous six months.

Results: Higher LCU scores were found to be linked to a higher incidence of illness over the next seven months.

Conclusion: The stress involved in the changes that life events bring is linked to an increased risk of illness.

Evaluation: The results are not representative of the population and can only be generalised to American Navy seamen. Also, the results don't explain individual differences in response to stress. There are also limitations associated with using correlational research. You can't assume a causal relationship between the variables — the correlation might be caused by a third unknown variable.   As well as this, there are problems with using the SRRS to rank stressful events (see below).

Additional study of events and illness — Stone et al (1987)

Stone et al (1987) asked married couples to complete a daily check list of desirable and undesirable events over a period of 3 months. They also kept a record of any illness they experienced.

It was found that undesirable events increased prior to illness, while desirable events decreased. These findings suggest that undesirable events may make individuals more prone to illness, while desirable events may act as a buffer, protecting against ill health.

Tip: Despite being small, these undesirable events (known as hassles in some studies) can have quite a large effect on us — see page 122 for more information.

Issues with the SRRS

The SRRS doesn't separate positive and negative life events. Stress and illness might be more linked to negative life changes. For example, a wedding might be stressful, but positive overall, while the death of a spouse might have a very negative stressful effect. A study by Michael and Ben-Zur looked into this:

Key study of life changing events and life satisfaction — Michael and Ben-Zur (2007)

Michael and Ben-Zur (2007) found that recently widowed individuals scored higher on life satisfaction before the loss of their spouse than afterwards. Not surprising — but they also found that divorced individuals scored higher after the divorce than before.

Although both groups are effectively losing a spouse (a big life adjustment), it seems that on the whole, the divorced people were a lot happier about it. Perhaps this is because they saw the divorce as a positive experience — they could start dating or living with a new partner, or they may have felt a sense of relief and viewed the divorce as a chance for a fresh start.

Long-term, minor sources of stress, such as everyday hassles at work (see pages 123-124), are not considered. Delongis et al (1998) designed a study to test this:

Key study of hassles and illness — Delongis et al (1998)

In a study by Delongis et al (1998), participants were asked to a complete questionnaire measuring major life events and a daily 'hassles and uplifts scale'. This scale was designed to measure minor events which happen to a person on a day-to-day basis.

The study found that there was no relationship between life events and illness, but a relationship between hassles and subsequent next day illness was observed. They concluded that the small hassles we experience everyday had a bigger impact on stress levels and health than the less frequent major life changing events.

Tip: 'Hassles' may include things like losing your keys, and getting stuck in traffic. 'Uplifts' may be things like receiving a compliment, or having an enjoyable evening with your partner.

Despite criticisms the SRRS was useful for showing that changes in life may link to stress and illness.

Correlational research

A lot of the research into the sources of stress is correlational, not experimental. Correlational studies aim to establish if two variables are related to each other. They're useful because they allow us to investigate relationships between stress and lots of other variables. For example, it's likely that our stress levels are the result of many interrelated factors, rather than one single factor. On the other hand, experiments aim to establish if a change in one variable causes a change in another. They have an advantage if we want to find out exactly what is causing stress.

Several of the life changes within the SRRS could be related to each other. For example, a big change in job conditions or getting fired are likely to affect a person's financial situation. Pregnancy or a change in personal habits and living conditions may affect personal health. This means that life changes could be both the cause and effect of stress.

Worked Exam-style Question

1 Describe evidence to show that life changes are a source of stress.
(6 marks)

There are a number of psychological studies which support the theory that life changes are a source of stress.

For instance, Holmes and Rahe (1967) found that hospital patients ■ were likely to have experienced life changes prior to becoming ill and that more serious life changes seemed to be more linked to stress and illness.

In a second study, Holmes and Rahe used the Social Readjustment Rating Scale (SRRS) to assess the number of major life changing events an individual had recently experienced. Their results showed that the more stress a person experienced, the more likely they were to suffer illness.

Similar results were produced in a study by Rahe et al (1970) on American Navy seamen. It was found that the stress involved in life changing events was linked to an increased risk of illness.

Exam Tip
You don't have to write everything you know about each study — just summarise the important bits that are relevant to the question being asked.

Summary Questions

Q1 a) Who were the participants in the study by Rahe et al (1970)?

    b) What was the problem with using this group of participants?

Q2 Give an example of a life changing event which could be found on Holmes and Rahe's Social Readjustment Rating Scale.

Q3 a) Describe the results of the study by Michael and Ben-Zur (2007).

    b) Give a possible explanation for these results.

Q4 Julia overslept, then couldn't find her keys and then got stuck in traffic. When she got to work her boss shouted at her and she had trouble getting her computer to work properly. A few days later Julia felt ill and then got a cold. Why might this have happened?

Learning Objectives:

- Understand daily hassles as a source of stress.
- Know about workplace stress including the effects of workload and control.

5. Sources of Stress — In Everyday Life

Exams, bad hair days, being a bit skint, losing your friend's hamster while they're on holiday — just some of the everyday hassles that stress you out...

Daily hassles

Daily hassles are everyday events that are stressful. Kanner et al (1981) suggested that stress is related to more mundane events than the major life events put forward by Holmes and Rahe. They named these daily hassles 'irritants'.

Examples

Having too much to do, misplacing objects and getting stuck in traffic.

Tip: For more information on using questionnaires in research see pages 63-64.

Key study of stress and daily hassles — Kanner et al (1981)

Method: 100 adults completed a questionnaire each month which asked them to choose which hassles they had experienced that month from a list of 117. They then had to rate each hassle to show how severe it had been for them. This was repeated for 9 months.

Results: Certain hassles occurred more frequently than others, such as worrying about weight, family health and the rising cost of living. They found that those with high scores were more likely to have physical and psychological health problems. They also found that scores on an uplifts scale (containing events that make you feel good, e.g. finishing a task or getting on well with a partner) were negatively related to ill health. These events may reduce stress or protect us from it.

Conclusion: Daily hassles are linked to stress and health, with a stronger correlation than that found with the SRRS (see page 119).

Evaluation: The weaknesses of correlational methods are relevant here — it isn't possible to establish a cause and effect relationship between the variables. Using questionnaires resulted in quantitative data, which is useful for making comparisons, but they don't allow participants to explain why certain experiences are stressful to them, so potentially useful data is missed. They rely on honesty in order for the results to be valid — participants may not be completely truthful about admitting mundane daily events that they find stressful. They also rely on the participants' recall being accurate.

Tip: To remind yourself about correlational research flip back to page 121.

Additional study of stress and daily hassles — Bouteyre et al (2007)

In a study by Bouteyre et al (2007), 223 first year psychology students at a French university completed a hassles scale and a scale ranking depression. It was found that 41% of students experienced depressive symptoms and that there was a positive correlation between hassles and depressive symptoms. This suggests that the hassles associated with the initial transition period at university could be a risk factor for depression.

Stress in the workplace

Unfortunately, most people need to work. Some aspects of the work they do, where they work, or who they have to work with, become a source of stress. This is important because if a person is very stressed at work they may be more likely to get ill. This is not only bad for them, but also for their employer because they will take more days off sick.

Stress in the workplace comes from five key areas:

- Relationships at work — our relationships with our bosses, colleagues and customers may be stressful. For example, we might feel undervalued and that we lack support.

- Work pressures — having a large workload, maybe with strict deadlines.

- The physical environment — where we work may be very noisy, overcrowded, or too hot or cold. Also, our work may involve health risks or unsociable working hours.

- Stresses linked to our role — worrying about job security or our prospects for promotion. Also, the range of our responsibilities may be unclear, and we may experience conflict, e.g. trying to please our bosses and the people who work for us.

- Lack of control — we may not have much influence over the type and amount of work we do, or where and when we do it. Check out the study by Marmot et al (1997) below.

Figure 1: *A large workload is a major cause of stress.*

Lack of control in the workplace

Lack of control in the workplace is stressful. Feeling that we don't have much influence over the type and amount of work we do can lead to stress. This can be seen in Marmot et al's (1997) study:

Key study of lack of control and illness in the workplace — Marmot et al (1997)	
Method:	Over 7000 civil service employees working in London were surveyed. Information was obtained about their grade of employment, how much control they felt they had, how much support they felt they had, etc.
Results:	When the medical histories of these employees were followed up 5 years later, those on lower employment grades who felt less control over their work (and less social support) were found to be more likely to have cardiovascular disorders. Participants on the lowest grade of employment were four times more likely to die of a heart attack than those on the highest grade.
Conclusion:	Believing that you have little control over your work influences work stress and the development of illness.
Evaluation:	The study only looked at 'white collar' work (office-type jobs), so the results may not apply to other jobs. Smoking was found to be common in those who developed illnesses. So, perhaps those who felt less control at work were more likely to smoke — and the smoking caused the heart problems rather than stress. Other factors (e.g. diet and exercise) may be linked to job grade and could be causing illness rather than the perceived lack of control.

Tip: Having a cardiovascular disorder increases your risk of having a heart attack. See pages 114-115.

The research is correlational, so it isn't possible to establish a cause and effect relationship between lack of control and illness. Data was obtained using questionnaires. This may have encouraged the participants to be more truthful than they would have been if interviewed. However, some people may have been concerned about admitting to experiencing stress at work in case it harmed their job prospects.

Tip: The presence of high levels of stress hormones (adrenaline and noradrenaline) in the urine and high blood pressure indicate activation of the sympathomedullary pathway. For a reminder see pages 110-111.

Tip: For more on ecological validity and why it's important see pages 62.

Key study of stress levels in sawmill workers — Frankenhaeuser (1975)

Method: Frankenhaeuser studied 2 groups of workers at a sawmill. One group had the repetitive task of feeding logs into a machine all day. The job was very noisy and the workers were socially isolated. They didn't have much control over their work as the machine dictated how quickly they should feed the logs in. The other group had a different task which gave them more control and more social contact. Stress levels were measured by testing urine samples and blood pressure.

Results: The workers who had minimal control and social contact had higher levels of stress hormones (adrenaline and noradrenaline) in their urine. They were more likely to suffer from high blood pressure and stomach ulcers.

Conclusion: A lack of control and social contact at work can lead to stress.

Evaluation: This was a field experiment, so it has high ecological validity. The findings are supported by Marmot's study. However, it doesn't take individual differences into account — some individuals may just be more prone to stress. The results could have been affected by extraneous variables, such as how much the workers were paid.

It's more likely that you would experience a combination of the factors causing workplace stress. Karasek and his colleagues looked into the relationship between workload and control at work:

Key studies of the relationship between workload and control — Karasek (1979) and Karasek et al (1982)

Tip: CHD stands for coronary heart disease — a medical condition resulting in restricted blood flow to the heart. For more information see page 114.

Karasek (1979) looked at the relationship between job demand (workload) and control. A model was produced stating that jobs with high demand and low control are more stressful than jobs involving low demand and high control.

A study by Karasek et al (1982) provided evidence for Karasek's (1979) model. 900 participants with a range of jobs were given self report questionnaires to measure the demand and control they experienced in their work. The study found that high job strain resulted from jobs with high demand and low control, and that participants with high job strain were more likely to develop CHD over a period of 10 years.

1   Peter is working as a pot washer in a hotel. He works at a noisy, hot dishwasher and on busy days the dirty pots pile up around him. The noise means he rarely speaks to anyone, and the speed of his work is dictated by how fast the dishwasher cycle finishes.

1   (a) Using your psychological knowledge, explain why Peter is feeling stressed. *(4 marks)*

1   (b) Outline one study investigating workplace stress. *(6 marks)*

(a) Peter has little control over his work. Feeling that he doesn't have much influence over the type and amount of work he does may cause Peter to feel stressed.

Peter works in a noisy and hot environment. This may cause him to feel stressed. Working in a noisy environment also means that Peter lacks social contact with his colleagues. This may leave him feeling isolated or lacking in support, again adding to his levels of stress.

On busy days the dirty dishes pile up around him. This large workload might make Peter feel as though he has too much work to cope with, which will further increase his stress levels.

(b) Marmot et al (1997) conducted a study investigating the relationship between lack of control and illness in the workplace. Over 7000 civil service employees working in London were surveyed. Information was obtained about their grade of employment, how much control they felt they had, how much support they felt they had, etc.

When the medical histories of these employees were followed up 5 years later, those on lower employment grades who felt less control over their work (and less social support) were found to be more likely to have cardiovascular disorders. Participants on the lowest grade of employment were four times more likely to die of a heart attack than those on the highest grade.

It was concluded that believing that you have little control over your work influences work stress and the development of illness.

Exam Tip
Read the scenario given to you carefully. Think about what each piece of information you are given is telling you.

Exam Tip
Don't worry if this isn't the study you would have picked to talk about. Just make sure you know enough about the study you do pick, and that it's relevant to the question that is being asked.

Summary Questions

Q1   What was the conclusion of the study by Kanner et al (1981)?

Q2   Who were the participants in the study by Bouteyre et al (2007)?

Q3   Name the five key areas that stress in the workplace comes from.

Q4   How were stress levels measured in the study by Frankenhaeuser (1975)?

Q5   Why did the experiment by Frankenhaeuser (1975) have high ecological validity?

Q6   Summarise the relationship between workplace stress, demand and control as described by Karasek's (1979) research.

6. Stress — Individual Differences

People are different, which means they experience and react to stress differently. Psychologists are interested in these 'individual differences.'

Personality types and stress

Psychologists love sticking people into groups. One theory about personality is that you can split everyone into three groups called 'Type A', 'Type B' or 'Type X'. People in each group show certain personality characteristics:

┌─ **Examples** ─────────────────────────────────

Type A people — competitive and ambitious.
Type B people — non-competitive, relaxed and easy-going.
Type X people — balance of Type A and Type B behaviours.

Friedman and Rosenman (1974) tested how these different types of personality affect the likelihood of CHD (coronary heart disease).

> ### Key study of personality type and illness — Friedman and Rosenman (1974)
>
> **Method:** Approximately 3000, 39-59 year old American males were assessed to class their personality characteristics into Type A, Type B or Type X using interviews and observation. At the start of the study none of them had CHD (coronary heart disease).
>
> **Results:** Eight years later, 257 of them had developed CHD. 70% of these were classed as Type A personality. This includes being 'workaholic', extremely competitive, hostile to others, and always in a rush. Participants classed as Type B were less competitive and less impatient. They were found to have half the rate of heart disease of Type A. These results were found even when the extraneous variables of weight and smoking were taken into account.
>
> **Conclusion:** Type A personalities seem to be at a higher risk of stress-related illnesses, such as CHD.
>
> **Evaluation:** Having only three personality types seems a bit simplistic. The study doesn't prove that personality characteristics can cause stress and illness. It could be the other way round. For example, Type A personality may develop as a response to being under stress (from work etc.). Also, the sample used in the study was quite limited — middle-aged, male Americans. This means that it's not that easy to generalise the results to the rest of the population. In addition, participants may not have been completely honest in their interviews so that their characteristics appeared desirable to the researcher (social desirability bias).

Later research also identified Type C personalities — mild-mannered, easy-going people who may not react well to stressful situations and suppress their emotions. These people seem to have a higher risk of cancer. Type D personalities were identified as very negative/pessimistic people who worry too much about things and lack social skills. These people seem more at risk from heart attacks.

Learning Objective:

- Know about personality factors, including Type A and Type B behaviour and hardiness.

Tip: Coronary heart disease is one of the most obvious effects of stress.

Tip: Extraneous variables are variables that could affect what you're trying to measure. In this study the dependent variable is developing CHD. Being overweight or a smoker can increase the risk of CHD, so these are extraneous variables that could affect the results. For more on variables see pages 67-68.

Additional studies of personality type and illness

Other researchers have found results which oppose those of Friedman and Rosenman (1974). In a longitudinal study of over 12 000 participants, Shekelle et al (1985) found no significant difference between Type A and Type B personalities when they looked at the number of people who developed heart disease after 7 years.

Myrtek (2001) conducted a meta-analysis of 35 studies investigating the link between Type A personality and cardiovascular disorders. It found that only one of the Type A personality traits — hostility — showed any correlation with coronary heart disease.

Tip: A meta-analysis is a study which combines the results of several studies all addressing a related topic.

Hardiness

Kobasa (1979) identified **hardiness** as an important individual difference. Kobasa described people as being hardy or non-hardy. There are three main characteristics of hardy personalities:

- Hardy personalities are very involved in what they do, and show a high level of commitment. This means that they work hard at relationships, jobs and other activities in life.

- They view change in a positive rather than a negative way, seeing it as an opportunity for challenge. Hardy personalities enjoy a challenge and see it as an opportunity to develop themselves.

- They have a strong feeling of control over their life and what happens to them. This is known as having an internal locus of control.

In comparison, non-hardy personalities view any life experiences in a much more negative way and feel that they're unable to cope with situations. They feel that external agencies have control over what happens to them and that it isn't worth trying to become more powerful. They give up easily and don't see any value in trying to change what's happening around them.

It's difficult to quantify what's meant by a hardy personality and therefore difficult to measure and test it. We also need to avoid making assumptions about cause and effect — it could be that some people have hardy personalities because of a lack of stress in their lives, rather than low stress being the result of personality. It could be that levels of hardiness fluctuate and may decrease when the person is experiencing lots of stress, such as after a bereavement.

Tip:

- **C**ommitment

- **C**hallenge

- **C**ontrol

These 3 **C**s form the hardy personality. The concept of the hardy personality is useful in stress management — see pages 133-134.

Key studies of stress and hardiness

There is evidence suggesting that people with a hardy personality are less likely to suffer from illness as a result of stress. For instance, a study by Maddi et al (1987) looked at employees of a US phone company that was reducing its workforce. During the downsize, two-thirds of the workforce suffered from stress-related health problems. However, the other one-third of the workforce thrived during the period. It was found that these people were much more likely to have a hardy personality.

Lifton et al (2006) measured the hardiness of 1432 students at five US universities. Students who displayed hardy personalities were significantly more likely to successfully complete their degrees. A large number of students who dropped out had low hardiness scores.

Gender and stress

Men and women are pretty different in loads of ways, so psychologists thought that maybe these differences could affect what kinds of things men and women find stressful and how they cope. They looked at how biological, social and cognitive differences between males and females influence their response to stress.

Biological explanation

Through evolution, men in their role of 'hunter-gatherer' may have developed a stronger 'fight or flight' response than women, who had the role of caring for children. In this way, males and females may have developed different physiological responses to stress.

Taylor et al (2000) suggest that women produce a calmer response to stress due to a hormone. Oxytocin is released in response to stress and has been shown to lead to maternal behaviour and social affiliation. Taylor called this the 'tend and befriend' response (instead of the 'fight or flight' response) and thought it might make females more likely to seek social support to help them cope with stress.

Social explanation

A Western stereotypical social role is that men are less open about their feelings than women. This means they're less likely to discuss stressful experiences with others and may use harmful coping methods instead, e.g. smoking and drinking.

Carroll (1992) found that women do generally make more use of social support to deal with stress. However, coronary heart disease has increased in women — but this could just be because a change in social roles means that it's now more acceptable for women to drink and smoke.

Cognitive explanation

Vogele et al (1997) claim that women are better able to control anger and therefore respond more calmly to stressful situations. Men may feel that anger is an acceptable way to respond, and feel stress if they cannot show it. These cognitive differences could be the result of biology or the roles we are taught to follow, or a bit of both.

Tip: Oxytocin is a hormone important during childbirth and breast feeding. It has also been shown to reduce feelings of anxiety by reducing corticosteroid levels in the body.

Culture and stress

Culture is a really vague term that is used to group people by beliefs, behaviours, morals or customs they share. It influences how people live and how others react to them. Variables such as low socio-economic status can lead to poor living conditions and experience of prejudice — which could lead to negative thinking. Also, some people believe that biological factors could influence the link between culture, stress and illness. For example, genetics may influence how some people react to stress and whether they get ill or not as a result of it.

Worked Exam-style Question

1 Outline and evaluate research into personality factors and stress.
(12 marks)

Friedman and Rosenman (1974) looked at the relationship between personality type and stress-related illness. They used interviews and observation to classify the personality types of approximately 3000

39-59 year old American males. Participants were classed as either Type A, Type B or Type X.

At the start of the study none of the participants had CHD (coronary heart disease). Eight years later it was found that 257 of them had developed CHD. 70% of these were classed as having a Type A personality. People classified as having a Type B personality were found to have half the rate of heart disease as Type A people. It was concluded that Type A personalities seem to be at a higher risk of stress-related illnesses, such as CHD.

The study used a large sample size and had high ecological validity. ■ It also took into account extraneous variables such as weight and smoking — factors which could have increased the risk of CHD.

Exam Tip
When evaluating a study remember to think about both its good points, and its bad points.

However, the methodology of the study has some problems. The study made use of interviews, and so participants may have shown social ■ desirability bias — they may not have been completely honest in their interviews so that their characteristics appeared more desirable to the researcher. Also, although the study used a large sample size, the sample itself was limited to middle-aged, male, Americans. This means that it's not that easy to generalise the results to the rest of the population.

Exam Tip
When you use psychological terms, like social desirability bias, make sure you show that you know what it means.

Also, the study doesn't prove that personality characteristics can cause stress and illness. It could be the other way round — Type A personality may develop as a response to being under stress (from work, etc.). Having only three personality types seems a bit simplistic too — later research also identified Type C and Type D personalities.

Other studies have found results which oppose those of Friedman and Rosenman (1974). In a longitudinal study of over 12 000 participants, ■ Shekelle et al (1985) found no significant difference between Type A and Type B personalities when looking at the number of people who developed heart disease after 7 years. Additionally, Myrtek (2001) conducted a meta-analysis of 35 studies investigating the link between Type A personality and cardiovascular disorders. It found that only one of the Type A personality traits (hostility) showed any correlation with CHD.

Exam Tip
Using other studies in your evaluations is a good habit to get into.

Summary Questions

Q1 Give two characteristics of the Type A personality.

Q2 Describe the hardy personality type.

Q3 a) What is an internal locus of control?

b) Which personality type has a strong internal locus of control?

Q4 Men and women have different responses to stress.

a) Which stress hormone did Taylor et al (2000) identify as being responsible for women's calmer response to stress?

b) Give a social explanation for gender differences in response to stress.

c) What did Vogele et al (1997) claim that women were better at doing than men, which allows them to respond more calmly to stressful situations?

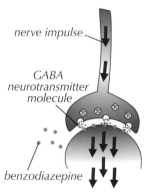

Learning Objective:

- Know about the biological methods of stress management, including drug therapy.

7. Stress Management — Biological Approach

Stress management is all about coping with stress. The biological approach uses physical methods like drug treatment, exercise and biofeedback.

Drug treatments

Drug treatments work in two ways:

1. They slow down the activity of the central nervous system (CNS).

Anti-anxiety drugs called benzodiazepines (BZs) increase the body's reaction to its own natural anxiety-relieving chemical GABA (gamma-aminobutyric acid), which slows down the activity of neurones and makes us feel relaxed — see Figures 1 and 2.

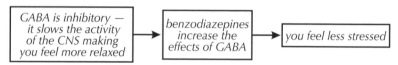

| GABA is inhibitory — it slows the activity of the CNS making you feel more relaxed | → | benzodiazepines increase the effects of GABA | → | you feel less stressed |

Figure 1: *Flow diagram showing how benzodiazepines increase the body's reaction to GABA.*

nerve impulse

GABA neurotransmitter molecule

benzodiazepine

Figure 2: *Benzodiazepines increase the body's reaction to GABA, making us feel more relaxed.*

2. They reduce the activity of the sympathetic nervous system (SNS).

The SNS increases heart rate, blood pressure and levels of the hormone cortisol. High levels of cortisol can make our immune system weak and also cause heart disease. The group of drugs called beta blockers reduce all these unpleasant symptoms.

> **Example**
>
> Beta blockers are sometimes used illegally in sports. A decrease in SNS activity results in decreased heart rate, blood pressure and breathing rate — this may give an edge over the competition in sports such as snooker, archery and darts, where a steady hand is needed.

Tip: The activity of the sympathetic nervous system is increased when the body is under stress — for a reminder see page 109.

Biofeedback

Biofeedback uses information about what's happening in the body — it gives people information about internal physical processes that they wouldn't otherwise be aware of, e.g. muscle tension. The idea is to give them more control over these internal processes and the ability to alter them.

For example, if they can modify the physical aspects of stress then this may make them more relaxed in stressful situations. The process takes place as training in a non-stressful environment, which the person is then encouraged to use in real-life stressful situations.

There are 4 steps involved:

1. The person is attached to a machine that monitors and gives feedback on internal physical processes such as heart rate, blood pressure or muscle tension.

2. They are then taught how to control these symptoms of stress through a variety of techniques. These can include muscle relaxation — muscle groups are tensed and relaxed in turn until the whole body is relaxed. This teaches people to notice when their body is becoming tense. Other techniques include actively clearing the mind using meditation, or breathing control exercises.

Figure 3: *Man undergoing biofeedback.*

3. This feeling of relaxation acts like a reward and encourages the person to repeat this as an involuntary activity.

4. The person learns to use these techniques in real-life situations.

Additional studies of biofeedback

Meuret et al (2004) found that biofeedback is effective in controlling breathing rate in people suffering from panic attacks.

Nestoriuc et al (2008) conducted a meta-analysis of 94 studies and showed biofeedback was effective in treating migraine, tension headaches, and symptoms of anxiety and depression.

Tip: A symptom of panic attacks is hyperventilation — an increased breathing rate. Biofeedback can help to slow this down.

Exercise

Exercise is another biological method of managing stress. Exercise and being physically active reduces the likelihood of stress-related illness. Morris (1953) compared bus conductors and bus drivers and found that the conductors had lower rates of cardiovascular problems. This could be the result of having a more active job, or not having the stress of driving. Or, it could be caused by any number of other variables. However, it's difficult to get a clear idea of the relationship because active people may be less likely to engage in harmful behaviours like smoking and drinking. Active people are likely to sleep better, which will have both a biological and a psychological influence on levels of stress.

Additional studies of stress and exercise

Berger et al (1988) found that a range of sports (including swimming, yoga and fencing) were effective in reducing stress levels.

Throne et al (2000) found that participating in a regular exercise programme reduced fire fighters' physiological response to stress.

Figure 4: *Exercise can reduce stress and improve mood.*

Strengths and weaknesses of the approach

1. Both drugs and biofeedback are effective:

Drugs are quick and effective in reducing dangerous symptoms such as high blood pressure. Kahn et al (1986) found that benzodiazepines were superior to a placebo (sugar pill) when they tracked around 250 patients over an 8-week period. Attanasio et al (1985) found that biofeedback helped teenagers and children with stress-related disorders to gain control over the symptoms of migraine headaches. They also showed an increase in enthusiasm and a more positive attitude.

2. Drugs and biofeedback treat symptoms rather than the underlying causes of stress:

Drugs only help with the symptoms and only so long as the drugs are taken. Biofeedback also aims to reduce symptoms, but using relaxation techniques can also give the person a sense of control and have more long-lasting benefits.

3. Drugs are easier to use than biofeedback:

Drugs are relatively easy to prescribe and use. Biofeedback needs specialist equipment and expert supervision. Some argue that the benefits of biofeedback could be gained from other relaxation techniques and so this is an unnecessary expense.

Tip: Placebos are pills that do nothing at all. They're used to test if any effect happens just because people think they're being treated.

4. Drugs have side effects, biofeedback doesn't:

Drugs can have minor side effects such as dizziness and tiredness or more serious effects such as blurred vision and changes in sex drive. Withdrawal symptoms when people come off medication, such as increased anxiety, seizures, tremors and headaches, can be distressing. Benzodiazepines can be addictive, and are generally limited to a maximum of 4 weeks' use.

There are no side effects of biofeedback — just relaxation. This method's advantage is that it's voluntary and not invasive.

Worked Exam-style Question

1 (a) Outline one biological method of stress management.

(4 marks)

1 (b) Evaluate the biological method of stress management you outlined in (a). *(6 marks)*

(a) One biological method of stress management is biofeedback. It gives people information about internal physical processes that they wouldn't otherwise be aware of, e.g. muscle tension. This gives them more control over these processes and the ability to alter them.

The person is attached to a machine that monitors and gives feedback on internal physical processes such as heart rate, blood pressure or muscle tension. They are then taught how to control these symptoms of stress through a variety of techniques. These can include muscle relaxation — muscle groups are tensed and relaxed in turn until the whole body is relaxed. This teaches people to notice when their body is becoming tense. Other techniques include actively clearing the mind using meditation, or breathing control exercises.

This feeling of relaxation acts like a reward and encourages the person to repeat this as an involuntary activity. The person then learns to use these techniques in real-life situations.

(b) A number of studies have found biofeedback to be effective. Nestoriuc et al (2008) conducted a meta-analysis of 94 studies and showed biofeedback was effective in treating migraine, tension headaches and symptoms of anxiety and depression. Meuret et al (2004) found biofeedback to be effective in controlling breathing rate in people suffering from panic attacks.

There are no side effects of biofeedback — just relaxation, which can give the person a sense of control and have more long-lasting benefits. It's also voluntary and not invasive.

However there are some drawbacks to biofeedback. It only treats the symptoms, rather than the underlying causes of stress. Also, it requires specialist equipment and expert supervision. Some argue that the benefits of biofeedback could be gained from other relaxation techniques and so it is an unnecessary expense.

Exam Tip
Try to be as accurate and concise as you can in the exam. It's important to think about what you want to say in your answer before you start writing.

Summary Questions

Q1 a) Which drugs slow down the activity of the CNS?

b) In what other way can drugs reduce stress?

Q2 a) Describe the findings of Morris et al's (1953) exercise study.

b) What did their findings suggest?

8. Stress Management — Psychological Approach

Learning Objective:

▪ Know about psychological methods of stress management, including stress inoculation therapy.

The psychological approach to stress management is all about learning to think differently...

Psychological methods of stress management

The psychological approach helps you to cope better by thinking differently about the stressful situation. The techniques have been shown to be effective and deal with the source of the problem rather than just the symptoms. They provide skills that have more lasting value — like the confidence to cope with future problems and the belief of being in control and seeing life as a challenge rather than as a threat.

Meichenbaum's stress inoculation training (SIT)

This works like immunisation. Just like you might be inoculated against any attack from disease, you can protect yourself from the harmful effects of stress. Training involves preparation so that you can deal with stress before it becomes a problem. Three steps are involved:

1. Conceptualisation: Identify fears and concerns with a therapist.

2. Skill acquisition and rehearsal: Train to develop skills like positive thinking and relaxation in order to improve self-confidence.

3. Application and follow-through: Practise the newly acquired skill in real-life situations with support and back-up from the therapist.

Meichenbaum (1977) found that SIT works both with short-term stressors such as preparing for public speaking, and longer-term stressors such as medical illness, divorce or work-related stress. SIT can be applied in many situations, ranging from treating phobias to increasing academic and sports performance.

Tip: Stress inoculation training can also be known as stress inoculation therapy.

Tip: When we're immunised against a disease we're often given a weakened form of the virus. This exposes our body to the disease, allowing us to build up a resistance to it, in case we're exposed to it for real. Meichenbaums's SIT is based on this principle.

Key studies of SIT

Sheehy and Horan (2004) gave first year law students weekly SIT sessions lasting for 90 minutes each. The sessions aimed to reduce their levels of anxiety and stress in order to increase their academic performance. After 4 weeks it was found that all participants had lower levels of stress and anxiety, and that many students improved their academic performance.

Zeigler et al (1982) found that SIT decreased cross country runners' stress levels and increased their performance.

Hardiness training

Kobasa suggests that a strong and hardy person shows 3 Cs:
Control over their lives, commitment (a sense of purpose in life) and challenge (life is seen as a challenge and opportunity rather than as a threat).
       Maddi introduced a training programme to increase hardiness, arguing that the more hardy the person, the better they cope with stress. This training has 3 steps:

1. Focusing: Learn to recognise physical symptoms of stress, e.g. increase in heart rate, muscle tension and sweating.

2. Reliving stressful encounters: Learn to analyse stressful situations to better understand possible coping strategies.

Tip: See page 127 for more on hardiness.

3. Self-improvement: Take on challenges that can be coped with and build confidence, thereby gaining a greater sense of control.

Key study of hardiness training — Maddi et al (1998)

Maddi et al (1998) compared the effectiveness of the hardiness training programme with other stress management techniques (e.g. a relaxation and meditation regime, a placebo, and a social support control group).

The 54 managers who went on the hardiness training programme recorded greater increases in hardiness and job satisfaction and greater decreases in strain and illness than the other stress management techniques and control groups.

Additional studies of hardiness training

Judkins et al (2006) found that nurse managers who took part in a hardiness training programme increased their levels of hardiness. A positive impact on staff turnover levels was also shown.

In a study by Green et al (2007) high school students were given life coaching sessions, which included hardiness training. After the coaching there was a significant increase in the students' hardiness levels. Other positive effects (e.g. decrease in depressive symptoms) were also reported.

Tip: Lower staff turnover levels shows that the nurse managers were less likely to leave their jobs. This suggests they were happier at work, potentially as a result of being less stressed due to their increased hardiness.

Weaknesses of the psychological methods

Despite proven effectiveness, there are weaknesses with the methods.

- Psychological methods only suit a narrow band of individuals who are determined to stick to the technique.

- Research tends to be based on white, middle-class business folk and so can't necessarily be generalised to others.

- The procedures are very lengthy and require considerable commitment of time and effort.

- The concepts may be too complex. For example, a lack of hardiness might be just another label for negativity. It could be argued that it's just as effective to relax and think positively.

Cognitive behavioural therapy (CBT)

Tip: See pages 196 for more on CBT.

CBT aims to alter thought processes. CBT techniques were developed to treat abnormality using concepts from the cognitive approach. The idea is that changing the way information is cognitively processed will result in a change in behaviour. These techniques can be used in stress management — by changing the way we think in stressful situations we can cope better and behave in ways that help to minimise or remove the stressor.

Rational-emotive therapy (RET)

Ellis (1962) suggested an ABC model. It begins with an activating event (A) which leads to a belief (B) about why this happened. This then leads to a consequence (C) (see Figure 1). If the beliefs are irrational, they will lead to maladaptive consequences — such as depression, anxiety or symptoms of stress.

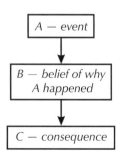

Figure 1: *C is a result of the person's belief system (B) —it's not a direct result of the event (A).*

For example, if somebody fails to get a promotion at work (A), they may believe that it happened because they're useless (B), and the emotional consequence (C) may be feeling depressed. RET focuses on encouraging people to change irrational beliefs into rational beliefs, for a more positive consequence. In this example, believing that they didn't get the promotion because it's not possible to always perform well in an interview may lead to a more positive cognitive mood and less stress.

Beck's cognitive restructuring therapy

Beck (1963) identified a cognitive triad of types of negative thought which can be applied to stress management. These are thoughts about:

- Themselves — "I'm useless at everything."
- The future — "Nothing will change and I won't improve."
- The world — "You need to be better than I am to succeed in life."

The therapist's goal is to disprove the negativity in a person's thinking. After a while they should be able to use different cognitive processes, leading to a more positive belief system. Beck initially developed the therapy for use with depression, but it's been adapted for use beyond this. For example, Proudfoot et al (1997) found that cognitive therapies were effective when used to deal with the psychological effects of unemployment.

Worked Exam-style Question

1 (a) Outline the process of stress inoculation training.
(6 marks)

1 (b) Outline **one** study supporting stress inoculation training.
(4 marks)

(a) Stress inoculation training (SIT) works like immunisation. Just like you might be inoculated against any attack from disease, you can protect yourself from the harmful effects of stress. Training involves preparation so that you can deal with stress before it becomes a problem. Three steps are involved. The first one is conceptualisation, where the person identifies fears and concerns with the help of a therapist. The second step is skill acquisition and rehearsal. This is where the person trains to develop skills like positive thinking and relaxation in order to improve self-confidence. The final step is application and follow-through. The person practises the newly acquired skill in real-life situations with support and back-up from the therapist.

(b) Sheehy and Horan (2004) gave first year law students weekly SIT sessions lasting for 90 minutes each. The sessions aimed to reduce their levels of anxiety and stress in order to increase their academic performance. After four weeks it was found that all participants had lower levels of stress and anxiety, and that many students improved their academic performance.

Exam Tip
This is worth 6 marks, so you need to do more than just naming the three steps. You need to add a bit of extra detail to each step too.

Exam Tip
Don't worry if the study you would have picked is different to the one here. If it shows hardiness training to be effective and you know enough about it, then it should be okay to use.

Summary Questions

Q1 Give the 3 Cs of a hardy personality.

Q2 a) Give an example of a study supporting hardiness training as a stress management technique.

b) Outline the findings of this study.

Q3 Give one weakness of the psychological approach to stress management.

Q4 What do the A, B and C stand for in Ellis' ABC model?

Q5 What is the goal of cognitive restructuring therapy?

Section Summary

- The biological approach is all about biology — psychologists try to explain behaviour in relation to what's going on in the body.
- Biological psychologists use experiments, correlational studies, questionnaires, interviews, case studies and brain scanning techniques.
- The nervous system and the hormonal system both play a big role in the stress response.
- Stress can be defined as 'the response that occurs when we think we can't cope with the pressures in our environment.'
- The hypothalamus is central to the physical stress response. It triggers an initial response via activation of the sympathomedullary pathway, and a long term response via the pituitary-adrenal system. These responses increase our physical ability to deal with the stressful situation.
- In modern day society the stress response is not really needed and can actually be harmful to our bodies. Hans Selye came up with a model for this effect, which he called the General Adaptation Syndrome. It has three stages — the alarm stage, the resistance stage and the exhaustion stage.
- There is a lot of evidence showing that the stress response can increase the risk of cardiovascular disorders, and decrease the effectiveness of the immune system.
- Sources of stress include life changing events. Holmes and Rahe measured these with their social readjustment rating scale.
- Daily hassles are also major causes of stress.
- The workplace is also a major source of stress — lack of control and a large workload can contribute to a person's levels of stress.
- Personality factors can influence how a person reacts to stress. Psychologists have attempted to classify people into different personality types. Friedman and Rosenman (1974) classified people as Type A or Type B personalities, while Kobasa identified 'hardiness' as a personality type. Studies have found links between personality types and resilience to stress-related illnesses.
- Gender and cultural differences can also influence how people cope with stress.
- The biological approach tries to manage stress using drug treatments, biofeedback and exercise. These methods have been shown to be effective, but often they only treat the symptoms of stress, rather than the underlying cause.
- The psychological approach to stress management helps people cope with stress by thinking differently.
- Meichenbaum's stress inoculation training helps people to deal with stress before it becomes a problem. Kobasa's hardiness training aims to increase hardiness, making people better able to cope with stress.
- Other psychological stress management techniques include cognitive behavioural therapy, rational-emotive therapy and cognitive restructuring therapy.

Exam-style Questions

1 (a)   Gena has started a job where she has to give presentations in front of large audiences. Just before she gives her presentation she experiences some unpleasant symptoms. Use your knowledge of the initial stress response to suggest what these symptoms may be.

(4 marks)

1 (b)   The doctor prescribes beta blockers to Gena. He explains that these drugs decrease the activity of the sympathetic nervous system.

Use your knowledge of the sympathomedullary pathway to explain why the doctor chose these drugs.

(3 marks)

1 (c)   Evaluate the use of drugs as a stress management technique.

(6 marks)

2   A recent psychological study asked participants to complete questionnaires recording their daily hassles and any illness they experienced over a 12 month period. The following graph shows the results.

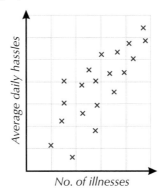

No. of illnesses

2 (a)   Identify the relationship shown by the graph.

(1 mark)

2 (b) (i)   Give **one** advantage of using questionnaires in psychological research

(1 mark)

2 (b) (ii)   Give **one** disadvantage of using questionnaires in psychological research.

(1 mark)

2 (c)   Outline **one** study showing the relationship between life changes and stress-related illness.

(6 marks)

3   Richard has found out that the company he works for will be reducing its workforce over the coming months. Richard is very worried about his job prospects. He feels that he has no control over what will happen to him and that he may as well give up now.

Outline **one** psychological stress management method that might help Richard.

(4 marks)

Learning Objectives:

1. The Social Approach

The social approach is all about the relationships between people.

Social psychology

Social psychology looks at how people affect each other:

Learning Objectives:

- Know about and understand the research methods used in social psychology.
- Know about and understand the ethical issues associated with social psychology.

- Social behaviour occurs when two or more people interact. People interact differently depending on the situation — so you may act differently with a parent, a friend, a stranger, or when you're in a group.

- Social psychology also considers how we think about other people. This is social cognition, which can involve things like stereotyping and prejudice.

- The influence of others can cause individuals to change their behaviour. Social psychologists have studied why people conform (change their behaviour to fit in with a group), and why they obey authority figures.

Research methods in social psychology

Social psychologists use loads of different research methods. Fortunately they're all methods that are used in some of the other approaches too.

Tip: There's more general stuff on research methods on pages 61-64. And more on ethical issues on pages 81-83.

Laboratory experiments

Laboratory experiments are conducted in artificial settings — e.g. Asch's study (pages 142-143).

Advantages

- They're highly controlled, so the effect of the independent variable can be measured. This also means that it's possible to establish cause and effect, and to replicate the method.

- Participants in different conditions can act as comparisons.

Disadvantages

- They use artificial environments, so studies have low ecological validity — most social interactions don't normally take place in labs. This means there are problems with generalising the results.

Tip: There are many advantages and disadvantages for each type of research method. Make sure you learn them in case you're asked to evaluate the method of a study in social psychology.

Field experiments

Field experiments are conducted in real-life settings — e.g. hospitals.

Advantages

- The variables are still highly controlled, so it should be possible to establish cause and effect.

- Studies take place in the participants' natural environments, so they're more likely to capture natural social behaviour. This means they have higher ecological validity than lab experiments.

- Demand characteristics are reduced if the participants don't know they're being studied.

Disadvantages

- It's very difficult to control all the variables in a natural environment, so the results can still be affected by confounding variables.
- Lots of field experiments involve using deception (see pages 61-62). This has ethical implications — you can't get informed consent, and it can be difficult to debrief participants.

Natural experiments

Natural experiments look at naturally occurring situations — the independent variable isn't manipulated.

Advantages

- Studies take place in the participants' natural environments, and nothing is manipulated, so they're likely to capture natural social behaviour. This means they have high ecological validity.
- Researchers can investigate variables that it would be unethical to manipulate.

Disadvantages

- Because none of the variables are controlled, experiments tend to have low internal validity. It's really hard to tell what actually caused the results. This means it's difficult to establish cause and effect.
- Natural experiments often involve deception, which raises ethical issues.

Figure 1: *Natural experiments use situations that occur without any manipulation. Football crowds are a great example.*

Naturalistic observation

Naturalistic observation is when the experimenter just observes behaviour, without manipulating any variables.

Advantages

- Participants are in a natural environment, and are often unaware they're being observed. This means that studies should have high ecological validity.
- Results from observations can be used to develop theories, which can then be tested in experiments.

Disadvantages

- Not controlling the independent variable means it's very difficult to establish cause and effect.
- The results are subjective — observers can be biased about what they record.
- Observation can involve deception, which brings up problems of gaining informed consent and debriefing participants. Ethically it's OK to observe people in places where they might expect to be observed by strangers — so you can watch them in the street, but you can't train a telescopic lens on their bedroom.

Tip: Don't forget to consider the ethical implications of using each type of research method.

Surveys

Surveys can include questionnaires and interviews. They can be really useful, but the problem is that there's no way of knowing whether people are telling the truth. Unless you rig them up to a lie detector like on Jeremy Kyle.

Questionnaires can include closed or open-ended questions.
Closed questions have a limited set of answers — e.g. yes or no.

Examples

Closed questions:

'Have you ever met the Queen?'
'How many exams will you sit at the end of the year?'

The answers to these questions are limited and short.

Open questions don't have a restricted set of answers.

Examples

Open questions:

'Describe a time when you did something nice for someone else.'
'What are your thoughts on recycling?'
'What do you think of Jeremy Kyle?'

These questions are likely to provide unique responses and there is no restriction on what can be said.

Interviews can be structured or unstructured. Structured interviews use pre-decided questions that are the same for all of the participants.
In unstructured interviews the interviewers give the participant more freedom, although they might still guide the conversation to cover certain topics.

Advantages

- With questionnaires you can gather lots of data quickly and cheaply. This means you can have a large sample, making the results more reliable.
- Closed questions and structured interviews produce quantitative data, which is really easy to analyse.
- Open questions and unstructured interviews produce qualitative data, which is really detailed.

Disadvantages

- Questionnaires and interviews rely on self-reporting. This means people can lie in order to show themselves in a good light — this is called social desirability bias.
- Interviews can be very time-consuming.
- It's easy to write bad questions. Researchers have to avoid leading questions (ones that lead the participants towards certain answers), or questions that can mean different things to different people.

Examples
Leading questions:

'Don't you agree that Kate and Matthew make a lovely couple?'
'Shaun stole the money, didn't he?'

These questions persuade people to respond in a certain way because of their wording. Often the phrasing can be subtle but can still influence how people answer.

Loftus and Palmer's (1974) study used the question:

'About how fast were the cars going when they smashed into each other?'

The word 'smashed' subtly implied that the cars were going quickly, leading participants to give higher answers than when the word 'contacted' was used.

Figure 2: *Questionnaires are a common research method in social psychology.*

Tip: Leading questions are really important to watch out for in eyewitness testimony (page 23). They can influence people's answers, especially when they are trying to remember something that happened in the past.

Worked Exam-style Question

1   Describe the strengths and limitations of using naturalistic observations to research social psychology.   *(12 marks)*

There are many different research methods that social psychologists use. Each method has many advantages and disadvantages and investigators often have to decide which would be best for their research.

Exam Tip
Introduce the idea that social psychologists have lots of research methods to choose from.

Naturalistic observations involve the experimenter just observing behaviour without interfering in any way. This means that the data recorded is highly realistic. These studies have a much higher ecological validity than other types of research. This is because the people being studied are often not aware of the experimenter and so their behaviour is much more realistic. Unlike surveys where people can often lie, naturalistic studies are more likely to produce accurate findings. The results from naturalistic studies can also be used to develop theories which can be tested in experiments.

Exam Tip
Show that you know what a naturalistic observation is — do this before you start evaluating the research methods.

Other research methods that social psychologists could use include laboratory experiments, field experiments or surveys. A laboratory experiment is a highly controlled research method. This means that the independent variable can be measured and cause and effect can be established. However, because of this control, laboratory experiments are very artificial and have low ecological validity. A naturalistic observation is much better in this way because it uses everyday situations to investigate behaviour. The results can then be generalised to large populations, which is something that laboratory experiments don't usually account for.

Field experiments are still controlled but a lot less artificial than laboratory studies since they use people in natural environments. However, it is hard to account for all of the different confounding variables. It is also difficult to ensure that the studies are ethical. Whilst naturalistic observations might have problems with ethics (often people are deceived or observed without giving their consent first), psychologists are allowed to observe people without their knowledge, but within reason.

Surveys are useful for getting lots of data quickly and cheaply. However, whilst they can get both qualitative and quantitative data, people can lie and sometimes questions can lead participants towards certain answers.

Exam Tip
It's a good idea to link the answer back to the question in your last paragraph.

Naturalistic observations do make it difficult to establish cause and effect, but many researchers believe getting realistic data with high ecological validity outweighs these disadvantages.

Summary Questions

Q1 Give two areas that social psychologists have studied.

Q2 Name a research method that can establish cause and effect.

Q3 Outline one disadvantage of natural experiments.

Q4 Give an example of an open question that could be used in a survey looking at people's religious beliefs.

2. Types of Conformity

There's more than one type of conformity, and unluckily for you, you need to learn them all...

Compliance

Compliance is where you go along with the majority, even if you don't share their views. You do this just to appear 'normal' — going against the majority might lead to exclusion or rejection from the group. This is called **normative social influence**.

┌─ **Example** ───────────────────────────────

- Employees at the same company tend to conform to the same dress code, e.g. no jeans or trainers.

- Supporters at a football match may all sing the same chant, even though they don't want to or don't like the chant.

- Someone may say they love a song that everyone else loves, even though they think it's pretty rubbish.

- Someone may laugh at a joke they don't understand, because everyone else is laughing.

Figure 1: *Normative social influence — employees conforming to a dress code.*

Internalisation

Internalisation is following along with the majority and believing in their views — you've accepted and internalised them so they're now your own too. This might happen if you're in an unfamiliar situation, where you don't know what the 'correct' way to behave is. In this situation, you'd look to others for information about how to behave. This is called **informational social influence**.

┌─ **Example** ───────────────────────────────

- A student who lives with animal rights activists while at Uni may become a vegetarian, and stay a vegetarian for the rest of their life.

- An adopted child may take on the religious beliefs of their parents.

- People tend to turn their headlights on in their cars just after they've seen others on the road turn theirs on.

- A person who doesn't know anything about football might begin to follow the team that their friends support, and then always support them.

Tip: An independent groups design is where there are different participants in each group (see page 69 for more). They're sometimes called independent measures, but they're just the same thing.

Key study of normative social influence — Asch (1951)

Asch designed an experiment to see whether people would conform to a majority's incorrect answer in an unambiguous task (one where the answer is obvious).

Method: Asch carried out a laboratory experiment with an independent groups design. In groups of 8, participants judged line lengths (see next page) by saying out loud which comparison line (1, 2 or 3) matched the standard line. Each group contained only one real participant — the others were confederates (who acted like real participants but were really helping the experimenter). The real participant always went last or last but one, so that they heard the others' answers before giving theirs. Each participant did 18 trials. On 12 of these (the critical trials) the confederates all gave the same wrong answer. There was also a control group, where the participants judged the line lengths in isolation.

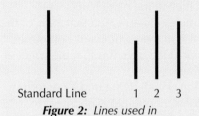

Standard Line   1   2   3

Figure 2: *Lines used in Asch's study.*

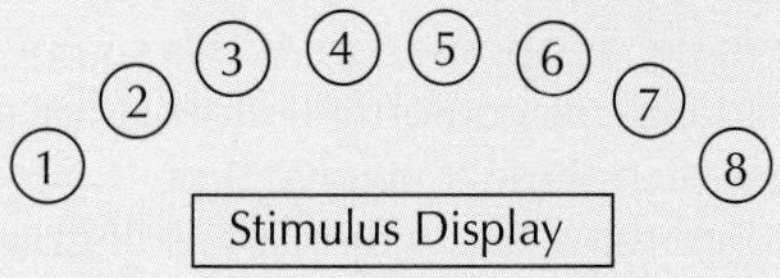

Figure 3: *Seating plan for Asch's study. The real participant was always in position 7 or 8 and the others were confederates.*

Real World Connection
The results of Asch's study have an important real life application. Tanford and Penrod (1986) discovered that 95% of the time, the vote of the first member of the jury matches the final outcome of the case. This is a strong suggestion that conformity is affecting the results. Other members of the jury may not want to appear to have different beliefs.

Results: In the control trials, participants gave the wrong answer 0.7% of the time. In the critical trials, participants conformed to the majority (gave the same wrong answer) 37% of the time. 75% conformed at least once. Afterwards, some participants said they didn't really believe their answers, but didn't want to look different.

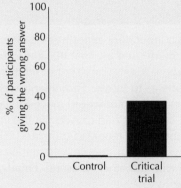

Figure 4: *Graph showing the results of Asch's experiment.*

Conclusion: The control condition showed that the task was easy to get right. However, 37% were wrong on the critical trials. They conformed to the majority — this was normative social influence.

Evaluation: This was a laboratory experiment, so there was good control of the variables. This minimises the effects of extraneous variables. Strict control of the variables also means that you could easily repeat the study to see if you get the same results. However, because the participants weren't in a natural situation, the study lacks ecological validity. Whether they were right or wrong didn't really matter to the participants — they might have been less likely to conform if their answer had had real-life consequences. In terms of ethics, the participants were deceived and might have been embarrassed when they found out the true nature of the study.

Tip: Extraneous variables can affect the variable that you're trying to measure. There's more about them on page 71.

Additional studies of normative social influence

Asch's study was carried out in America in the early 1950s. Other psychologists were interested to see whether the results were a product of the time and the American culture when the research was carried out, or whether the same results would be shown over time and in different places.

Neto (1995) carried out the same study over forty years later to see if he got the same results as Asch. This time, the experiment was carried out in Portugal. Another difference was that all the participants were female, as opposed to Asch's sample of males. Neto found that 59% of the participants conformed at least once. 28% of the participants conformed between three to twelve times. Neto concluded from this that the effect of conforming to a majority is still observable.

However, Lalancette and Standing (1990) didn't find a conformity effect when they made some changes to Asch's original experiment to make the stimuli more ambiguous. This could show that conformity to a majority is an inconsistent effect.

Informational social influence

Sherif researched whether people are influenced by others when they're doing an ambiguous task (one where the answer isn't clear).

Key study of conformity and the autokinetic effect — Sherif (1935)

Method: This was a laboratory experiment with a repeated measures design. Sherif used a visual illusion called the **autokinetic effect**, where a stationary spot of light, viewed in a dark room, appears to move. Participants were falsely told that the experimenter would move the light. They had to estimate how far it had moved. In the first phase, individual participants made repeated estimates. They were then put into groups of 3 people, where they each made their estimate with the others present. Finally, they were retested individually.

Results: When they were alone, participants developed their own stable estimates (personal norms), which varied widely between participants. Once the participants were in a group, the estimates tended to converge and become more alike. When the participants were then retested on their own, their estimates were more like the group estimates than their original guesses.

Conclusion: Participants were influenced by the estimates of other people, and a group norm developed. Estimates converged because participants used information from others to help them — they were affected by informational social influence.

Evaluation: This was a laboratory experiment, so there was strict control of the variables. This means that the results are unlikely to have been affected by other variables, so it should be possible to establish cause and effect. It also means that the method could be replicated. The repeated measures design meant that participant variables that could have affected the results were kept constant. However, the method is flawed because the participants were being asked to judge the movement of a light that wasn't moving — this rarely happens in real life. This study is less successful than Asch's in demonstrating the effects of conformity — the answer in Asch's study was obvious, so the only reason his participants conformed was to avoid standing out.

This experiment created an artificial situation, so the study lacks ecological validity. As well as this, the sample used was quite limited — all of the participants were male, so the results can't be generalised to everyone. An ethical problem with this study was deception — the participants were told the light was moving when it wasn't.

Tip: A lot of the time, the sample used within experiments can be biased. A certain type of person is chosen by the researchers, or certain types of people volunteer for psychology experiments and so we have to consider this when evaluating the findings.

Additional studies of informational social influence

Jenness (1932) carried out the first study into conformity. He used an ambiguous task, where participants had to look at a glass bottle filled with beans. The participants were individually asked to estimate how many beans they thought were in the bottle. The participants were then put into a group, and were asked to discuss the number of beans and come up with a group estimate. Finally, the participants were asked to estimate the number individually again, and were asked if they'd like to stick with their original estimate or whether they'd like to use the group's estimate. Jenness found that nearly everyone changed their individual guesses so that they were closer to the group estimate.

Rohrer et al (1954) carried out a repeat of Sherif's (1935) experiment, but the difference was that the participants were re-tested up to a year later. Rohrer et al found that even a year later, the participants carried on using the group estimate, rather than using their original individual estimate. So, even when the group doesn't exist any more, and is no longer present, it can still influence behaviour.

Conformity to assigned roles

Zimbardo et al (1973) carried out a study to see whether people could conform to assigned roles. They set up a mock prison to see if people would conform to the assigned roles of prisoner or guard.

The Stanford Prison Experiment — Zimbardo et al (1973)

Method: Male students were recruited to act as either guards or prisoners in a mock prison. They were randomly given the roles of prisoner or guard, and their behaviour was observed. The prisoners were 'arrested' at home, taken to 'prison' and given uniforms and numbers. The guards also wore uniforms and mirrored sunglasses.

Results: Initially, the guards tried to assert their authority and the prisoners resisted by sticking together. The prisoners then became more passive and obedient, while the guards invented nastier punishments. The experiment was

Figure 5: A guard and prisoners in Zimbardo's study.

abandoned early because some prisoners became very distressed.

Conclusion: Guards and prisoners adopted their social roles quickly. Zimbardo claims this shows that our social role can influence our behaviour — seemingly well-balanced men became unpleasant and aggressive in the role of guard.

Evaluation: This was a controlled observation, so there was good control of variables. However, because it was an artificial environment, the results can't really be generalised to real-life situations. In terms of ethics, some participants found the experience very distressing. There's also a problem with observer bias, as Zimbardo ran the prison himself, and later admitted that he became too personally involved in the situation. This experiment doesn't take individual differences into account — not all of the participants behaved according to their new roles.

Tip: Psychologists have to design their experiments to meet ethical guidelines, otherwise they can't be carried out — see pages 81-82 for the guidelines produced by the British Psychological Society.

Additional study of assigned roles — Orlando (1973)

No-one has ever replicated Zimbardo's prison study. This has been down to design problems, such as making it an ethically sound experiment. However, there have been other studies into assigned roles though. One of these was done by Orlando (1973).

Orlando (1973) set up a mock psychiatric ward in a hospital for three days. 29 staff members of the hospital volunteered to be 'patients', and were held in the ward. Another 22 staff members were involved, but they were just asked to carry out their normal daily roles.

It only took a little while for the 'patients' to start behaving like real patients of the hospital. It became very difficult to tell them apart — they seemed to be conforming to the roles that had been assigned to them. Many showed signs of depression and withdrawal, and six even tried to escape from the ward. After the study, the mock patients reported that they had felt frustrated, anxious and despairing. Some felt that they'd lost their identity, that their feelings weren't important, and that they weren't being treated as people.

Real World Connection
Studies like this can give really useful information about how real patients might feel in a hospital. Orlando's (1973) study lead to more of an effort by the staff to respect the patients, and improved the relationship and cooperation between them.

Reicher and Haslam (2006)

Reicher and Haslam (2006) developed Zimbardo's ideas. In the Holocaust during World War Two, approximately 6 million Jews were horrifically murdered by the Nazis. Psychologists had different theories about the soldiers who'd carried out the killings. Some thought they must be 'evil' individuals, but others thought they were 'normal' people who'd committed atrocities because of the social role they were in.

Zimbardo's (1973) study showed that normal people will shape their behaviour in order to fit into a social role, even if it's only been randomly assigned. It seemed that the participants' behaviour was situational (due to the social situation they were in), rather than dispositional (due to their internal characteristics). Reicher and Haslam (2006) recreated a similar situation to Zimbardo's experiment, but they were particularly interested to see how the group dynamics changed over time.

Tip: Experiments in psychology are often carried out to develop and test the results and ideas of previous research.

The BBC Prison Study — Reicher and Haslam (2006)

Method: This was a controlled observation in a mock prison, which was filmed for television. The participants were 15 male volunteers who had responded to an advert. They were randomly assigned to 2 groups of 5 guards and 10 prisoners. They had daily tests to measure levels of depression, compliance with rules, and stress.

The prisoners knew that one of them, chosen at random, would become a guard after 3 days. An independent ethics committee had the power to stop the experiment at any time in order to protect the participants.

Results: The guards failed to form a united group and identify with their role. They didn't always exercise their power and said they felt uncomfortable with the inequality of the situation. In the first 3 days, the prisoners tried to act in a way that would get them promoted to guard status. After one was promoted, they became a much stronger group because they knew there were no more chances of promotion. The unequal system collapsed due to the unwillingness of the guards and the strength of the prisoner group. On Day 6 the prisoners rebelled and the participants decided to live in a democracy, but this also collapsed due to tensions within the group. Some of the former prisoners then wanted to set up a stricter regime with them as leaders. The study was abandoned early on the advice of the ethics committee, as the participants showed signs of stress.

Conclusion: The participants didn't fit into their expected social roles, suggesting that these roles are flexible.

Evaluation: In contrast to Zimbardo's findings, Reicher and Haslam's prisoners were a strong group, and the guards were weak. However, it's possible that this was because Reicher and Haslam's guards were not as empowered as Zimbardo's, who were actively encouraged to maintain order. This study has been criticised for being made for TV — many people (including Zimbardo) argued that elements of it were staged and the participants played up to the cameras. Because this was an artificial situation, the results can't be generalised to real life. The ethics of this study were good — the participants were not deceived, so they were able to give informed consent. The participants were protected by the ethics committee and the study was abandoned as soon as they appeared to be becoming stressed. They were also debriefed and offered counselling afterwards.

Figure 6: *A still from the BBC Prison Study.*

Exam Tip
If you're evaluating a study it's a good idea to think about the participants. Here, they were all male. Female participants might have produced totally different results.

Worked Exam-style Questions

1   Outline the difference between internalisation and compliance.
(2 marks)

Internalisation means accepting the majority's views as your own — you believe and accept their views. Compliance is where you go along with

Exam Tip
This question is really just asking for definitions of the two terms. It's only worth 2 marks, so you only need to make two key points.

the majority, even if you disagree with their views, to appear normal.

---

2 (a) What is normative social influence? *(1 mark)*

(b) Give an example of normative social influence. *(1 mark)*

(c) Outline and evaluate research into the effects
of normative social influence. *(12 marks)*

(a) Normative social influence is where someone goes along with the majority even if they don't share their views in order to appear normal.

(b) An example of normative social influence is where employees at the same company conform to the same dress code.

(c) Asch (1951) carried out a study into normative social influence. He wanted to find out whether people would conform to a majority's incorrect answer in an unambiguous task.

His study was a laboratory experiment with an independent groups design. In groups of 8, participants were asked to judge line lengths. They had to say out loud which of three comparison lines matched a given standard line. However, each group only contained one real participant. The others were confederates. The real participant always spoke last, or second to last, so that they heard the confederates' answers first. Each participant did 18 trials. On 12 of these trials, the confederates all gave the same wrong answer. These were the critical trials. There was also a control group where the participants judged the line lengths in isolation.

In the control trials, Asch found that participants gave the wrong answer 0.7% of the time. In the critical trials, participants conformed to the majority almost 40% of the time. 75% of participants conformed at least once. When the participants were interviewed afterwards, some of them said that they didn't really believe their answers but that they hadn't wanted to look different.

The control condition showed that the task was easy to get right. So Asch concluded that normative social influence was being demonstrated on the critical trials.

The fact that the study was a laboratory experiment means that there was good control of the variables. This minimises the effect of extraneous variables, and also means that the study could easily be replicated. However, the participants weren't in a natural situation so the study lacks ecological validity. The participants may have been less likely to conform if the answer had real-life consequences. In terms of ethics, the participants were deceived as to the true nature of the study, and so they may have been embarrassed afterwards. Also, the sample only included males, so the results can't be generalised to females.

Asch's carried out his study in America in 1951. It might be that his results are a product of the time and the culture when the research was carried out. Different results might be shown over time and for studies carried out in different places.

Neto (1995) carried out the same study several decades later to see if he could replicate Asch's results. However, this time, the experiment was carried out in Portugal, and only used female participants. Neto found that 59% of the participants conformed at least once. 28% of the participants conformed between three to twelve times. Neto

Exam Tip
There are lots of possible answers to this question. If your answer is different to this it doesn't mean it's wrong.

Exam Tip
Don't forget to give the conclusion. Don't just stop at the results — say what they mean.

concluded from this that the effect of conforming to a majority is still observable.

However, Lalancette and Standing (1990) didn't find a conformity effect when they made some changes to Asch's original experiment to make the stimuli more ambiguous. This could show that conformity to a majority is an inconsistent effect, and so reduces the support for Asch's original results.

Exam Tip
It's a good idea to use other research in your evaluation. It doesn't matter if the research supports or disagrees with the results of the main study you're discussing — it's all useful in an evaluation.

Summary Questions

Q1 What is the difference between normative social influence and informational social influence?

Q2 What was different about the critical trials in Asch's (1951) study of conformity?

Q3 What is the autokinetic effect?

Q4 Comment on the ecological validity of Sherif's experiment.

Q5 Who were the participants in Zimbardo's (1973) prison experiment?

Q6 Did Zimbardo's study show that the participants' behaviour was situational or dispositional?

Q7 Who carried out the BBC prison study?

Q8 What was the conclusion of the BBC prison study?

3. Independent Behaviour and Social Change

There are lots of factors that influence whether we conform or resist.

Situational factors that affect conformity

Asch's participants (see pages 142-143) were influenced by situational factors:

Group size

You might expect that the bigger the majority is, the more influential it will be. If that was the case, it would be easier to resist conforming when there were fewer people to influence you. To test this, Asch (1956) conducted his conformity experiment (pages 142-143) with different numbers of confederates as the majority.

With only two confederates, the real participant conformed on only 14% of the critical trials. With three confederates, conformity rose to 32%. There was little change to conformity rates after that — no matter how big the majority group got. So, very small majorities are easier to resist than larger ones. But influence doesn't keep increasing with the size of majority.

Social support

Asch absolutely loved doing his conformity experiment, so he ran yet another version of it to test the effect of having a supporter in the group. When one of the confederates agreed with the participant rather than with the other confederates, the rate of conformity fell to 5.5%. A fellow dissenter (someone who disagrees with the majority) made it easier for the participant to resist the pressure to conform.

Other factors that affect conformity

Confidence, expertise and gender could also have an effect on conformity:

Confidence and expertise

When Asch debriefed his participants, he found a common factor of confidence in the people who hadn't conformed. If someone felt confident in their judgements, they were more able to resist group pressure.

- Wiesenthal et al (1976) found that if people felt competent in a task, they were less likely to conform.

- Perrin and Spencer (1980) thought that Asch's results might just reflect the social trends in America during the 1950s. They replicated Asch's line task, but used a group of engineering students. They found that there was almost no effect of conformity in the students. This could have been due to the fact that engineers had confidence in their skills in making accurate observations.

  In a follow-up study, the participants were a group of young people on probation, and their probation officers were used as the confederates. This time round, the level of conformity was very similar to Asch's results. So, it looks like it isn't as simple as time and place affecting conformity. It doesn't seem like it's a stable behaviour — there are other factors, such as expertise, personality and power relationships that can affect results.

Gender

Until the mid-1970s the dominant view was that females conform more than males. Then Eagly and Carli did a load of research that suggests it might not be as simple as all that...

Learning Objectives:

- Understand social influence in everyday life.

- Be able to give explanations of independent behaviour, including how people resist pressures to conform.

- Understand the influence of individual differences on independent behaviour, including locus of control.

- Know how social influence research helps us to understand social change, including the role of minority influence.

Figure 1: *The conformity rates measured in engineering students were very different to Asch's findings.*

Eagly (1987) argued that men and women's different social roles are responsible for the difference in conformity rates — women are more concerned with group harmony and relationships, so they're more likely to agree with the opinions of others. Assertiveness and independence are valued male attributes, so maintaining your own opinion under pressure fits with the perceived male social role. This ties in with Becker's (1986) findings that women conform more than men in public settings, but not when their opinions are private.

Eagly and Carli (1981) did a meta-analysis of conformity research, where they re-analysed data from a number of studies. They did find some sex differences in conformity, but the differences were inconsistent. The clearest difference between men and women was in Asch-like studies where there was group pressure from an audience.

Tip: There's more about meta-analyses on page 171. They're a good way of bringing a lot of results together to look for a general trend.

Eagly and Carli (1981) also pointed out that male researchers are more likely than female researchers to rate female participants higher on conformity. This could be because male researchers use tasks that are more familiar to men (so they don't need to look to others as much for help). This is an example of gender bias.

Additional study of gender — Sistrunk and McDavid (1971)

Sistrunk and McDavid reviewed research into conformity from the 1950s and 1960s. This research had almost always reported that women conform more than men. However, when Sistrunk and McDavid looked further, they found that the psychologists conducting these studies were always male... So, they carried out their own study into gender differences. They came up with a questionnaire full of statements that had been judged to be 'masculine', 'feminine' or 'neutral' (e.g. a feminine statement would be "cake is easier to make than pie"). Each statement started with a 'majority response' (e.g. "most American's agree that").

The questionnaires were given to male and female participants and they were asked to agree or disagree with the statements. It was found that women and men tended to conform when it was a subject that they were not familiar with. However, for neutral statements, conformity was very similar.

It could be that the earlier results were down to the fact that the male researchers had unintentionally designed their studies in a masculine way, using topics unfamiliar to women.

Tip: Gender is a factor in lots of areas of psychological research — for example, look back to the stress research on page 128.

Aspects of personality

Parts of someone's personality can affect whether they'll conform or show independent behaviour. Rotter (1966) developed a questionnaire to measure a personality characteristic called **locus of control**. It indicates how much personal control people believe they have over events in their lives. The questionnaire involved choosing between paired statements like these ones:

1. Misfortune is usually brought about by people's own actions.

2. Things that make us unhappy are largely due to bad luck.

If you agree with the first statement, you have an **internal locus of control**. This is categorised by a belief that what happens in your life results from your own behaviour or actions. For example, if you did well in a test you might

Tip: Questionnaires are a popular research method — see pages 63-64 for more about them.

put it down to how much work you did for it.

If you agree with the second statement, you have an **external locus of control**. This is a belief that events are caused by external factors, like luck or the actions of others. For example, if you did well in a test you might put it down to good questions coming up, or a lenient examiner.

People with an internal locus of control feel a stronger sense of control over their lives than people with an external locus of control. This means that they're more likely to exhibit independent behaviour. People with an external locus of control may be more likely to conform.

Minority influence

Tip: In the exam, always make it clear whether you're talking about majority influence or minority influence.

Obviously people don't always go along with the majority — if they did, nothing would ever change. Sometimes small minorities and even individuals gain influence and change the way the majority thinks. In **minority influence**, it seems that a form of internalisation (see page 142) is taking place. Members of the majority actually take on the beliefs and views of a consistent minority — rather than just complying.

Moscovici et al (1969) did some research into minority influence that compared inconsistent minorities with consistent minorities.

Key study of minority influence — Moscovici (1969)

Method: This was a laboratory experiment into minority influence using 192 women. In groups of 6 at a time, participants judged the colour of 36 slides. All of the slides were blue, but the brightness of the blue varied. Two of the six participants in each group were confederates. In one condition the confederates called all 36 slides 'green' (consistent) and in another condition they called 24 of the slides 'green' and 12 of the slides 'blue' (inconsistent). A control group was also used which contained no confederates.

Results: In the control group the participants called the slides 'green' 0.25% of the time. In the consistent condition 8.4% of the time participants adopted the minority position and called the slides 'green'. In fact, 32% of the participants called the slides 'green' at least once. In the inconsistent condition the participants moved to the minority position of calling the slides 'green' only 1.25% of the time.

Conclusion: The confederates were in the minority but their views appear to have influenced the real participants. The use of the two conditions illustrated that the minority had more influence when they were consistent in calling the slides 'green'.

Evaluation: This study was a laboratory experiment so it lacked ecological validity because the task was artificial. The participants may have felt that judging the colour of the slide was a trivial exercise. They might have acted differently if their principles were involved. Also, the study was only carried out on women so doesn't allow for gender differences and the results can't be generalised to men. However, owing to the use of a control group, we know that the participants were actually influenced by the minority rather than being

Exam Tip
Don't worry if you find that you can't remember the exact figures in the exam — as long as you can remember the trend in the results then that's enough to get you some marks.

independently unsure of the colour of the slides. In a similar experiment, participants were asked to write down the colour rather than saying it out loud. In this condition, even more people agreed with the minority, which provides more support for minority influence.

Additional study of minority influence — Nemeth (1986)

Nemeth has carried out a lot of research into minority influence since Moscovici's study. Nemeth (1986) came up with a cognitive explanation for minority influence. She thought that a minority within a group, particularly one that disagrees, can have the effect of making the majority question their views. The majority is encouraged to think about the minority's opinions, which can bring about new ways of thinking.

Minority influence and social change

There are many examples in history of things changing because the ideas of a few have taken hold. Try these for starters:

The Suffragettes

In the early 1900s in Britain, a small minority began to campaign for women to be allowed to vote. This was called the suffragette movement. Suffragettes chained themselves to railings outside Downing Street and Buckingham Palace. The suffragettes' campaign involved violent methods such as assault and arson. In 1913 a suffragette threw herself under the feet of the King's horse. She died from her injuries. Eventually the majority was influenced by the suffragettes' point of view and in 1928 women were finally given the right to vote on the same terms as men.

Martin Luther King

In the 1950s in America, black people did not have the same rights as white people. For example, in parts of America, buses were segregated and black people had to give up their seats to white people. Reverend Martin Luther King challenged the views of the majority to bring about political and social rights for black people. He and other activists used peaceful protests like marches and sit-ins. This was known as the Civil Rights Movement. His ideas were so unpopular that during this time his home was bombed by activists, he was subjected to personal abuse, and he was arrested. In the end though, the actions of civil rights activists influenced the majority. Nowadays there are laws that ensure people are given equal rights regardless of racial origin, and in 1964 Martin Luther King was awarded the Nobel Peace Prize.

Gay Rights Movements

Homosexuality was once illegal in the UK. It was decriminalised in England and Wales in 1967 — but the age of consent was 21 (higher than for heterosexual people) and homosexuals were still treated negatively. Over the last decade, there have been moves towards equality as a result of Gay Rights Movements. These minorities have successfully changed attitudes. For example, the Equality Act (Sexual Orientation) 2007 made it illegal to discriminate against gay people in the provision of goods and services.

Figure 2: *Protests and marches are often part of a minority's campaign.*

Tip: These are just three examples from many — you may have learnt about other ones too.

Worked Exam-style Questions

1 (a) Outline one study into minority influence. *(6 marks)*

   (b) James and Asif want to change the system at their school for voting for the head boy because they think the current system is unfair. Other people in their class are happy to remain using the current system. Explain how a change to the system might be made, even though James and Asif are in the minority. *(4 marks)*

Exam Tip
The question only asks for an outline of the study — so don't waste time evaluating it — you won't get any marks for this.

(a) Moscovici (1969) carried out a laboratory experiment into minority influence. 192 female participants were tested in groups of six, but only four people in each group were real participants. The other two were confederates. The participants had to judge the colour of 36 slides, which were all blue. In one condition, the two confederates said that all of the slides were green. In another condition, they said that 24 of the slides were green and 12 of the slides were blue. A control group was also used which used no confederates.

The participants in the control group said that the slides were green 0.25% of the time. When the confederates were consistent, the participants followed the minority and called the slides green 8.4% of the time. When the confederates were inconsistent, the participants only followed the minority 1.25% of the time.

Moscovici thought that this showed that even though the confederates were in the minority, their views had an influence on the real participants. Using a consistent and an inconsistent condition showed that the minority had more of an effect when they were consistent in saying that the slides were green.

Exam Tip
You need to make sure that you talk about James and Asif — don't just talk about minority influence and change in general.

(b) James and Asif could carry out a campaign to explain why they feel that the current system is unfair and how the system should be changed. However, they would need to promote their views in a very consistent way to the majority group, rather than changing their mind about things. Moscovici's research into minority influence in 1969 supports this — conformity rates were higher with a consistent minority rather than an inconsistent minority.

Exam Tip
Bring in other research to support your points wherever you can.

In minority influence, it seems that a form of internalisation takes place. This is where members of the majority actually adopt and believe the views of a consistent minority. So James and Asif might be able to influence the majority with their ideas and change their views. This could lead to a change in the system, if enough people take on their ideas and become the majority.

Summary Questions

Q1 How might confidence affect conformity?

Q2 What did Eagly and Carli (1981) find about gender in their meta-analysis?

Q3 What is minority influence?

Q4 Moscovici (1969) carried out a famous study into minority influence. Who else studied minority influence?

Q5 Give one example of minority influence causing social change.

4. Obedience to Authority

Obedience and conformity are similar concepts but be careful not to confuse the two. Both involve people changing their behaviour but **obedience** *happens after a direct order, while* **conformity** *is from an indirect influence.*

Milgram's (1963) study of obedience

Following the events of the Holocaust during World War II many people were put on trial because of the atrocious crimes they had committed. Lots of them tried to plead 'not-guilty' saying their actions were just a result of following orders. In 1961 Stanley Milgram began his research after hearing about one of these cases. He wondered whether there was any truth in their claims — and whether people actually do extraordinary things when told to by an authority figure. He devised a series of experiments to test his ideas and ended up creating one of the most shocking and important studies within psychology.

Learning Objective:
- Know about obedience to authority, including Milgram's work and explanations of why people obey.

Key study of obedience — Milgram (1963)

Method: Milgram conducted laboratory experiments to test factors thought to affect obedience. One 'remote learner' condition tested whether people would obey orders to shock someone in a separate room. It took place at the prestigious Yale University. 40 men took part, responding to newspaper adverts seeking volunteers for a study on 'learning and memory'. They received payment for attending, which didn't depend on them proceeding with the experiment. The experimenter wore a grey technician's coat. Each participant was introduced to a confederate (acting like a participant, but who was really part of the experimental set-up). They drew lots to see who would act as 'teacher' and 'learner', but this was fixed so the participant was always the teacher.

       The participant witnessed the confederate being strapped into a chair and connected up to a shock generator in the next room (see Figure 1). It didn't actually give electric shocks, but the participants thought it was real.

The switches ranged from 15 volts (labelled 'Slight Shock') to 450 volts (labelled 'XXX'). The participant taught the learner word-pairs over an intercom. When the learner answered incorrectly, the participant had to administer an increasing level of shock. As the shocks increased, the learner started to scream and ask to be let out. After the 330 V shock, he made no further noise. If participants

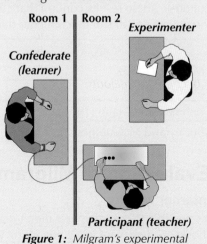

Figure 1: Milgram's experimental set-up involved a teacher (participant), a learner (confederate) and the experimenter.

Tip: Milgram's study is also known as the 'remote learner' experiment.

Exam Tip
Milgram's study was a laboratory experiment. So, in the exam you could use the advantages and disadvantages of lab experiments (page 61) to evaluate the methodology of this study.

hesitated, the experimenter told them to continue. Debriefing included an interview, questionnaires and being reunited with the 'learner'.

Results: 26 participants (65%) administered 450 V and none stopped before 300 V (when the learner started protesting). Most participants showed obvious signs of stress during the experiment, like sweating, groaning and trembling.

Conclusion: Ordinary people will obey orders to hurt someone else, even if it means acting against their consciences.

Variations on Milgram's experiment

Milgram carried out his experiment in loads of slightly different ways to investigate the effect that certain conditions would have on the results.

Some of Milgram's variations on this experiment	Percentage administering 450 V
Male participants	65%
Female participants	65%
Learner's protests can be heard	62.5%
Experiment run in seedy offices	48%
Learner in same room as participant	40%
Authority (experimenter), in another room, communicating by phone	23%
Other teachers (confederates) refuse to give shock	10%
Other participant (a confederate) gives shock instead	92.5%

Tip: We couldn't replicate Milgram's study today — there are too many ethical issues.

Studies in different countries

Milgram's experiments were only conducted on American citizens. Other researchers wanted to investigate whether these findings would also exist in other countries, so many different studies were conducted all over the world. As the table below shows, obedience levels do change across different cultures. These results confirm that cultural differences do exist, but overall, the figures are all still much higher than we might expect.

Study	Country	Obedience rate
Milgram (1963)	USA	65%
Mantell (1971)	Germany	85%
Kilhman and Mann (1971)	Australia	54%
Burley and McGuinness (1977)	UK	50%

Real World Connection

Milgram's findings have been really influential within the real world. When teaching business ethics, students are now warned about the unfair requirements sometimes put upon them by their bosses. When people are aware of what happens when they are told to do something by an authority figure, they are more likely to question whether they agree with carrying out the request in the first place.

Evaluation of Milgram's experiment

Internal validity

It's possible that participants didn't really believe they were inflicting electric shocks — they were just going along with the experimenter's expectations (showing demand characteristics). But Milgram claimed participants' stressed reactions showed they believed the experiment was real.

Ecological validity

Milgram's participants did a task that they were unlikely to encounter in real life (shocking someone). So the study lacks ecological validity. However, because it was a laboratory experiment there was good control of the variables, so it's possible to establish cause and effect.

Ethical issues

The participants were deceived as to the true nature of the study. This means they couldn't give informed consent. They weren't informed of their right to withdraw from the experiment. In fact, they were prompted to continue when they wanted to stop. The participants showed signs of stress during the experiment, so they weren't protected. However, they were extensively debriefed and 84% of them said they were pleased to have taken part. As well as this, at the time of the experiment there weren't any formal ethical guidelines in place, so technically Milgram didn't breach any. There's more general stuff on ethics on pages 81-83.

Tip: Ecological validity is a really important concept that comes up a lot in psychology. You can always comment on the ecological validity of any type of study.

Factors affecting obedience

Milgram identified several factors that appeared to affect obedience.

Presence of allies

When there were 3 teachers (1 participant and 2 confederates), the real participant was less likely to obey if the other two refused to obey. Having allies can make it easier to resist orders than when you're on your own.

Proximity of the victim

Milgram's results suggest an important factor was the proximity (closeness) of the learner. In the 'remote learner' condition, 65% gave the maximum shock. This dropped to 40% with the learner in the same room, and 30% when the participant had to put the learner's hand onto the shock plate. Figure 2 clearly shows how more people are likely to obey orders when they can only hear the victim, compared with when they have to see or touch the victim. Proximity made the learner's suffering harder to ignore.

Proximity of the authority

When the authority figure gave prompts by phone from another room, obedience rates dropped to 23%. When the authority figure wasn't close by, orders were easier to resist.

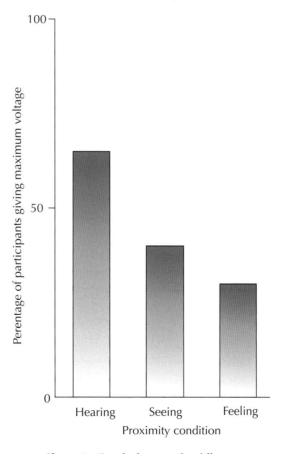

Figure 2: *Graph showing the difference in obedience levels depending on proximity.*

Tip: The variations in Milgram's experiments show that obedience isn't clear cut. There are loads of factors that can affect how obedient people are.

Milgram's agency theory (1973)

Milgram came up with his **agency theory** to explain obedience. When people behave on behalf of an external authority (do as they're told), they're said to be in an **agentic state**. This means they act as someone's agent, rather than taking personal responsibility for their actions. The opposite of this is behaving autonomously — not following orders. Milgram claimed that there were some binding factors that might have kept his participants in the agentic state:

- Reluctance to disrupt the experiment — participants had already been paid, so may have felt obliged to continue.

- The pressure of the surroundings — the experiment took place in a prestigious university. This made the experimenter seem like a legitimate authority.

- The insistence of the authority figure — if participants hesitated they were told that they had to continue the experiment.

Before his study, Milgram believed that people were autonomous and could choose to resist authority. His **agency theory** shows Milgram's findings changed his mind about how much impact legitimate authority figures have.

Figure 3: *People frequently follow orders of authority figures, especially if the authority figure or setting is prestigious.*

Evaluation of agency theory

There's lots of experimental evidence to support agency theory — Milgram's participants often claimed they wouldn't have gone as far by themselves, but they were just following orders. Sometimes people resist the pressure to obey authority. This can be because of the situation, or because of individual differences (see pages 161-162). Agency theory doesn't explain why some people are more likely to exhibit independent behaviour than others.

Milgram's findings

Milgram's findings tell us about why people obey.

Agentic state

Milgram's agency theory stated that when we feel we're acting out the wishes of another person (being their agent), we feel less responsible for our actions. This effect is seen in Milgram's studies. Some participants were concerned for the welfare of the learner and asked who would take responsibility if he were harmed. When the experimenter (authority) took responsibility, often the participant would continue.

This agentic state was also in the experiment's set-up. The participants voluntarily entered a social contract (an obligation) with the experimenter to take part and follow the procedure of the study. People can start off acting in an autonomous way (thinking for themselves), but then become obedient. This is known as an agentic shift. When Milgram's participants arrived for the experiment they were in an autonomous state, but as soon as they started following orders they underwent an agentic shift, and entered an agentic state.

Exam Tip
If you talk about the good and bad points of Agency Theory and reference it to Milgram's study, the examiner will be really impressed. For example, participants would not have gone all the way to 450 V by themselves — they were in an agentic state due to the commands of the experimenter.

Example

There are many everyday situations when people are in the agentic state:

- At work people often follow orders from their boss regardless of how unreasonable they may be. This could be because they feel their boss 'knows best.'

Gradual commitment

Gradual commitment means agreeing to something gradually — in small steps. It makes it harder to refuse the next request. In Milgram's study, participants were asked to deliver only a 15 volt shock at the start. This was gradually built up to very large shocks. Participants might have been more reluctant to obey if they'd been asked to deliver the 450 volt shock at the start. They obeyed at the lower levels, so it was harder for them to justify disobeying the later requests.

Gradual commitment is also known as the **'foot-in-the-door' effect**. Once you've gone along with a minor request, the request could be gradually increased until you're doing something you might never have agreed to in the first place.

> **Real World Connection**
> The foot-in-the-door effect can be seen in real life situations. For example, charity collectors often stop people in the street and ask for a moment of their time. If the person agrees, they may then be asked to sign a petition, and after a conversation about the charity, they might then agree to giving a certain amount of money per month. If the collector had asked them out right for the money, they would have been more likely to just say no.

Key study of the foot-in-the-door effect — Schwarzwald, Bizman and Raz (1983)

Method:	The study used an independent design with two conditions to investigate people's fundraising behaviours. One group was asked to sign a petition two weeks before being asked to make a donation (foot-in-the-door condition). The other group was just asked to make a donation with no petition mentioned (control condition).
Results:	More people made donations from the foot-in-the-door condition (if they had signed a petition) than those in the control condition. They also donated more money.
Conclusion:	The foot-in-the-door effect can be effective within fundraising, in increasing donations.
Evaluation:	Other studies have provided mixed evidence for the foot-in-the-door effect. For example, in a similar experiment into fundraising, Bell (2003) found no effect.

> **Exam Tip**
> Many studies are repeated in similar ways by other psychologists. They often provide contradictory results. It's worth being able to give an example if you can.

┌ **Example** ──────────────

The foot-in-the-door effect can happen in lots of situations:

- Asking for a homework extension of one day followed by then asking for an extension of two days.
- Asking your parents if you can drive their car after asking if they will drive you to the shops.

People as justified authorities

We're socialised to recognise the authority of people like parents, police officers, doctors, teachers etc. These kinds of people are justified authorities — they're given the right to tell us what to do. This means we're more likely to obey them. When Milgram re-ran his study in some run-down offices, obedience rates were lower than when the study was run in the university. He argued that the experimenter's authority was higher in the university situation because of the status of the university.

Bickman (1974) conducted a field experiment where researchers ordered passers-by to do something like pick up a bit of litter. They were dressed either in a guard's uniform, as a milkman, or just in smart clothes. Bickman was interested to see whether the perceived differences in authority would affect levels of obedience.

> **Tip:** A lot of the experiments into the foot-in-the-door effect have looked at pro-social behaviour. This is behaviour which usually benefits another person or group of people.

Key study of justified authorities — Bickman (1974)

Method:	Researchers in New York dressed up as a guard, a milkman or a normal citizen. They then approached people on the street and asked them to pick up litter, move up from a bus stop or give money to a stranger.
Results:	Approximately 90% of participants obeyed the guard figure, but only 50% obeyed the civilian (Figure 4).
Conclusion:	People are much more likely to follow orders from a perceived authority figure.
Evaluation:	This study had high ecological validity as being stopped by a guard or passerby could naturally happen in real life. However, there are ethical issues due to a lack of informed consent.

Figure 5: Seeing someone in uniform can be enough to make people obey.

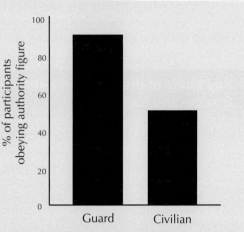

Figure 4: Graph showing the percentage of orders obeyed from different authority figures.

Additional study of justified authorities — Sedikides and Jackson (1990)

Sedikides and Jackson (1990) looked at the influence of authority figures. The experiment was set in a zoo where the researchers were dressed as a zoo keeper (high strength) or visitor (low strength). They asked 208 people to stand away from the railings of an exhibit and then either waited next to them (high immediacy condition) or left them alone (low immediacy condition). Those in the high strength / high immediacy condition were more compliant than those in the low strength / low immediacy condition. It would seem that uniform and presence both influence conformity rates.

Buffers

Buffers are things that protect us — in this case from the consequences of our actions. Milgram's participants were more obedient in conditions where they could not see or hear the victim receiving the shocks. When they were in the same room as the learner, there wasn't any buffer. So... losing the buffer made it harder for Milgram's participants to act against their conscience and go along with someone's unjust orders to hurt the learner.

Resisting the pressure to obey authority

Some people can resist the pressure to obey authority. This can be affected by several factors, including the situation and individual differences.

The situation

More of Milgram's participants resisted orders if there were other participants present who refused to obey (see page 157). This suggests that people find it easier to stand up to authority if they have support from others, because they no longer have to take full responsibility for rebelling.

Key study of resisting obedience — Gamson et al (1982)

Method:	Gamson et al studied groups of participants to look at whether people were more likely to obey authority than conform to group norms. The individuals were asked to sign a document agreeing to the unfair dismissal of a fictional employee at a local company. They were told the document would be used in a court trial. The discussions were filmed. At several points filming stopped and groups were again encouraged to sign the document agreeing to the sacking.
Results:	Participants rebelled against the unjust authority figure. This happened through a process of minority influence — with one or two people resisting the authority's requests at first. This rebellion then spread to the whole group. Out of 33 groups, 16 complete groups rebelled against the authority and voiced their own views despite being told not to and another 9 groups partially disobeyed.
Conclusion:	The presence of allies and collective action seemed to help the participants in their resistance.
Evaluation:	Because participants did not know they were taking part in an experiment, this study has high ecological validity. But, there are many ethical issues due to deception and lack of informed consent (see pages 81-83 for more on ethics).

Real World Connection
Resistance to authority underlies a lot of important events within history. The US Civil Rights Movement and the anti-apartheid movement in South Africa are two examples where people have defied authority and stood up for what they believe in.

Figure 6: *Nelson Mandela was imprisoned on Robben Island for his defiance of authority against the apartheid in South Africa.*

This ties in with Asch's research on conformity. He found that participants were more likely to resist the pressure to conform if one of the confederates agreed with them (page 150). It seems that people are more likely to display independent behaviour if they've got support from others. It doesn't really make sense to call this behaviour independent, seeing as it depends on having someone else there to agree with you... But just go with it...

Around 25% of participants in Asch's original study did not conform while 35% of Milgram's participants disobeyed the authority figure. As further studies have shown, situational factors may impact how people view authoritarian demands. Milgram found that when he conducted his experiment in a more run-down setting, obedience rates dropped. This could be because participants are more likely to question the status of the authority figure after assessing their surroundings.

Tip: Situation and disposition are important factors in psychology. A person's situation is the context and environment that they're in. Their disposition is their internal characteristics and tendencies.

The role of individual differences

If an individual has a high level of moral reasoning (thinking about right and wrong) they may be more able to resist an order that goes against their conscience. One of Milgram's participants had experienced a Second World War concentration camp. She refused to administer any level of shock, because she didn't want to inflict pain on another person. Those who resisted may have still felt personally responsible — they weren't in an agentic state.

Tip: Individual differences can account for a lot of variation within psychological findings. They include things like personality, age and gender.

Key study of individual differences and defying authority — Kohlberg (1969)

American teenagers from all across the country were presented with a moral dilemma. They each had to write down a rationale and solution to the problem. Kohlberg then analysed their answers to assess their obedience levels. He found that there were six different stages of moral development. Those who fell within the advanced stages were more likely to disobey authority figures.

Rotter (1966) claimed that people could be categorised as having an internal or external locus of control (pages 151-152). People with an internal locus of control take responsibility for their actions more than people with an external locus of control. This means that they're more likely to exhibit independent behaviour — they're less likely to conform, or be obedient, than people with an external locus of control.

Key study of locus of control — Schurz (1985)

Schurz's experiment was conducted in Austria using a similar method to Milgram. Each participant was asked to press a button releasing a painful stimulus to a 'learner' everytime they got the wrong answer. There were 20 switches, each one increasing in intensity. Participants also received a measurement of their locus of control. 80% of the participants pressed all 20 switches. Locus of control did not appear to influence obedience. But, independent people were much more likely to take responsibility for their actions.

Sometimes people feel that they're being pushed too far or a rule restricts them too much. In this situation they might react by doing the opposite of what they're told. This is known as the **'boomerang effect'**.

Worked Exam-style Questions

1 (a) Describe and evaluate a theory explaining obedience.
(8 marks)

(b) Outline one piece of research that shows why people may disobey authority.   *(6 marks)*

(a) Milgram came up with his agency theory in order to explain obedience. He developed the theory to account for the agentic state — the state in which a person acts out the wishes of another person and so feels less responsible for their actions. He suggests that people follow orders from someone else merely because of their authority status. When in this state, people act as an agent and do as they're told.

There are several ways which help people stay in such a state. Milgram calls these 'binding factors' and they include a general reluctance to disrupt the environment, the pressure from surroundings and the insistence of an authority figure.

The findings from Milgram's (1963) study appeared to support this idea. Participants often continued to shockingly high levels of obedience when the experimenter took responsibility for any harm caused to the learner.

However, despite this evidence for agency theory, there may be other factors which may influence obedience rates. Agency theory can't explain why people are more likely to show independent behaviour and why some people don't obey. So, other theories are needed to explain this. Individual differences, such as locus of control and moral reasoning, can provide alternative explanations, and the situation can also play a role.

(b) One piece of research that effectively illustrates why people may disobey authority is a study by Gamson et al (1982). He studied groups of participants who were asked to discuss and sign a document agreeing to the unfair dismissal of a fictional employee. The discussions were filmed and on several occasions the groups were directed to sign the document against their views and say they were in favour of the sacking. They were told the document would later be used in court.

Gamson et al found that the majority of the groups refused to do this. At first, only one or two people rebelled, but then this spread to the rest of the group by a process of minority influence. Many of the groups rebelled against the authority and voiced their own opinions despite being told not to. The study clearly showed that the presence of allies and collective action seemed to help the participants in their resistance against authority figures.

Exam Tip
When a question asks you to outline a study, just write the method, results and conclusion. You don't need to give any evaluation.

Summary Questions

Q1 Give two reasons why Milgram's study was unethical.

Q2 List three variations that Milgram did of his original experiment.

Q3 What is the agentic shift?

Q4 Outline the foot-in-the-door condition used in the study by Schwarzwald, Bizman and Raz (1983).

Q5 Cyril is fundraising for a global climate change charity. How could he use the foot-in-the-door technique to raise more money?

Q6 a) Outline the methodology used in Bickman's (1974) study.
    b) Describe the results of Bickman's (1974) study.

Q7 What was the conclusion of Sedikides and Jackson's (1990) study?

Q8 Who were the participants in Kohlberg's (1969) study of the effect of individual differences on defying authority?

Q9 In the study by Schurz (1985) what percentage of participants pressed all 20 switches?

Q10 Give an example of the 'boomerang effect'.

Tip: For Milgram's full study see pages 155-156.

5. Research into Conformity and Obedience

We can learn a lot from the revolutionary experiments of people like Milgram. Although their studies couldn't be conducted today, they have stimulated many theories and have wider applications within the real world.

The impact of Milgram's (1963) findings

Before the study Milgram asked different experts on human behaviour (e.g. psychiatrists) to predict the results. They thought the maximum average shock that participants would go up to was 130 V, and that only someone with a psychopathic personality disorder would administer a 450 V shock. He actually found that 65% of participants went up to 450 V, even when they clearly didn't want to.

Milgram's study completely changed what people thought about obedience, and it's had a huge impact ever since. It showed that his participants deferred responsibility for their actions onto the authority figure. Milgram found the highest rate of obedience when the experiment took place in a university and he wore a lab coat. This exposed the huge amount of trust that people have in justified authorities. Hofling et al (1966) also showed this when they got nurses to break hospital rules because they thought they were following a doctor's orders.

Key study of obedience — Hofling et al (1966)	
Method:	In this naturalistic experiment, 22 real night nurses were telephoned by a fake doctor who asked them to administer 20 mg of an unauthorised drug called *Astroten*. It was actually a fake drug. The nurses knew that the maximum dose allowed was 10 mg and that they were not allowed to receive instructions from doctors over the telephone.
Results:	21/22 (95%) of the nurses carried out the doctor's request. When a similar group of nurses were asked how they would act, 21/22 said they wouldn't do it.
Conclusion:	People are highly influenced by authority even in real life settings. The findings by Hofling et al also further support the results given by Milgram in his experiments.
Evaluation:	Although the ecological validity of this experiment is high, there is evidence of population and cultural bias as the sample of nurses comes from America in the 1960s. This population might have been more likely to obey.

Figure 1: Hofling's study highlights how easy it is to obey authority within a work environment.

We often have no choice but to place our trust in experts, but with this comes the potential for abuse of power. A contemporary example of this is the case of Harold Shipman — a doctor who murdered patients by injecting them with huge overdoses. He was able to do this because his patients trusted him, and he's thought to have got away with killing over 200 of them before anybody became suspicious. Scary...

Zimbardo and the effect of deindividuation

Deindividuation is when people lose their personal identity (stop feeling like individuals), and identify with a group.

Key study of deindividuation — Zimbardo (1970)

Zimbardo (1970) replicated Milgram's experiment and examined the effect of different conditions. He compared participants who wore their own clothes and were treated as individuals, to ones who wore hoods covering their faces and were spoken to as a group. He found that the average level of electric shock doubled when the participants were wearing a hood.

Figure 2: Wearing clothes that hide features is a classic example of becoming more anonymous.

When the participants were deindividuated, they became more obedient and more antisocial. Zimbardo later demonstrated this in the Stanford Prison Experiment (1973) (pages 145-146). The prison guards wore uniforms and sunglasses, and they quickly became aggressive towards the prisoners. It seems that they stopped taking personal responsibility for their actions, and changed their behaviour to fit into their social role.

Deindividuation in large crowds

Many experiments have looked at deindividuation in crowds.

Key study of deindividuation in crowds — Mann (1981)

Method:	Mann looked at newspaper coverage of suicide attempts. It focused on crowds that gathered below when someone was threatening to jump off a tall building or bridge.
Results:	The newspaper reports showed that people in large crowds were likely to start jeering and telling the person to jump. This was even more common when it was dark.
Conclusion:	Mann concluded that the anonymity you get in a big group can lead to more extreme behaviour, because the sense of personal responsibility is shifted onto the group.

These studies help explain problems like police brutality and rioting behaviour. Zimbardo's research suggests there are ways of combating the negative effects of deindividuation — he found that when participants wore name tags instead of hoods, they gave less severe electric shocks. This has implications for social change — e.g. hoodies are banned in some public places. It could be that wearing hoodies makes people more likely to behave in an antisocial way. Or it could be that people find hoodies threatening because the people wearing them can't be identified. Or it could just be a load of rubbish.

People in groups

Sherif (1935) and Asch (1956) (pages 142-144) showed that participants' responses to tasks changed when they were in a group. In Sherif's study this was because they were in an unfamiliar situation, so they looked to other people for information on how to behave. Asch's participants felt pressure from the group to give the wrong answer, just so they would fit in. These findings have wider implications for society, as we rely on groups to make important decisions.

Real World Connection

The riots in London in 2011 are a good example of deindividuation within large crowds. Many of the rioters reported afterwards that they got caught up in the action as they were part of a larger group. These feelings of anonymity from the larger group meant people felt they wouldn't get caught, leading to deindividuation and antisocial behaviour.

┌─ Examples ────────────────────────

Groups we rely on to make decisions include:

Governments, juries, friendship groups, work colleagues and religious organisations.

Janis (1972) found that groups having to make important decisions can be guilty of **Groupthink**. This happens especially in very cohesive groups, which are isolated from other influences, and have very powerful leaders — e.g. governments. Janis saw that members of the group converge their thinking so that it falls in line with what they imagine the general view of the group is. This leads to a unanimous decision that doesn't actually reflect what everyone in the group wants. It happens because individuals want to preserve the unity of the group. Groupthink is most common in situations where there's lots of pressure to make a quick, important decision.

Janis proposed ways of combating Groupthink:

- Initially, group leaders shouldn't express their opinions, so other members won't feel pressured to agree with them.
- One member should be given the role of devil's advocate (always expressing the opposite argument) to make sure that all possibilities are explored.
- Objective people outside of the group should be consulted.

┌─ Examples ────────────────────────

Groupthink situations have come up a lot in the past:

- Just before the attacks on Pearl Harbour, the US military were sent lots of warnings. They chose to ignore these messages and were not prepared enough for the 'surprise' invasion.
- The Challenger spacecraft was launched despite the concerns of the engineers. It shortly exploded after take off much to the horror of all involved.

Figure 4: *The Challenger spacecraft disaster highlights the dangers of Groupthink.*

Ethical implications

There are loads of ethical issues surrounding studies like Milgram's. The participants were deceived and put under stress. However, it's important with every study to do a **cost / benefit analysis** — consider whether the cost to the participants was worth the benefit of the findings to society. Despite feeling pressured during the studies, a high proportion of Milgram's participants said they were pleased to have taken part. This was because they felt they'd learned valuable lessons about themselves.

Research into conformity and obedience can lead to social change. Studies like Milgram's raised awareness of the possible negative outcomes of blind obedience. Janis's ideas on Groupthink showed that some conflict within a group is necessary, not destructive. His ideas have been taken on board by group leaders to help ensure they make the best decisions.

Worked Exam-style Questions

1   Vic's teacher asked her to go to the staff room to collect the register, an area that students are not normally allowed into. Use social psychological findings to explain why Vic might obey her teacher.   *(12 marks)* ■

Exam Tip
It is a good idea to jot down some notes of what your answer will cover at the start of a question. Then you can make sure your answer stays focused and is in a logical order.

Vic has been asked to do something, normally forbidden, by a person she would see as an authority figure. Social psychological findings can explain why Vic might go against the rules to obey her teacher. These include obedience to authority, agency theory and the role of justified authorities.

Vic has carried out an action that she wouldn't normally do. She is going to the staff room which is a place she wouldn't normally be allowed to go. As Milgram (1963) showed, people can exhibit behaviour that is usually against their moral judgement when they're under the instruction of an authority figure (e.g. Vic's teacher). Hofling (1966) carried out a similar study which found around 95% of nurses obeyed a doctor's orders over the telephone, despite knowing that this was forbidden. The study was useful in showing that obedience does happen in real life settings.

Exam Tip
Applying knowledge of psychology to the real world is required in this question. You need to do more than just recall everything you know. Refer back to the question scenario in your answer.

Milgram (1973) suggested that agency theory was one way of explaining why people obey certain authority figures. He explained that in certain situations people are placed in the 'agentic state' which leads them to do as they are told and act out the wishes of another person without feeling personal responsibility. ■ *In Vic's case, she has been told to go to a place she wouldn't normally be allowed. However, because her teacher has told her to do it, Vic may feel she has no personal responsibility if she gets into trouble with another teacher for going to the staff room.*

Exam Tip
Support your answer with references to psychological studies.

Justified authorities also make a huge difference in obedience levels. Milgram re-ran his obedience experiment in different settings and with different conditions and he found that we are more likely to obey authority figures who are socially recognised, such as teachers. Vic is therefore more likely to obey her teacher than a fellow student. Bickman ■ *(1974) showed that this is the case when he ran an experiment to investigate justified authorities. He showed that people were more likely to follow orders from a guard or milkman than another passerby.*

Exam Tip
Finish your answer with a short conclusion, summarising all of your points. If you can, include one or two evaluative comments.

As social psychology has shown, there are many explanations for ■ *why Vic obeyed her teacher and went to the staff room. Whilst some of the research lacks ecological validity, there are many findings which can be applied to real life and they are useful in helping us understand why people obey authority figures.*

Summary Questions

Q1   Give an example of a naturalistic experiment investigating obedience.

Q2   a)   What happens when people are deindividuated?

   b)   How were the prison guards in Zimbardo's experiment deindividuated?

   c)   What effect did this have on their behaviour?

Q3   Name three types of group where Groupthink might happen.

Q4   Alastair is conducting an experiment into conformity. In terms of ethics, why would he have to conduct a cost / benefit analysis?

Section Summary

- Social psychology is all about the relationships between people — it looks at things like stereotyping, prejudice, conformity and obedience.

- The social approach uses many research methods — these include laboratory experiments, field experiments, natural experiments, naturalistic observations and surveys.

- There are two types of conformity — compliance and internalisation.

- Compliance is where you go along with the majority even if you don't believe in their views. You do this to appear normal and to avoid rejection from the rest of the group — this is called normative social influence.

- Internalisation is where you accept the views of the majority. This may be because you're in an unfamiliar situation and look to others for how to behave — this is called informational social influence.

- Asch (1951) carried out a study to demonstrate normative social influence and Sherif (1935) demonstrated informational social influence.

- Zimbardo et al (1973) conducted an experiment in a prison which showed people conform to the roles assigned to them.

- Reicher and Haslam (2006) carried out the BBC Prison Study and found different results to Zimbardo et al (1973) — their participants didn't identify with the roles assigned to them.

- Factors that influence whether we conform or resist orders include situational factors such as group size and social support. Other factors such as confidence, expertise and gender also have an effect.

- Rotter (1966) developed a measure of a person's locus of control. People either have an internal locus of control (they take responsibility for their actions) or an external locus of control (they blame fate or luck for their behaviour). It's thought that these personality characteristics could influence conformity.

- Moscovici (1969) studied minority influence. He showed that a small consistent group can cause people to change their views or behaviour.

- Minority influence can cause social change. Examples in the real world include the suffragette movement, the Civil Rights Movement and the Gay Rights Movement.

- Milgram (1963) studied obedience in his famous 'remote learner' experiment. 65% of the participants obeyed the experimenter and administered 450 V to a learner.

- Milgram created lots of variations of his study to investigate obedience in different situations. There were no differences between males and females, but clear differences depending on presence of allies and the proximity of the victim or authority figure.

- Milgram (1973) came up with agency theory to account for his high obedience results. People in an agentic state feel less responsible for their actions because they are just obeying an authority figure.

- Bickman (1974) found people in uniform were more likely to be obeyed — this is because they are seen as authority figures.

- People do disobey, and this could be because of individual differences or because of the situation.

- People may conform when in a group because of deindividuation or Groupthink.

- Deindividuation is when people lose their personal identity within a group and are more likely to show antisocial behaviour.

- Groupthink happens in very cohesive groups — the members of the group converge their thinking with what they feel the general view of the group should be. This can result in decisions being made that conflict with what the individuals actually believe.

Exam-style Questions

1   Rachel is conducting a questionnaire investigating how people comply to social influence in the workplace. Evaluate the method Rachel is using to collect her data.

(4 marks)

2 (a)   Describe how normative social influence can explain why someone might conform.

(2 marks)

2 (b)   Describe how informational social influence can explain why someone might conform.

(2 marks)

3   Outline and evaluate research into the effects of informational social influence.

(12 marks)

4 (a)   Outline what is meant by 'locus of control'.

(6 marks)

4 (b)   Describe how locus of control can affect conformity and independent behaviour.

(2 marks)

5   Describe how studies into minority influence have helped psychologists to understand social change.

(12 marks)

6   Dave is carrying out an investigation into conformity.
He has decided to test his participants in the laboratory.

6 (a)   State **two** advantages of carrying out an investigation in a laboratory.

(2 marks)

6 (b)   State **two** disadvantages of carrying out an investigation in a laboratory.

(2 marks)

7 (a)   Outline Milgram's work into obedience.

(8 marks)

7 (b)   Consider reasons why someone might disobey an authority figure.

(6 marks)

8   In Milgram's study, participant A couldn't see the learner.
Participant B had to place the learner's hand on the electric shock pad.
Describe and explain the difference you might see in their obedience levels.

(4 marks)

9   Ben has very strong views against animal testing but his teacher at school has asked him to take part in the school debate team where he has to argue against his morals.
Explain why Ben might obey his teacher despite it being against his views.

(3 marks)

1. The Individual Differences Approach

Everybody is different and the individual differences approach in psychology looks at how, why and what this means.

What is the individual differences approach?

Individuals differ in their psychological characteristics. The individual differences approach studies how psychological characteristics, like aggression and memory span, differ from person to person. Psychologists argued for ages about whether an individual's personality is influenced by nature (inherited factors) or nurture (environmental factors). This is known as the nature-nurture debate. It's now thought most likely that both have an effect and interact with one another, so there shouldn't be much more debate over which one is solely responsible.

> **Example**
>
> The nature-nurture debate can be used as an explanation for intelligence:
>
> Elaine is very intelligent. This could be due to genetic reasons (nature) as her parents are also very intelligent. Or it could be due to her environment as she was encouraged to read a lot from a young age.

Different perspectives

There are lots of different perspectives within the approach. These will be covered in more detail further on in the section, but for now, here's a brief overview...

The biological approach (see pages 180-184)

This approach explains behaviour in terms of physiological or genetic factors. It focuses on physical treatments for psychological disorders, e.g. using drugs or electroconvulsive therapy.

The psychodynamic approach (see pages 186-189)

The psychodynamic approach puts abnormal behaviour down to underlying psychological problems, often caused by past events and experiences. Treatment comes in the form of psychoanalysis, where the therapist tries to find and sort out these underlying problems.

The behavioural approach (see pages 190-194)

The behavioural approach claims that all behaviour, including abnormal behaviour, is learned. It's believed that old behaviours can be 'unlearned' — treatment of abnormal behaviour is based on this.

The cognitive approach (see pages 195-197)

This approach puts abnormality down to irrational and negative thoughts. So, as you can probably guess, treatment focuses on changing the way a person thinks about things.

Figure 1: *Drugs can be used to treat disorders, as proposed by the biological approach.*

Research methods

Several different research methods are used in the individual differences approach. These include:

Case studies

In a case study you use interviews and observation to collect information about an individual or group. You can study behaviour over a long period of time — this means you could observe some behaviours that might not be seen in another type of study. Also, it's often possible to observe behaviour in a natural setting. However, in a natural setting it's harder to control all variables, and it's mighty tricky to replicate the study.

Meta-analyses

This is where you analyse the results from loads of different studies and come up with some general conclusions. They're a good way of bringing together data (which is a general aim of the scientific process), and by doing this they reduce the problem of sample size. However, one problem is that there are loads of conflicting results out there, which obviously makes doing a meta-analysis a bit tricky...

Correlational studies

These use statistics to compare two variables. For instance, you might give a questionnaire to all participants to measure their stress levels on a scale. They'd then do another task, e.g. a memory test, for which they'd also get a score. A correlation would compare the scores to see if there is a relationship between stress and memory. But you couldn't use this to show that one causes the other. There might be other variables involved.

Physiological studies

These include methods such as brain scanning, which can produce a detailed picture showing up any structural abnormalities. This means psychologists can make links between structures in the brain and behavioural abnormalities. However, scanning is a pretty expensive process, so it's not always possible.

> **Examples**
>
> Devices that are used in physiological studies include:
>
> - MRI scanners.
> - Technology that measures heart beat, brain waves, the amount of sweat on the skin, pupil dilation and eye movement.

Classifying people

The DSM-IV is the fourth edition of the American Psychiatric Association's Diagnostic and Statistical Manual of Mental Disorders. It contains all known mental health disorders, and offers a new method of classification — a multiaxial classification:

- Individuals can be rated on multiple axes/dimensions. Diagnostic categories are used, for example organic mental disorders, personality disorders etc.
- DSM-IV made diagnosis more concrete and descriptive than it had been.
- Classifications are useful to acquire new information about a disorder. This can help in the development of new treatments and medication.
- This type of classification has been criticised for stigmatising people and ignoring their 'uniqueness' by putting them in artificial groups.

Real World Connection
Conner et al (2008) conducted a meta-analysis looking at the relationship between depression and drug use. They collected the results of 60 studies which had looked at this relationship and found that, overall, there was a small but significant positive correlation between depression and drug use.

Tip: There's more about case studies and correlational studies on pages 63-64.

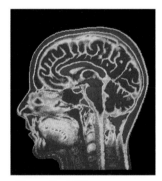

Figure 2: *MRI scanners are used often in physiological studies to show brain abnormalities.*

Tip: There are also other manuals that psychologists use to classify people, such as the ICD-10.

The DSM-IV is divided into five different axes that allow health professionals to take into consideration a patient's symptoms along with any personal or environmental influences (see Figure 3). This allows a whole picture to be formed of the patient and their disorder.

Axis	Description	Example
I	Acute symptoms that require treatment.	Schizophrenic episode.
II	Personality and development disorders.	Antisocial personality disorders.
III	Physical influences that worsen Axis I disorders.	HIV/AIDs can worsen depression.
IV	Psychosocial factors.	Loss of a family member.
V	Level of functioning.	The ability to cope with everyday life.

Figure 3: Table showing the multiaxial DSM-IV.

The DSM-IV is only used in the diagnosis of mental health disorders. Patients must meet certain criteria before they can be officially diagnosed. Often, this can take a long time as symptoms have to be monitored over a few weeks, or sometimes even months.

Example

To diagnose a person with schizophrenia, the following symptoms must be reported:

- Two or more symptoms from the following list. Each symptom should have been present for a significant amount of time over the course of one month:
    1. Delusions
    2. Hallucinations
    3. Disorganised speech
    4. Disorganised or catatonic behaviour
    5. Negative symptoms — e.g. lack of emotion
- A clear impact on a person's social relationships, self-care and academic or work ability.

Key study of psychiatric classification — Rosenhan (1973)

Method 1: In a field study, eight 'normal' people tried to be admitted to 12 different psychiatric hospitals around the USA, with only one symptom — claiming they heard voices, saying 'empty', 'hollow' and 'thud'.

Results 1: Seven were diagnosed with schizophrenia and all eight were admitted to psychiatric hospital.
On admission, they said they were sane and had faked symptoms to get admitted, but this was seen as a symptom itself. It took, on average, 19 days before they were released, usually with a diagnosis of 'schizophrenia in remission'. Other, real patients could tell that these people were not mentally ill.

Method 2: Rosenhan later told staff at a psychiatric hospital that one or more pseudopatients (normal people pretending to have schizophrenia) were trying to be admitted to the hospital.

Results 2: No pseudopatients appeared, but 41 genuine patients were judged to be pseudopatients by staff.

Conclusion: Medical staff could not distinguish the sane from the insane (although many of the real patients could).

Evaluation: Being a field study, it wouldn't have been possible to control all variables, and so the results lose some of their reliability. Staff would probably not expect 'normal' people to try to gain admission to a psychiatric hospital, and so this might explain why the participants were initially admitted. 'Schizophrenia in remission' is a diagnosis that is rarely used, which suggests the psychiatrists concerned may not have believed they were really suffering from schizophrenia. There are ethical considerations in this study — people had their freedom taken away, mentally healthy people may have received treatments, professionals were deceived, and the study risked genuine patients not being treated.

Figure 4: *Rosenhan's study is directly relevant to real-life admittance to psychiatric wards.*

Worked Exam-style Question

1 Jon wants to see if an individual's stress level has a direct relationship with exam performance.

1 (a) Which research method should he use? *(1 mark)*

1 (b) Give one limitation of using this method. *(2 marks)*

(a) Jon should use a correlational study to look at the relationship between stress levels and exam performance within his participants. ∎

(b) One limitation of using this method is that Jon's results would only show if the two variables are correlated and not if one causes the other. This means that he could not conclude that stress <u>causes</u> a difference in exam performance — it may be that there are other factors that affect both stress and ability which haven't been studied in his experiment.

Exam Tip
There are other research methods that might be appropriate here, but this one fits the example best.

Summary Questions

Q1 What is the nature-nurture debate?

Q2 What does the cognitive approach suggest is the cause of abnormality?

Q3 Name two research methods used in the individual differences approach.

Q4 Rosenhan (1973) conducted experiments into psychiatric classification.

    a) His first experiment involved eight 'normal' people trying to be admitted to 12 different psychiatric hospitals. What results did he see?

    b) Outline the method and results of his second experiment.

Real World Connection

Sometimes rare and eccentric behaviour is dependent on the culture in which it happens. Once a year in Gloucestershire, a small community of people take part in a cheese rolling festival. Whilst running down a hill chasing a round of cheese might not be 'normal' behaviour to some people, it's a cultural event to others.

Tip: The x-axis shows a numerical measure of the behaviour, e.g. the number of hand washes per week.

Figure 2: *Mild depression is categorised as an abnormal behaviour by psychiatrists, yet statistics show that it is fairly frequent.*

2. Defining Abnormality

Abnormality is a term used to describe something as not being normal. However, defining what's normal and what's not is trickier than it might seem...

1. Deviation from social norms

All societies have their standards of behaviour and attitudes. Deviating from these can be seen as abnormal. But cultures vary, so there isn't one universal set of social 'rules'. One problem with defining abnormality as deviation from social norms is that it can be used to justify the removal of 'unwanted' people from a society. For example, people opposing a particular political regime could be said to be abnormal.

The concept of deviation from the majority can be expressed statistically in terms of the **normal distribution**:

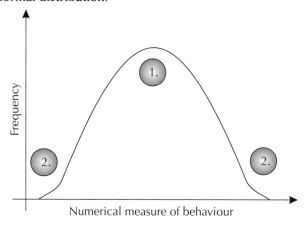

1. Statistically frequent behaviours. People who behave in the average way make up the middle of the bell-shaped curve.

2. Statistically infrequent behaviours. Those people who behave 'abnormally' make up the tail ends of the bell curve — this behaviour is rare (statistically infrequent).

Figure 1: *Graph showing a general population's deviation from the norm.*

Limitations

However, there are problems with defining abnormality simply in terms of statistical infrequency:

- It doesn't take account of the desirability of behaviour, just its frequency. For example, a very high IQ is abnormal, as is a very low one, but having a high IQ is desirable whereas having a low IQ is undesirable.

- There's no distinction between rare, slightly odd behaviour and rare, psychologically abnormal behaviour.

- There's no definite cut-off point where normal behaviour becomes abnormal behaviour.

- Some behaviours that are considered psychologically abnormal are quite common, e.g. mild depression. Hassett and White (1989) argue that you cannot use statistical infrequency to define abnormality because of this. Using the statistical infrequency idea, some disorders would not be classed as anything unusual.

Interestingly, as recently as 1974, homosexuality was classified in the DSM as a disorder. However, the diagnosis was dropped because it was found that homosexuality wasn't as infrequent as previously thought, and that homosexuals don't differ from heterosexuals in terms of psychological well-being.

2. Failure to function adequately

Failure to function adequately is another definition of abnormality. You can't function adequately if you can't cope with the demands of day-to-day life. Various criteria are used for diagnosis, including:

- Dysfunctional behaviour — behaviour which goes against the accepted standards of behaviour.

- Observer discomfort — behaviour that causes other individuals to become uncomfortable.

- Unpredictable behaviour — impulsive behaviour that seems to be uncontrollable.

- Irrational behaviour — behaviour that's unreasonable and illogical.

- Personal distress — being affected by emotion to an excessive degree.

If you can tick the box for more than one of the criteria above, the person's behaviour is considered to be abnormal. It does seem a bit unfair though — we've probably all done stuff that could fit under these categories at some point. (People are always uncomfortable around me, but that could be because I've got fleas...)

Limitations

There are also limitations to this definition of abnormality:

- Psychologists haven't been able to define exactly what 'function' or 'adequately' mean — it depends on who decides whether someone can or can't do something.

- This definition depends on the culture which the person is in at the time.

- Sometimes the behaviour can be beneficial. For example, someone might risk their life to save someone else.

3. Deviation from ideal mental health

Jahoda (1958) identified six conditions associated with good mental health. They were:

- Positive self-attitude
- Self-actualisation (realising your potential, being fulfilled)
- Resistance to stress
- Personal autonomy (making your own decisions, being in control)
- Accurate perception of reality
- Adaptation to the environment

Limitations

- It's hard to meet all the standards set in this list, and they're subjective (ideas of what is required for each will differ from person to person).

- A violent offender, for example, may have a positive self-attitude and be resistant to stress etc. — yet society wouldn't consider them to be in good mental health.

- Once again, cultural factors may determine what we see as normal or abnormal and what is good or bad mental health.

Exam Tip
You could be asked about any of the three definitions of abnormality (deviation from social norms, failure to function adequately and good mental health) so make sure you can describe them all along with their limitations.

Tip: Cultural dependency comes up as a limitation in all definitions of abnormality. There's more on this on page 176.

Real World Connection
Cultural factors may influence our definition of abnormality, especially in what deviates from ideal mental health. Many Eastern countries tend to attribute ill health to physical ailments rather than mental ones.

Variation across time and culture

The idea of ideal mental health varies across time and between cultures. What's considered mentally 'healthy' at one time, wouldn't necessarily be at another. For example, in some cultures today, it's considered abnormal for women to enjoy sex — they may be forced to have their clitoris surgically removed to prevent their enjoyment. In Victorian times here, women who enjoyed sex were deemed abnormal and hence Freud coined the term 'nymphomania'. There's still influence from this today — there are still double standards about male and female sexual activity. But the idea of 'ideal' mental health can be a useful one because it moves away from focusing on mental 'illness'.

┌─ **Examples** ─────────────────────────────────

Norms change all the time, and this can be because of the influence of the law, relationships with other people and the ever-changing world we live in.

- It used to be the norm that you didn't wear a seatbelt in a car. Now, this is against the law and is considered to be dangerous.
- Women used to wear gloves all the time. In Western culture, this would be seen as against the norm in the middle of summer.

Tip: The DSM-IV classifies mental illnesses using symptoms described by the patient (see pages 171-172).

Symptoms associated with mental illness

The Department of Health provides a guide to assess symptoms associated with mental illness. To be classified as a mental illness, there should be one or more of the following (not temporary) symptoms:

- Impairment of intellectual functions, such as memory and comprehension.
- Alterations to mood that lead to delusional appraisals of the past or future, or lack of any appraisal.
- Delusional beliefs, such as of persecution or jealousy.
- Disordered thinking — the person may be unable to appraise their situation or communicate with others.

Figure 3: *This Namibian woman's outfit wouldn't be considered as normal in our society. But that doesn't make it abnormal in Namibia.*

Cultural relativism

The concept of abnormality varies from one culture and time to another. **Cultural relativism** means that judgements made about abnormality are relative to individual cultures. That's because what's normal in one culture is sometimes considered to be abnormal in another. So definitions of abnormality are limited because they're culturally specific. It's important to work out whether an abnormality is absolute, universal, or culturally relative.

- Absolute — occurring in the same way and frequency across cultures.
- Universal — present in all cultures, but not necessarily with the same frequency.
- Culturally relative — unique to a particular culture.

Many physical conditions are absolute. The same goes for some mental conditions. However, social norms vary from one culture to another. This can affect how these conditions are perceived. For example, in some cultures it's considered normal to experience hallucinations, but in other cultures it can be seen as a symptom of schizophrenia. Some abnormal behaviours are universal, e.g. depression occurs in all cultures, but is more common in women and in industrial societies. Some abnormal behaviours are culturally relative — these are known as culture-bound syndromes.

'Witiko' is an example of culturally relative behaviour. It is a culture-bound syndrome, suffered by native Canadians, who lose their appetite for ordinary food, feel depressed and believe they are possessed by the Witiko, who is a giant man-eating monster. This can result in cannibalism, murder or pleas for death from the sufferer. It is thought to be an extreme form of starvation anxiety.

Biased definitions

Attempts to define abnormality may be biased. There are often problems when it comes to defining abnormality — these often relate to stereotypes.

Gender

Factors such as biological or hormonal differences, and the different ways that men and women are brought up, could lead to gender differences in the frequencies of disorders. However, the gender stereotype can lead people to believe that women are generally moodier, and men generally more violent and antisocial. This could be a factor in clinicians tending to diagnose more mood disorders in women and more antisocial disorders in men — the clinicians expect to find them.

Race

Several studies have found that very large numbers of black people in Britain are being diagnosed with schizophrenia. Surveys of inpatients by Bagley (1971) and Cochrane (1977) found that immigrant groups in Britain are more likely to be diagnosed as schizophrenic than native-born people. This is particularly so for people originating in Africa, the Caribbean and Asia. It was first thought that this could be explained in terms of genetic or biological factors, except that the same rates of occurrence were not found in the countries of origin. Therefore, possible reasons include racial stereotypes in diagnosis and greater stress. Stress could be due to poorer living conditions, prejudice, or the general stress of living in a new culture.

Even if stereotypes alone are to blame for a diagnosis, the person could 'develop' the disorder. Once a person is labelled with a mental disorder, they may begin to behave in the expected way due to the label. The diagnosis then becomes a **self-fulfilling prophecy**.

Problems with classification systems

A major problem with systems for classifying abnormality is that they can lead to pigeon-holing people into certain categories. This leads to practical, theoretical and ethical considerations.

- Diagnosis — when people report how they feel 'psychologically', these are subjective feelings. One person's "I'm extremely depressed" may mean the same as someone else's "I'm fed up". A more idiographic approach would be useful — that is, focusing on each unique case and viewing patients on their merits.

- There are many different theories of abnormality — psychodynamic, learning, cognitive, etc. They all have their own definitions and ideas of what causes abnormality.

- There's little evidence of validity — how much any of the classification systems measure what they're supposed to. It's hard to find a central cause (aetiology) for most disorders. And, if patients have more than one disorder, it can be difficult to spot symptoms of one disorder.

Real World Connection

Johnstone (1989) argued that social class was a factor that directly affected how someone was diagnosed with a mental illness. She reported how, when people from different class backgrounds reported the same symptoms, they received different diagnoses. If patients were from a lower social class they were more likely to be labelled as schizophrenic, whereas those in higher social classes were diagnosed with depression. This study highlights possible issues with diagnoses in real life.

Tip: A self-fulfilling prophecy is when predicted events, circumstances or actions 'come true' due to a person changing their behaviour to make it happen.

- Psychiatrists may not always agree from category to category, so classification systems may not always be reliable.

- Treatment — grouping patients can be useful for prescribing treatments, but treatment often depends on diagnosis. Therefore, if the diagnosis is subjective initially, the treatment may not be correct.

- Labelling theory (Scheff, 1966) argues that if people are treated as mentally ill, their behaviour will change and become more like that expected from their diagnosis.

- Szasz (1974) said that psychiatric labels were meaningless. He said illness was a bodily problem, so 'mental' illness could not exist. He believed the term was used to exclude non-conformists from society.

- Finally, it's hard to say where normality ends and abnormality starts.

Figure 4: *It's hard to distinguish when a behaviour such as dieting turns into an eating disorder.*

Exam Tip
It's a good idea to illustrate your answer with appropriate examples where possible.

Worked Exam-style Question

1 (a) Outline **one** definition of abnormality. *(4 marks)*

1 (b) Discuss the limitations of the definition of abnormality you outlined in part (a). *(4 marks)*

(a) Abnormality has been defined in several ways. One of these ways is through the 'deviation from social norms' theory. This says that each society and culture has a set of standard behaviours and attitudes. If people deviate a lot from them they fall into the category of 'abnormal'.

■ *For example, if we were to record the exam results from the AS-Level psychology exam, most candidates would get marks within the middle range and a few would do either really well or really badly. This definition can be shown using a normal distribution curve.*

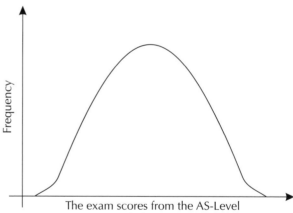

The exam scores from the AS-Level psychology paper.

Exam Tip
There are three definitions to chose from. Write about the one you feel most comfortable with. However, make sure you know about all three though in case you get questions about a specific one in the exam.

■ *The majority of people and their 'normal' behaviour are represented by the large middle part of the curve. People who deviate from the rest of the population are represented at the extreme ends of the curve. A graph like this shows that the norms are what the majority of people within a population live by.*

(b) The deviation from social norms definition of abnormality only looks at how frequently a behaviour or action happens, not whether it is desirable. For example, having a high IQ might be statistically abnormal, but that doesn't mean it is undesirable. This links to the idea that it is

very hard to define what abnormal actually is, as it does not necessarily mean it is something bad. There is no distinction within this definition of where something goes from being rare and slightly odd, to rare and psychologically abnormal — there is no exact cut-off point between when something should be defined as normal or abnormal. Some behaviours which are defined as abnormal may actually happen a lot within society. For example, mild depression is common in the Western world but it's still categorised and defined as an 'abnormal' behaviour.

Summary Questions

Q1 What role does the Department of Health have in defining abnormality?

Q2 What does 'cultural relativism' mean in terms of abnormal behaviour?

Q3 Give an example of a culture-bound syndrome.

Q4 James went to a class with no shoes on. For each of the definitions of abnormality, decide whether James's behaviour would be defined as being abnormal or not.

Q5 What did Scheff (1966) say about psychiatric labels?

Learning Objective:

- Know about the biological approach to psychopathology.

- Know about biological therapies, including drugs and ECT.

Tip: 'Aetiology' just means 'the cause' of an illness. It crops up a lot within abnormal psychology since there are so many different possible causes.

Tip: If you know some examples for each of the assumptions, it not only makes the assumptions easier to learn, but it shows the examiner you know what you're talking about.

Tip: Neurotransmitters are chemicals found in the brain that send messages from one neuron to another. Take a look back at page 109 to read more about them.

Figure 1: *The flu virus has been linked to certain psychological disorders.*

3. The Biological Model of Abnormality

One of the ways we can look at abnormality is through the biological model. It's one of many different models used to look at symptoms and treatments of abnormality, and focuses on the physical side of things.

The assumptions of the biological model

The biological (or medical or somatic) model assumes that psychological disorders are physical illnesses with physical causes. In principle they're no different from physical illnesses like flu, except they have major psychological symptoms. When the same symptoms frequently occur together, they represent a reliable syndrome or disorder. The cause or 'aetiology' may be one or more of the following:

Genetics

Faulty genes are known to cause some diseases that have psychological effects.

┌─ **Examples** ─────────────────────────────

There are many illnesses shown to have genetic causes. Evidence of a genetic cause has been seen in:

- Huntington's disease — which leads to a deterioration of mental abilities.

- Schizophrenia — which can lead to symptoms such as hallucinations, delusions and disorganised behaviour.

Neurotransmitters

Too much or too little of a particular neurotransmitter may produce psychological disorders.

┌─ **Examples** ─────────────────────────────

The use of drugs which target particular neurotransmitters suggests that these may be related to psychological disorders.

- An increased level of dopamine is linked to schizophrenia — drugs like cocaine, which increase dopamine levels, can lead to schizophrenia-like symptoms.

- Depression can be effectively managed and often treated with drugs called SSRIs, which manage serotonin levels in the brain.

Infection

Disorders may be caused by infection.

┌─ **Examples** ─────────────────────────────

- General paresis is a condition involving delusions and mood swings, leading to paralysis and death. It is caused by syphilis, and can now be treated.

- Brown et al (2004) investigated the link between pregnant women getting the flu and their child having schizophrenia. They found that pregnant mothers who were exposed to the flu virus during the first few months of their pregnancy were more likely to have a child that later develops schizophrenia than those who didn't get the flu.

Brain injury

Accidental brain damage may produce psychological disorders.

Examples

Case studies and other psychological investigations have been useful in showing a link between brain injuries and abnormality.

- In 1848 an explosion sent an iron rod through Phineas Gage's head, destroying parts of his frontal lobes (see Figure 2). He survived, but he became more impulsive and disorganised, couldn't plan for the future and had a strangely different personality.

- Alcohol abuse can often cause brain damage, which can lead to a brain disorder called Korsakoff's syndrome. The main symptom is memory loss.

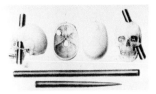

Figure 2: *Phineas Gage experienced mental health problems following his severe brain injury.*

The genetic basis of schizophrenia

Research has been done into the genetic basis of schizophrenia.

Twin Studies

Identical twins share 100% of their genes. They occur when one zygote splits and forms two embryos. Non-identical twins occur when two separate eggs are fertilised by two separate sperm. They only share 50% of their genes.

So in theory, if schizophrenia has a purely genetic basis, if one identical twin suffers from schizophrenia then the other twin will too. The risk of both non-identical twins suffering should be lower.

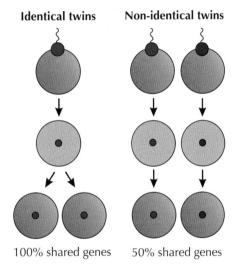

Identical twins   Non-identical twins

100% shared genes   50% shared genes

Figure 3: *Shared genes in twins.*

Tip: A zygote is another way of saying 'fertilised egg'.

Key study of schizophrenia rates in twins — Gottesman (1991)

Method: Gottesman carried out a meta-analysis of approximately 40 twin studies.

Results: It was found that having an identical twin with schizophrenia gave you a 48% chance of developing the condition. This reduced to 17% in non-identical twins.

Conclusion: Schizophrenia has a strong genetic basis.

Evaluation: The meta-analysis was carried out on field studies, giving the research high ecological validity. Because identical twins share 100% of their genes, it might be expected that both twins would always suffer from the same conditions. The fact that both twins had developed schizophrenia in only about half of the cases means that another factor must also be involved. Identical twins tend to be treated more similarly than non-identical twins, and so the family environment might play a large role.

Tip: A meta-analysis is a type of research method which statistically summarises the results from lots of different studies that are all looking at the same relationship.

Additional study of schizophrenia rates in twins — Heston (1970)

Heston (1970) conducted an investigation into the concordance rates of schizophrenia amongst identical twins. He found that in people who had an identical twin with schizophrenia, 90% of them reported some form of mental health disorder.

However, siblings are often raised in very similar environments. So, there could be other factors that might cause and influence the onset of schizophrenia and other issues. Biology may not be the only cause. Also, Heston's study included schizoid disease as well as schizophrenia, which is possibly why there is such a high concordance rate.

Adoption studies

Adoption studies have found evidence for a genetic basis of schizophrenia.

Key study of schizophrenia rates in adoption — Heston (1966)

Method: 47 adopted children whose biological mothers had schizophrenia were studied. The control group consisted of 50 adopted children whose biological mothers didn't suffer from schizophrenia. The children were followed up as adults and were interviewed and given intelligence and personality tests.

Results: Of the experimental group, 5 of the 47 became schizophrenic, compared to 0 in the control group. Another 4 of the experimental group were classified as borderline schizophrenic by the raters.

Conclusion: The study supports the view that schizophrenia has a genetic basis.

Evaluation: Interview data can be unreliable and affected by social desirability bias. However, interviews are a good way of getting data in a naturalistic way. The adopted children whose mothers didn't suffer from any conditions might have not shown any symptoms of schizophrenia yet — it can't be completely ruled out.

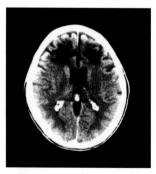

Figure 4: *As this CT scan shows by the dark areas, the front part of the brain has been separated from the rest of the brain to alleviate depressive symptoms.*

Biological therapies

The biological model says that once the physical cause of a psychological disorder has been identified, a physical (biological) therapy is needed to treat the physical problem. One or more of the following may be used:

Psychosurgery

Psychosurgery is brain surgery involving destruction or separation of parts of the brain. Moniz developed the 'frontal lobotomy' in the 1930s to separate parts of the frontal lobes from the rest of the brain. This reduced aggression and generally made people more placid. However, it's not a cure, but a change — the irreversible changes to personality may have just made patients easier to manage. Psychosurgery is now only a last resort treatment for some disorders, e.g. very serious depression.

Drugs

Drugs can be used to change neurotransmitter levels in the brain. For example, phenothiazines reduce levels of dopamine and can therefore relieve symptoms of schizophrenia.

In depression, drugs called Selective Serotonin Re-uptake Inhibitors (SSRIs) are used to manage the levels of serotonin within the brain. Research has shown that people with depression appear to have less serotonin than the average person. SSRIs work by making more serotonin available in the depressed person's brain. They do this by stopping the synapses taking up the serotonin once it's released (see Figure 5).

Tip: The side effects for drugs such as phenothiazine can often be very unpleasant. Doctors and psychiatrists weigh up the pros and cons of giving patients drugs before they start treatment.

Tip: In depression, drugs don't always work. So we can't say for certain that all mental illnesses are purely biologically based. However, the fact that drugs can sometimes be used to help psychological illnesses suggests there must be some sort of biological background to these types of disorders.

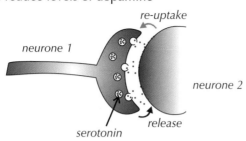

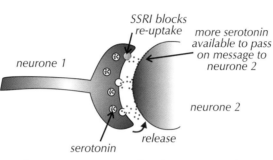

Figure 5: SSRIs are used in the treatment of depression to manage serotonin levels.

Electroconvulsive therapy (ECT)

During ECT, an electric shock of around 225 volts is given to a person's brain. This can help to relieve depression, but can also produce memory loss. Although quite commonly used in the past, it's now only used as a last resort therapy. It's not really clear exactly how ECT works, which is why it's only used in extreme cases.

To carry out ECT on a patient, it's important that the procedure is controlled and carefully monitored. The patient is first anaesthetised, injected with muscle relaxants and has electrodes attached to their head. These transmit a brief electrical shock to the brain which causes a seizure lasting up to a minute. They usually have a rubber stop placed in their mouth so they don't bite down on their tongue during the procedure. The patient wakes up from the anaesthetic around 20 minutes later.

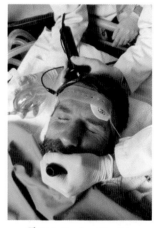

Figure 6: A patient is sedated during ECT to make sure they don't harm themselves.

Strengths and weaknesses of the biological model

Strengths

It has a scientific basis in biology and a lot of evidence shows that biological causes can produce psychological symptoms. It can be seen as ethical because people are not blamed for their disorders, they just have an illness. Biological therapies have helped relieve conditions (e.g. schizophrenia) that could not be treated very well previously.

Exam Tip
As with every model in psychology, there are strengths and weaknesses. Make sure you know these so you can evaluate the model in the exam.

Key study of relapse rates — Leucht (2003)

Method: Leucht (2003) conducted a meta-analysis which looked at how effective new-generation (atypical) antipsychotic drugs were at preventing relapse in people with schizophrenia. In the studies, half of the participants were given the newer antipsychotic drugs and half were given a placebo or conventional (typical) antipsychotics.

Results: Leucht found that overall, patients who had taken the new-generation antipsychotics had a significantly lower rate of relapse than those who had taken the placebo drug or the conventional antipsychotics.

Conclusion: New-generation antipsychotic medicine is thought to be an effective method of preventing relapse.

Weaknesses

Biological therapies raise ethical concerns. Drugs can produce addiction and may only suppress symptoms rather than cure the disorder. The effects of psychosurgery are irreversible. Psychological disorders may not be linked to any physical problem. Psychological therapies can be just as effective as biological treatments, without any interference to biological structures.

Worked Exam-style Questions

1   Outline one way in which the biological approach
    explains psychopathology.   *(3 marks)*

The biological model says that if someone has too much or too little of certain neurotransmitters, this could lead to a psychological disorder. For example, an increase in the amount of dopamine in the brain can lead to schizophrenia and a decrease in serotonin can lead to depression. The amount of neurotransmitters in the brain can be modified by drugs. For instance, in depression, SSRIs are used to block the re-uptake of serotonin, making more available in the brain.

2   Describe and evaluate biological methods
    for treating abnormality.   *(12 marks)*

There are three main treatments that the biological approach to abnormality uses in dealing with psychological illnesses. These are drugs, psychosurgery and electroconvulsive therapy (ECT).

■   *Drugs are used to change neurotransmitter levels in the brain. For example, some people with schizophrenia have been found to have higher dopamine levels, whilst it's thought that people with depression have lower serotonin levels. Drugs can adjust these levels and relieve symptoms. A meta-analysis by Leucht et al (2003) showed that drugs really do seem to make a difference in patients with schizophrenia. They found that patients who were given the new-generation (atypical) antipsychotic drugs had a significantly lower rate of relapse than those who were given a placebo or conventional antipsychotic drugs.*

Psychosurgery is another method that can be used to treat psychological illnesses. This involves permanently destroying or separating parts of the brain. One form of psychosurgery which involved separating the front part of the brain from the rest was developed by Moniz in the 1930s to make people less aggressive. However, this is just a change and not a cure for mental illness — it often had significant effects on the personalities of the people who underwent the surgery. It is now only used in really severe cases of mental illness.

Finally, ECT involves giving an electric shock of around 225 V to the brain. This causes the person to have a seizure whilst under a general anaesthetic. It is not clear exactly how it works, and it can produce memory loss, so like psychosurgery it is only used as a last resort.

Biological methods have helped to relieve conditions, and there's a lot of evidence to show that biological causes can produce psychological symptoms. However, whilst these are three good methods to treat psychological illness, biological therapies are not always the most effective methods. Often psychological therapies can work just as well and these don't interfere at all with biological structures. There may also be ethical concerns to using biological treatments. Drugs can sometimes be addictive and some produce negative side effects. They might also only suppress symptoms and not cure the disorder. Also psychosurgery is a permanent change to the brain — the personality changes might just make the patient easier to manage rather than being a cure. Therefore, it is useful to understand that whilst biological methods can be used to treat psychological illnesses, there are also alternatives that should be considered.

Exam Tip
Describe and evaluate each biological method in a separate paragraph. Structuring your answer clearly makes it much easier for the examiner to read and mark.

Exam Tip
Finish your answer by having an overall summary — it clearly shows you've answered the evaluation part of the question.

Summary Questions

Q1   What does the biological model assume about psychological disorders?

Q2   According to the biological approach, what are the four possible causes of abnormality?

Q3   Give an example of where a brain injury has produced a psychological disorder.

Q4   How can twin studies help in the biological approach to abnormality?

Q5   How do SSRIs work?

Q6   Outline what happens during ECT.

Tip: Take a look back at page 170 for a reminder about the psychodynamic approach.

Tip: If something is innate, it means we are born with it.

Tip: The Oedipus complex (and the Electra complex for girls) were described by Freud. He suggested that during the phallic stage, children develop unconscious sexual desires for the opposite sex parent. At the same time, they start to rival the same sex parent, showing jealous hatred.

4. The Psychodynamic Model of Abnormality

The psychodynamic model is based on Freud's theories. It suggests that psychological illnesses develop from our own personalities.

Conflict in development

The psychodynamic model is based on Freud's idea of conflict in development and also his division of personality into the **id**, **ego** and **superego**.

The id, ego and superego are different levels of consciousness and govern the way we think and act. A way to see the relationships between these three aspects of the personality is by thinking of an iceberg. The tip of the iceberg is the conscious part of the mind made up of the ego and part of the superego. The majority of our personality, however, comes from our unconscious mind which is below the surface — it's made up of our id, a little of our ego and the rest of our superego (see Figure 1).

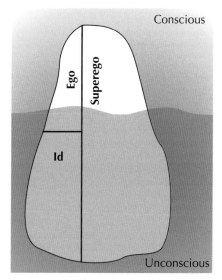

Figure 1: *Iceberg diagram to illustrate the parts of the personality.*

- The id is the 'pleasure principle' and is found in the unconscious part of the mind. It's our innate drive to do what we want to satisfy ourselves. It appears at birth.

- The ego exists in both the conscious and unconscious parts of the mind and acts as a rational part known as the 'reality principle'. It develops within the first three years after birth and balances the id and the superego to keep our behaviour in line.

- The superego is in both the conscious and unconscious parts of the mind. This is the part of the mind that takes our morals into consideration. It develops around four to five years of age.

The psychodynamic theory also uses Freud's stages of development — the oral, anal, phallic, latency and genital stages. Each of these stages has certain characteristics (see Figure 2).

Stage of development	Age	Characteristics
Oral	0 - 18 months	sucking behaviour
Anal	18 months - 3.5 years	keeping or discarding faeces
Phallic	3.5 - 6 years	genital fixation — Oedipus complex
Latency	6 years - puberty	repressed sexual urges
Genital	puberty - adult	awakened sexual urges

Figure 2: *Table outlining Freud's stages of development and their characteristics.*

If a child fixates on any of these behaviours during their development, Freud claimed this would lead to a conflict and then a psychological issue.

The model suggests that conflict and anxiety may occur during childhood because the ego is not yet developed enough to deal with the id's desires, understand real-world issues or cope with the superego's moral demands (e.g. knowing right from wrong). Psychological disorders may also come from conflict or anxiety which happens in a certain stage of development.

Examples

During the anal stage, conflict may occur during potty training. If a child experiences too much punishment during this stage, it can lead to a conflict and a fixation. Freud claimed this could lead to one of two types of personality:

- Anal retentive personality — a stubborn perfectionist obsessed with cleanliness and tidiness.

- Anal expulsive personality — a messy and carefree person with a lack of self-control.

During the oral stage, a conflict could occur when being weaned off breast feeding. This could lead to a fixation in later life, characterised by traits such as nail biting, smoking or abnormal eating behaviours.

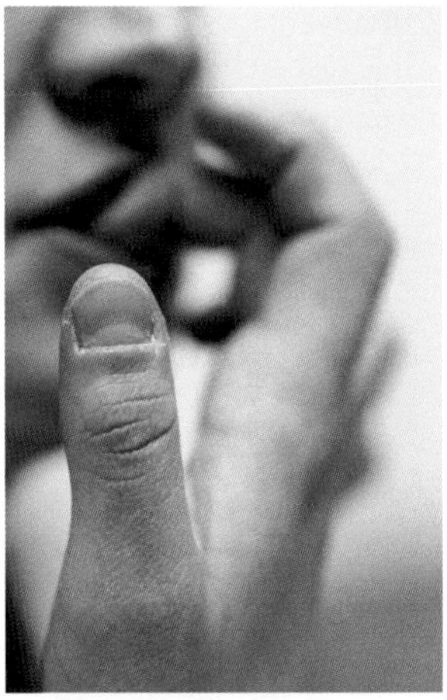

Anxiety from the conflicts is repressed into the unconscious mind. Stress or trauma in adulthood may 'trigger' the repressed conflicts, leading to psychological disorders.

Figure 3: *Nail biting is a behaviour that Freud claimed is caused by an oral fixation.*

Key study of Little Hans — Freud (1909)

Method: Freud carried out a case study of a child called Hans who had a phobia of horses. Hans was observed by his father, who made notes of Hans's dreams and stuff he said, and then relayed his findings to Freud for analysis.

Results: Hans was afraid of horses because he thought they might bite him or fall on him. During the study he developed an interest in his 'widdler'. His mum had told him not to play with it or she'd cut it off. Hans told his dad about a dream where he was married to his mum and his dad was now his grandfather.

Conclusion: Freud's interpretation of these findings was that Hans had reached the phallic stage of development and showed evidence of the Oedipus complex — he wanted to have an exclusive relationship with his mother and was jealous of his father. Hans had sexual feelings for his mother, shown partly by his dream of marrying her.

The horse symbolised Hans's father because, to him, they both had big penises. His fear of horses is an example of displacement — a defence mechanism that protected him from his real fear of his father. Hans suffered from castration anxiety. He was afraid that he would be castrated by his father if he found out about his feelings for his mother. This was symbolised by Hans's fear that a horse would bite him.

Evaluation: This was a case study, meaning that it provided lots of detailed data about the subject. The findings provided evidence to support Freud's theories. However, the results were based entirely on observation and interpretation.

Tip: Freud's ideas were very subjective with little scientific basis. This makes the reliability of his findings and theories pretty questionable.

This means they could have easily been caused by a third variable (e.g. Hans's castration anxiety might have come from his mother threatening to cut his penis off...). Also, before the study Hans had been frightened by a horse falling down in the street, which could explain his fear of them. Freud analysed information from Hans's father, so the results could be biased. As this was a study of one person, the results can't be generalised.

Figure 4: *Freud was the founder of psychoanalysis.*

Psychoanalysis

Freud introduced **psychoanalysis** as a treatment in the early twentieth century. Its aim was to allow the patient to access repressed thoughts and unconscious conflicts — Freud called this '**insight**'. Patients were then encouraged to deal with the conflicts. Freud recognised that this process would be painful and cause anxiety, and that people would be resistant at first. However, patients were encouraged to focus on the feelings that the repressed thoughts brought about.

Freud used three psychoanalytic techniques to uncover his patients' repressed thoughts:

Hypnosis

Hypnosis is an altered mental state, involving deep relaxation. Freud believed that people could access repressed thoughts whilst in this state. He gradually lost interest in the technique for two main reasons — he found it difficult to hypnotise people, and also found that people become very suggestible when hypnotised.

Free association

In free association, the patient is given a cue word and is asked to say any ideas or memories that come into their mind. Freud believed that by doing this repressed thoughts would eventually emerge, giving an insight into the unconscious problems causing abnormal behaviour.

Dream analysis

Dream analysis was also used by Freud. It was thought that a certain part of the mind keeps repressed thoughts in the unconscious and that this part is less active during sleep. Therefore, Freud believed that repressed thoughts are likely to appear in dreams.

Strengths and weaknesses

The psychodynamic approach also has strengths and weaknesses.

Strengths

- It's quite a unique approach to abnormality, suggesting that disorders may be linked to unresolved conflicts related to biological needs.

- It offers methods of therapy which may also uncover unconscious conflicts. The client can then understand the causes of their problems and so resolve them and release their anxieties.

- It was the first theory to focus on psychological causes of disorders. Before this, the focus had been on physical causes or things like possession by evil spirits.

Weaknesses

- Freud's claims are based on his subjective interpretations of his patients' dreams, etc. Therefore they're hard to scientifically test and so can't be proved right or wrong.

- Psychoanalysis may take a long time and so be very expensive.

- The childhood conflicts that are 'uncovered' may be emotionally distressing and possibly inaccurate, depending on the reliability of the patient's memory, the techniques used to uncover them and the analyst's interpretations.

- The focus is on the patient's past, rather than on the problems that they are currently suffering.

Figure 5*: Psychoanalysis was conducted in Freud's office where the patient could lie down.*

Worked Exam-style Question

1   Outline psychological therapies used to treat abnormality.

(6 marks)

In the twentieth century, Freud developed several techniques to treat certain psychological disorders. He called this psychoanalysis and it allowed the patient to access repressed thoughts and unconscious conflicts which they could then deal with. There were three main techniques he used in psychoanalysis.

Firstly he used hypnosis, which involved putting the patient in a deep state of relaxation. The patient would then be able to access repressed thoughts in this state.

Secondly, he used free association. This allowed Freud to explore a patient's subconscious mind. He would give each patient a cue word and ask them to say whatever entered their mind when they heard the cue word. He thought this would give a better insight into their repressed thoughts and unconscious problems.

Finally, dream analysis was also used by Freud. It was thought that a certain part of the mind keeps repressed thoughts unconscious. This part was thought to be less active during sleep, and so Freud believed that by analysing people's dreams he would have access to these repressed thoughts.

Exam Tip
The question asks you to 'outline' the techniques, so all you have to do is give a little bit of information about each one. Since it doesn't ask you to evaluate them, you don't need to talk about the strengths and weaknesses of each therapy.

Exam Tip
This question is quite broad — this is great as it gives you a chance to write about something you really understand. But just make sure you stay focused on what the question wants.

Summary Questions

Q1 What is the id?

Q2 Name Freud's five stages of development in order.

Q3 Susie bites her nails. How would Freud explain this?

Q4 What is the aim of psychoanalysis?

Q5 a) Give two strengths of the psychodynamic model when explaining psychopathology.

   b) Give two weaknesses of the psychodynamic model when explaining psychopathology.

Learning Objectives:

- Know about psychological approaches to psychopathology, including the behavioural approach.

- Know about psychological therapies, including systematic desensitisation.

Tip: Classical conditioning is all about learned associations.

Tip: Phobias can be created when the natural fear response is associated with a particular stimulus.

5. The Behavioural Model of Abnormality

The behavioural model gives us another explanation for abnormality. It's based on the idea that all our behaviours are learnt.

The behavioural model of abnormality

Behaviourists argue that abnormal behaviours are learnt in the same way that all behaviours are learnt — through classical and operant conditioning. These pages are all about their take on the matter.

Classical conditioning

Behaviourists reckon that classical conditioning can be used to explain the development of many abnormal behaviours, including phobias (see Figure 1) and taste aversions (see next page).

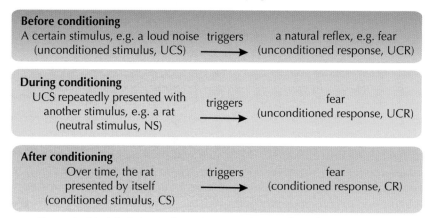

Before conditioning
A certain stimulus, e.g. a loud noise (unconditioned stimulus, UCS) triggers → a natural reflex, e.g. fear (unconditioned response, UCR)

During conditioning
UCS repeatedly presented with another stimulus, e.g. a rat (neutral stimulus, NS) triggers → fear (unconditioned response, UCR)

After conditioning
Over time, the rat presented by itself (conditioned stimulus, CS) triggers → fear (conditioned response, CR)

Figure 1: Model of classical conditioning showing how fear can develop.

Watson and Rayner (1920) experimented with an 11-month-old boy, 'Little Albert', producing fear of a white rat by associating it with a loud, scary noise. This is a classic, old-school crazy study.

Key study of Little Albert — Watson and Rayner (1920)

Method: The participant was an 11-month-old boy called 'Little Albert'. He showed no fear of white fluffy objects such as rats or rabbits. The researchers tried to create a conditioned response to these objects.
A white rat was placed in front of Little Albert. As he reached out for it, a metal bar was struck loudly behind his head. This was repeated twice at first, then 5 more times a week later.

Results: When Little Albert was shown a rat, he would start to cry. This also extended to other white fluffy objects, such as a white Santa Claus beard.

Conclusion: A fear response to white fluffy objects had been conditioned in Little Albert, showing that abnormal behaviour can be learned.

Evaluation: The experiment was extremely unethical — such an experiment couldn't be repeated today. Also, not everyone goes on to develop a fear or phobia after a negative situation, so learning theory can't be the full story.

Taste aversions are often developed if you're ill after a certain food or drink. Its taste will become a CS, producing a CR of nausea. This can even be the case if the illness wasn't actually caused by the food or drink.

Example

A lot of cancer patients experience nausea following treatment. But they also need to eat. Associating the two together can create a taste aversion.

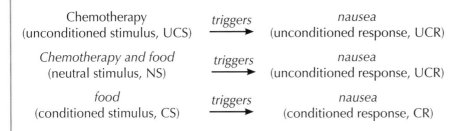

Chemotherapy (unconditioned stimulus, UCS) — *triggers* → nausea (unconditioned response, UCR)

Chemotherapy and food (neutral stimulus, NS) — *triggers* → nausea (unconditioned response, UCR)

food (conditioned stimulus, CS) — *triggers* → nausea (conditioned response, CR)

Operant conditioning

Operant conditioning is learning from the consequences of actions. Actions which have a good outcome through **positive reinforcement** (reward) or **negative reinforcement** (removal of something bad) will be repeated. Actions which have a bad outcome (punishment) will not be repeated.

Examples

- Maintaining phobias — we get anxious around phobic stimuli (heights, spiders etc.) and avoid them. This prevents the anxiety, which acts as negative reinforcement.

- Bulimics feel guilt and disgust, so make themselves sick. The removal of these feelings is negative reinforcement.

- Anorexics desire to lose weight, or to have more control of their life, so not eating is positively reinforced.

- Schizophrenia patients are rewarded for socially acceptable behaviour through token economy systems. This is positive reinforcement.

Figure 2: Animal trainers often use positive reinforcement to shape behaviour.

Behavioural therapies

Behavioural therapies are based on changes through conditioning. Behaviourists try to identify what reinforces unwanted behaviours and try to change them through conditioning.

Operant conditioning therapies are often used in psychiatric hospitals. They control abnormal behaviour by removing the reinforcements which maintain the behaviour, and giving new reinforcements for better behaviour. For example, psychiatric patients might receive tokens for behaving 'normally'. These can be exchanged for reinforcements, such as sweets or being able to watch TV. This is called a **token economy**.

Key study of token economy — Paul and Lentz (1977)

Method:	Using an independent design experiment, Paul and Lentz (1977) set up a token economy system for the schizophrenic patients in a local psychiatric hospital. One group of patients took part in the token economy system whilst the other group (the control group) didn't. Tokens were given as rewards when patients were 'well behaved' and they were taken away if patients acted 'strange' or 'bizarre'. The patients could exchange their tokens for luxury items such as chocolate or cigarettes.
Results:	After a time, those in the token economy group showed fewer abnormal behaviours than those in the control group. Only around 50% of the control group were able to be released compared to just under 100% of the group that took part in the token economy system.
Conclusion:	Token economy systems are effective in shaping behaviours.
Evaluation:	There are problems with the ethics of this study as it's based on denying people items such as chocolate and cigarettes which could be seen as too controlling.

Tip: Lots of studies have looked at token economy systems and shown that they don't have huge success rates in the long term. Bear this in mind when evaluating this type of research.

Behavioural therapies can also use classical conditioning to change behaviour, for example...

Aversion therapy

This stops an undesired behaviour by associating it with unpleasant feelings.

Tip: Remind yourself of the differences between conditioned and unconditioned responses on pages 190-191.

Examples

Aversion therapy has useful applications in real life:

- Alcoholics are given alcohol at the same time as a drug that naturally produces nausea. Nausea becomes a conditioned response to alcohol, so they should then feel no urge to drink, but instead feel sick at the idea of it.

- A special nail varnish has been created for nail-biters which has a foul tasting coating. Each time a person goes to bite their nails, they taste the coating until they eventually learn to associate biting their nails with a horrible taste.

Systematic desensitisation

This is a treatment for phobias.

- First, the phobic person makes a 'fear hierarchy'. This is a list of feared events, showing what they fear least (e.g. seeing a picture of a spider) through to their most feared event (e.g. holding a spider).

- When put in the situation of their least feared event, they're anxious.

- Then they're encouraged to use a relaxation technique.

- Relaxation and anxiety can't happen at the same time, so when they become relaxed and calm, they're no longer scared.

- This is repeated until the feared event is only linked with relaxation.

- This whole process is repeated for each stage of the fear hierarchy until they are calm through their most feared event.

Real World Connection
Since the 1990s, computer-based courses have grown in popularity. They have been used increasingly for systematic desensitisation particularly in helping to cure fears of animals, heights and flying. Carlin et al (1997) managed to successfully cure a 37 year old woman's spider phobia through a 12 week virtual reality programme of systematic desensitisation.

Many people have a phobia of spiders. A fear hierarchy allows them to
visualise each step of the way to help them overcome their fear.
Steps may include:

1. See a picture of a spider $\longrightarrow$ relaxation $\longrightarrow$ calm, no anxiety

2. See a tank containing a spider $\longrightarrow$ relaxation $\longrightarrow$ calm, no anxiety

3. Imagine holding a spider $\longrightarrow$ relaxation $\longrightarrow$ calm, no anxiety

4. See a real spider out of a tank $\longrightarrow$ relaxation $\longrightarrow$ calm, no anxiety

5. Hold a real spider $\longrightarrow$ relaxation $\longrightarrow$ calm, no anxiety

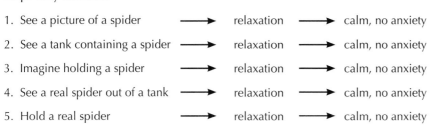

Figure 4: One stage of
systematic desensitisation is
confronting the fear.

Systematic desensitisation is based on conditioning principles. By creating
relationships between stimuli and responses, new behaviours can be formed
(see Figure 3).

Before **Stimulus** $\longrightarrow$ **Anxiety**

Systematic desensitisation

After **Stimulus** $\longrightarrow$ **Relaxation**

Figure 3: Systematic desensitisation reduces anxiety by developing
behavioural associations.

Key study of systematic desensitisation — Wolpe (1961)

Method:	Wolpe carried out systematic desensitisation on 39 people who, altogether, reported 62 different phobias. The phobias included spiders, bright lights and storms, amongst many others. Wolpe took each patient through three stages — muscle relaxation, the development of a fear hierarchy and then unlearning their anxiety.
Results:	He successfully managed to partly or wholly cure 35 out of 39 patients.
Conclusion:	Systematic desensitisation, as a behavioural therapy, can be effective in treating phobias.

Tip: Wolpe's (1961)
study provides results
to back up the idea that
behavioural therapies
can be effective in
treating phobias.

Strengths and weaknesses

The behavioural model has strengths and weaknesses.

Strengths

- It's a scientific approach — it has clear testable concepts, which have
  been supported in many experiments.

- Behavioural therapies can be very effective for treating phobias, eating
  disorders, obsessions and compulsions.

Weaknesses

It cannot explain all behaviours because it neglects:

- The influence of genetics and biology — or example, how brain
  functioning affects behaviour.

- The influence of cognitions — how thought processes contribute to
  disorders (see pages 195-196).

Behavioural therapies are not effective for all disorders, e.g. conditioning
doesn't cure schizophrenia. The procedures sometimes raise ethical issues,

e.g. aversion therapy may be quite distressing. It only treats the behaviour, so doesn't address any underlying causes for it.

Worked Exam-style Question

Exam Tip
Scribble a quick plan of action before you start. That way, you'll present your answer in a much clearer way.

1   Describe and evaluate the use of behavioural therapies in abnormal psychology.   *(12 marks)*

The behavioural therapies used in abnormal psychology either use operant conditioning or classical conditioning to help change behaviour. For example, token economies use operant conditioning, and aversion therapy and systematic desensitisation use classical conditioning to try to change behaviour. However, as with therapies from other approaches, behavioural therapies have strengths and weaknesses in treating abnormal behaviour.

Exam Tip
Don't forget to include studies to back up your points.

Token economies are based on operant conditioning and are used mainly within psychiatric wards. Patients are usually given rewards (positive reinforcement) for good behaviour, and the rewards taken away (punishment) when they show 'bad' behaviour. As Paul and Lentz (1977) concluded, this can be effective in changing the behaviours of many patients, such as those with schizophrenia. However, often this technique does not last in the long term, and there are ethical implications in denying people basic items such as food.

Classical conditioning forms the foundations for aversion therapy and systematic desensitisation. Aversion therapy removes undesired behaviour by pairing it with unpleasant feelings. For instance, if someone wanted to stop biting their nails, then by painting their nails with a horrible tasting varnish, they would soon learn to associate a disgusting taste with their bad habit.

Systematic desensitisation has successfully been used in treating phobias. Patients make a list of feared events called a fear hierarchy and then create calming and relaxing thoughts to associate each stage of their fear with. This is repeated until the feared event is only linked with relaxation. Wolpe (1961) had success with this technique and partly or wholly cured 35 out of 39 phobic people. However, in systematic desensitisation, it could just be exposure that helps people overcome their fear, not conditioning.

Exam Tip
You might have given evaluative comments about the individual therapies earlier, but finish with an overall summary to round off your answer.

Behavioural therapies have been shown to be effective. Because it is a scientific approach, the therapies can be tested to see how reliable and useful they are. However, they aren't effective for all psychological disorders, and they only treat the observable behaviours, not the causes.

Summary Questions

Q1 Outline the results and conclusion of Watson and Rayner's (1920) case study.

Q2 What is the difference between classical and operant conditioning?

Q3 When Cat was younger she was really ill after eating some haggis. She now immediately feels nauseous if she even just smells haggis. How would the behavioural model of abnormality explain this?

Q4 Give two weaknesses of the behavioural model of abnormality.

6. The Cognitive Model of Abnormality

Learning Objectives:
- Know about psychological approaches to psychopathology, including the cognitive approach.
- Know about psychological therapies, including Cognitive Behavioural Therapy.

This is the final model of abnormality — the cognitive model.
It claims that abnormal behaviour is a direct result of faulty thinking.

Thoughts and beliefs

The cognitive model assumes that behaviours are controlled by thoughts and beliefs. So, irrational thoughts and beliefs cause abnormal behaviours. A few different versions of the model have been suggested:

Ellis's (1962) ABC model

The 'ABC model' claims that disorders begin with an activating event (A) (e.g. a failed exam), leading to a belief (B) about why this happened. This may be rational (e.g. 'I didn't prepare well enough'), or irrational (e.g. 'I'm too stupid to pass exams'). The belief leads to a consequence (C). Rational beliefs produce adaptive (appropriate) consequences (e.g. more revision). Irrational beliefs produce maladaptive (bad and inappropriate) consequences (e.g. getting depressed).

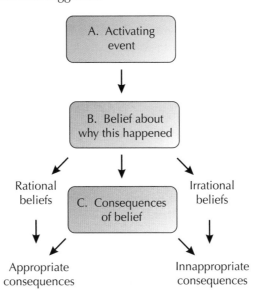

Figure 1: *Flowchart outlining Ellis's 'ABC model'.*

Real World Connection
There are many instances of where people can either rationally or irrationally account for events. This leads us to have either an appropriate or inappropriate reaction. In the example below, Matteo's irrational belief that he is a bad person leads to a depressed mood, whilst the rational belief that he didn't have enough lessons would lead him to take appropriate action.

Beck's (1963) cognitive triad

Beck (1963) identified a 'cognitive triad' of negative, automatic thoughts linked to depression (see Figure 2). He said they have negative views:

- about themselves (e.g. that they can't succeed at anything),
- about the world (e.g. that they must be successful to be a good person),
- and about the future (e.g. that nothing will change).

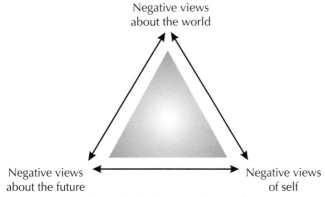

Figure 2: *Beck's cognitive triad.*

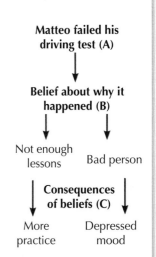

Tip: There's more about these two models on pages 134-135.

Changing faulty cognitions

Cognitive therapies assume that we can treat psychological disorders by eliminating or changing the original faulty thoughts and beliefs. They're used to treat a wide range of conditions, and can be particularly helpful with problems such as depression and anxiety. They've also been shown to be as effective as medication for some conditions.

Tip: Take a look back at page 134 to read more about Cognitive Behavioural Therapy.

This is generally what happens during cognitive behavioural therapy:
- The therapist and client identify the client's faulty cognitions (thoughts and beliefs).
- The therapist then tries to show that the cognitions aren't true.

--- Example ---

Mandy is terrified of germs and is constantly scared of becoming ill. Her therapist asks her to think about her thoughts and feelings and write down her negative and irrational thoughts. Mandy then must write down a more rational explanation.
- Negative thought: "I'm going to get ill and die if I don't clean the work surface everyday".
- Rational explanation: "Other people live in less clean conditions and they don't die".

Tip: Cognitive therapies are often very interactive and frequently depend on the patient having 'homework' and writing things down.

- Together, they then set goals to think in more positive or adaptive ways. This could be focusing on things the client has succeeded at and trying to build on them.

--- Example ---

Steve gets anxious about public speaking but he has been asked to give a speech at his best friend's wedding.
- His therapist will set him small goals, such as speaking in front of his colleagues at work, speaking on the telephone and rehearsing what he is going to say. He can then build upon these small but successful steps.

- Although the client may occasionally need to look back to past experiences, the treatment mainly focuses on the present situation.
- Therapists sometimes encourage their clients to keep a diary — they can record their thought patterns, feelings and actions.

Cognitive therapies

Examples of cognitive therapies are Hardiness Training and Meichenbaum's Stress Inoculation Training (SIT), which, as you can probably guess, was developed to reduce stress (see pages 133-134).

Hardiness Training

Hardiness Training was developed by Kobasa and Maddi (1977). It's based on the idea that the more hardy people are (able to cope with certain events), the less stressed they are likely to get.

Figure 3: *Olympic swimmers performed better after Hardiness Training.*

There are three steps to Hardiness Training:

1. Focusing	**2. Reliving stressful encounters**	**3. Self-improvement**
recognise physical symptoms of stress	analyse situations	take on challenges and gain control

Hardiness Training has been successful in various sports. Fletcher (2005) used it on Olympic swimmers and found they improved their performance following training.

Stress inoculation training (SIT)

Meichenbaum's (1985) SIT also has three different phases:

1. Conceptualisation
identify fears and concerns with help of a therapist
$\longrightarrow$
2. Skill acquisition and rehearsal
e.g. positive thinking, relaxation
$\longrightarrow$
3. Application and follow-through
practise new skills in real-life situations

Whilst SIT has been successful, it often takes a long time and requires an intensive training process.

Strengths and weaknesses

Strengths

- The cognitive model offers a useful approach to disorders like depression and anorexia. This is because it considers the role of thoughts and beliefs, which are greatly involved in problems like depression.

- Cognitive therapies have often successfully treated depression, anxiety, stress and eating disorders.

- It allows a person to take control and make a positive change to their behaviour.

- There is lots of research to support the cognitive approach. Gustafson (1992) showed that people with depression, schizophrenia and other psychological disorders did show faulty thinking processes.

Weaknesses

- Faulty cognitions may simply be the consequence of a disorder rather than its cause. For example, depression may be caused by a chemical imbalance in the brain, which causes people to think very negatively.

- Cognitive therapies may take a long time and be costly. They may be more effective when combined with other approaches, e.g. cognitive-behavioural methods.

- The treatments work better with some conditions than others, e.g. it's an effective treatment for depression and panic disorders but less effective for severe depression where antidepressants may be needed as well.

- The person could begin to feel like he or she is to blame for their problems.

So, you're probably getting the point by now. All these different models and approaches are great in some ways, but are actually kind of dodgy in other ways. It makes it tricky to see which model best explains abnormality, or whether they're all partially right.

Worked Exam-style Questions

1   Outline how cognitive therapies are used as treatments in psychopathology.   *(8 marks)*

Cognitive therapies aim to change faulty cognitions. Faulty cognitions are irrational thoughts and beliefs that people have which can then lead to abnormal behaviour. Cognitive therapies allow the therapist to challenge these faulty cognitions so that the abnormal behaviour can be changed.

Tip: It is very difficult to generalise the findings from Hardiness Training because all the research is based on a limited population. Most participants were middle class and white — and what is stressful to them might not be to other people.

Real World Connection
SIT is used a lot within the sporting world and has proven highly successful in improving athletes' performances. Mace et al (1986) gave a female gymnast 8 sessions of stress inoculation training. Afterwards, she was found to have higher self esteem and perform better.

Exam Tip
Start your answer with a short introduction to outline what you're going to say in your answer. It'll help to keep you on track and it'll also show that you know what you're talking about.

For instance, a patient with anxieties might go to their therapist because they are worried something disastrous will happen if they don't keep everything really clean. The patient and their therapist will identify that this is a faulty cognition and that obsessive cleaning will not make any difference in whether something will happen to them or not.

The therapist will then try to show that their beliefs are not true. Using the same example, they will tell the patient that lots of people live in conditions that are not immaculate and they live without disastrous consequences. They would then set goals to think in more positive ways, and the therapist might encourage the patient to keep a diary of their thoughts and behaviours.

2   Outline the limitations of the cognitive approach to psychopathology.   *(4 marks)*

There are several limitations of the cognitive model of abnormality. It could be that faulty cognitions are actually the consequences of a disorder, not the cause of it. For example, if someone has depression their negative thoughts may be due to the levels of serotonin and chemical imbalances in their brains, and not a cause of the illness.

■   Secondly, therapies can often take a long time to work and can be expensive. Therapies also work better for some disorders than others. Therefore, investing lots of time and effort into a therapy which has a limited use could be seen as wasteful.

■   Finally, a person with a psychological illness may go through therapy and feel that they are to blame for their illness because the approach focuses on the problem being the patient's own faulty cognitions.

Summary Questions

Q1 How does Ellis (1962) explain abnormality?

Q2 What is Beck's (1963) cognitive triad?

Q3 What do cognitive therapies assume?

Q4 Give two strengths of the cognitive approach when explaining psychopathology.

Section Summary

- The individual differences approach looks at how psychological characteristics differ from person to person.

- The individual differences approach uses different perspectives — the biological, psychodynamic, behavioural and cognitive approaches — to look at how everyone is different.

- Several research methods are used, including case studies, meta-analyses, correlational studies and physiological studies.

- The DSM-IV is the American Psychiatric Association's Diagnostic and Statistical Manual of Mental Disorders. It contains all known mental health disorders.

- Defining abnormality can be difficult. It can be defined as a deviation from social norms, as a failure to function adequately or as a deviation from ideal mental health.

- Time, culture, race and gender are all factors which might influence and change our definitions of what is abnormal.

- Classifying people can lead to pigeon-holing people into certain categories, and there are problems with the reliability and validity of classification systems.

- The biological approach assumes that psychological disorders are physical illnesses. It suggests the cause of disorders as being genetic, from infections, from an imbalance of neurotransmitters or as a result of a brain injury.

- Twin studies and adoption studies are used to look into genetic causes.

- Biological therapies include psychosurgery, drugs and electroconvulsive therapy (ECT).

- The psychodynamic approach assumes that conflict in development accounts for psychological problems in later life.

- Freud divided personality into three parts — the id, ego and superego. He also suggested we have five stages of development — oral, anal, phallic, latency and genital. He believed that if conflicts between the parts of the personality arose during any of the five stages of development, this would lead to fixations and then psychological problems in adulthood.

- Psychoanalysis was invented by Freud as a way to delve into the unconscious mind. Freud used hypnosis, free association and dream analysis to try and uncover patients' repressed thoughts and unconscious conflicts which he said caused abnormal behaviour.

- The behavioural approach claims behaviours are all learnt through classical conditioning and operant conditioning.

- Aversion therapy and systematic desensitisation are behavioural therapies which can be used to treat abnormal behaviours.

- The cognitive approach suggests that faulty cognitions (irrational thoughts and beliefs) can account for abnormality.

- Two variations of the cognitive model of abnormality include Ellis's (1962) ABC model and Beck's (1963) cognitive triad.

- Therapies aimed to change faulty cognitions include cognitive behavioural therapy, hardiness training and stress inoculation training (SIT).

- All of the approaches have strengths and weaknesses. No one approach can fully explain abnormality.

Exam-style Questions

1   Rozanne is investigating to see if depression has a genetic basis.
Give **two** other biological causes which could explain psychological disorders.

(2 marks)

2   Outline the assumptions of the behavioural approach of abnormality.

(6 marks)

3   Catherine conducted research into hand-washing behaviour.
She found that people, on average, tend to wash their hands five times a day.

3 (a)   How might deviation from social norms describe why someone who
only washes their hands once a day could be seen as abnormal?

(2 marks)

3 (b)   Evaluate the deviation from social norms definition of abnormality using
this example.

(4 marks)

4   Compare the biological and cognitive approaches to abnormality.

(12 marks)

5   Sandra has been diagnosed with severe depression. Her doctor has given
her the option of having electroconvulsive therapy (ECT) or cognitive therapy.

5 (a)   Outline what ECT involves.

(3 marks)

5 (b)   Outline what cognitive therapy involves.

(3 marks)

6   Aston the postman has a fear of dogs. Describe and evaluate one method
that a behavioural psychologist might use to treat his phobia.

(8 marks)

7   Praveen has been told that her nail-biting habits are due to a conflict during
her oral stage of development.

7 (a)   Which psychological model has Praveen's therapist applied to explain
her behaviour?

(1 mark)

7 (b)   Give **one** weakness of this model.

(1 mark)

7 (c)   Give **two** treatment methods that Praveen's therapist might use.

(2 marks)

Exam Help

Exam Help

You'll have done loads and loads of exams before, but that doesn't mean you know every secret to doing well. This section is crammed full of useful tips to make sure that you're fully prepared for the big day.

The exam papers

You'll have to do two exams for AS Psychology — Unit 1 and Unit 2. So far so good. Both exam papers are broken down into sections.

Unit 1

Unit 1 is broken down into just **two** sections, like this:

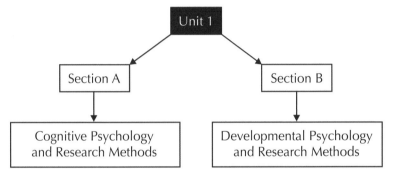

You get 1 hour 30 minutes to answer the questions in this exam.

You get mainly shortish answer questions, but one whopping 12 mark question. There are 72 marks up for grabs in Unit 1.

Unit 2

Unit 2 has **three** wonderful sections:

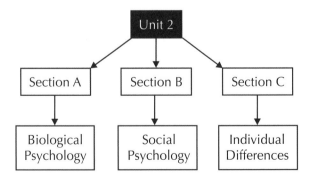

You get 1 hour 30 minutes to answer the questions in this exam.

This unit also has mainly shortish answer questions — but there could be a couple of 8 mark questions. There'll also be one or more big 12 mark questions. There are 72 marks up for grabs in Unit 2.

Exam Tip
Make sure you know exactly what each unit covers — you don't want any surprises on the day of the exam.

Exam Tip
You won't be asked anything on cognitive psychology, research methods or developmental psychology in the Unit 2 exam. Similarly, none of the Unit 2 stuff will come up in your Unit 1 exam. This means you can learn it in two separate chunks. However, if you really want to impress the examiner in your Unit 2 exam, you could bring things from Unit 1 into your evaluations. They have to be relevant things, of course...

Exam Tip
In the Unit 1 and Unit 2 exams, you get 1 hour 30 minutes for 72 marks. If you do the maths, that works out at just over 1 minute per mark — worth bearing in mind when you're deciding how much to write for each question.

Command words

Exam questions contain content words and command words. The content words give away what the topic of the question is. A command word gives you an instruction of exactly what you need to do to answer the question. It's really vital that you know what they mean so that you can write the correct things in your answer.

Exam Tip
Some questions may not use the command words, instead asking what, why, etc. Here, look at the number of marks available to judge how much to write.

Command word:	What it means:
Give/Name/State	Give a brief one or two word answer, or a short sentence.
Describe	Give details of something — it might be a theory, concept or a study.
Outline	This requires less detail than 'describe' — it's more of a brief summary of something. Just give details of the main or important features. You don't need to go into too much depth.
Identify	This will often just require a single point without any explanation. Sometimes 'state' might be used instead.
Explain	If a question asks you to explain something, it means you need to give reasons for it and say why it is the case.
Discuss	This is asking for an answer that is a bit like a debate. The idea is that you'll build up an argument for and against something. You need to give evidence and examples for what you're saying, and support your points with explanations. This sort of question tends to be worth quite a lot of marks.
Evaluate	Evaluating something means weighing it up. You need to weigh up the advantages and disadvantages, positives and negatives, or strengths and weaknesses. It's important to keep your answer balanced — don't just concentrate on the one side.
Consider	This is quite similar to 'evaluate' — your answer will involve weighing up the point that you've been asked to consider. Again, keep your comments balanced.

Exam Tip
The more questions you practise, the quicker you'll get at figuring out what you need to do.

Command words can sometimes be combined together in a question. For example, examiners will often ask you to 'outline and evaluate' or 'describe and explain' something. Don't let this put you off — just break the question down into bits. Start your answer with the outline or describe bit, and then move on to your evaluation or your explanation.

How much to write

The number of marks that a question is worth gives you a pretty good clue of how much to write. You get one mark per correct point made, so if a question is worth four marks, make sure you write four decent points. There's no point writing a massive answer for a question that's only worth a few marks — it's just a waste of your time. For the longer essay-style questions, make sure that you've written enough to cover the 12 marks, but don't just waffle.

Exam Tip
For higher scoring questions, marks will be given in bands. You'll start by getting marks for the breadth of knowledge you show, but then also for the depth and quality of your answer.

1 Outline the key features of the multi-store model of memory. *(6 marks)*

The multi-store model proposes that memory is made up of three stores. These three stores are a sensory store, a short-term store and a long-term store. Sensory memory holds the information that is constantly being taken in from the environment, such as visual and auditory information. If you don't pay attention to this information, it will be lost from the sensory store. However, if you do pay attention to it, it will pass into short-term memory. Short-term memory has a limited and temporary capacity, but if the information in it is rehearsed, it will be transferred into long-term memory, which theoretically has an unlimited capacity and duration.

The model has three features, and the question's worth 6 marks. So, you'd just need to write enough to get you two marks for each feature. The answer might look short, but it's all you'd need to write.

It's important to remember that it's not just a case of blindly scribbling down everything you can think of that's related to the subject. Doing this just wastes time, and it doesn't exactly impress the examiner. You only get marks for stuff that's relevant and answers the question. So, make sure you read over the question a couple of times before you start writing so that you really understand what it's asking.

Exam Tip
The same applies to evaluation questions too. If a question worth 6 marks asks you to evaluate a theory or model, then you should give three marks worth of positive points, and three marks worth of negative points.

Planning an answer

Examiners will stick to their mark scheme pretty strictly. So they won't give you extra marks for writing loads if it doesn't answer the question — to them it's just pointless and irrelevant information.

Also, when you're writing your answers, try to structure them in an organised way. If there's one thing that examiners find worse than a load of pointless information, it's being unable to make head nor tail of an answer — it just makes it really difficult for them to mark.

Before you start, it's worth jotting down a quick plan of what you want to write so that you don't just end up with a really jumbled answer.

— Example —

If a question asks you to outline and evaluate a study, your plan might look something like this:

1.   Brief description of the method, results, conclusion
2.   Strengths of the study design
3.   Weaknesses of the study design

Exam Tip
It's fine to write a plan like this before you start the question. Just put a line through it when you're done so that the examiner knows that it's not part of your answer.

Time management

This is one of the most important exam skills to have. How long you spend on each question is really important in an exam — it could make all the difference to your grade.

It doesn't matter if you leave some questions out to begin with. For example, if you're stuck on a question that's worth only a few marks, don't spend ages trying to answer it — you can always come back to it if you have time left at the end when you've bagged loads of other marks elsewhere.

Figure 1: *Keep an eye on the time in exams.*

Applying your knowledge

You need to be able to apply your knowledge to questions in the exam.

Exam Tip
Exam questions are often put into a context — you'll need to work out which bit of your psychological knowledge to use in your answer.

Example

You could be asked how learning theory can be used to explain attachment. It's no good just explaining what learning theory is — you won't get very many marks. You need to talk about learning, associations and reinforcers in relation to a child and its caregiver.

You'll have gathered that to get the higher grades, your answer needs to show detailed and accurate knowledge. Basically, you need to show the examiner that you understand stuff really well. Picking out studies and theories to support your answers is great — but keep it all relevant to the question.

Quality of written communication (QWC)

In some of these questions, you get marks for QWC. It assesses things like:

- whether your scribble, sorry, writing is legible
- whether your spelling, punctuation and grammar are accurate
- whether your writing style is appropriate
- whether you organise your answer clearly and coherently
- whether you use specialist psychology vocabulary where it's appropriate.

On the front of the paper, you'll be told which of the questions this is being assessed in. However, stop right there. This doesn't mean that you don't need to think about it in all the other questions though. If your writing is easy to read and your answers make sense it makes the examiner's job much easier.

Assessment objectives

Tip: The questions in the exam won't be labelled AO1, AO2 or AO3, but you can use the information on these pages to work out which assessment objective a question covers.

In the exams, you need to meet certain assessment objectives. There are three assessment objectives — AO1, AO2 and AO3.

AO1 is about the facts and theories

These questions cover the knowledge and understanding of science and How Science Works. You get marks by recalling and describing psychological knowledge, such as theories, studies and methods. For example, you might get asked to describe a theory of memory. To get the marks, you'd simply need to describe what the theory proposed and describe its key features. What you don't need to do is evaluate the theory — that'd just be a waste of time that you could use elsewhere, and you won't get any extra marks.

Exam Tip
If a question only has AO1 marks, there's no point writing anything that would get you AO2 or AO3 marks — for example, if a question asked you to outline the experimental design of a study, don't give its strengths and weaknesses. It won't get you any more marks as it's not actually answering the question.

Examples

AO1 Questions

- Outline the response of the pituitary-adrenal system to long-term stress.
- Outline Ainsworth's 'strange situation' study.

AO2 gets you to apply your knowledge

AO2 questions are slightly different in that they get you to apply your knowledge and understanding of science and How Science Works. It's likely that these questions will begin with 'analyse' or 'evaluate'. Rather than just recalling stuff, e.g. listing relevant experiments, you've got to apply your knowledge to the situation in these questions. So, you'd need to use the experiments you've come up with to support your argument. You also might have to apply your knowledge to situations you've not come across before. For example, you could be asked to assess the validity, reliability or credibility of a study that's new to you.

Exam Tip
It's really important to pay attention to the command words in questions — they tell you exactly what's needed by your answer. To make sure you know what they all mean, have a look at page 202.

---Examples---

AO2 Questions

- Evaluate Atkinson and Shiffrin's multi-store of memory.
- Sally has developed CHD. Use Friedman and Rosenman's (1974) study to explain how this could be a result of her personality.

AO3 is about 'How Science Works'

'How Science Works' focuses on how scientific research is carried out. You need to be able to suggest a suitable experimental design and know how to make sure measurements and observations are accurate and precise. You could also be asked to analyse and evaluate the methodology and results of a study described in the exam. When you're doing this, don't forget about things like practical and ethical problems.

Tip: Have a look at pages 5-8 for more on How Science Works and Unit 1: Section 3 for more on research methods.

---Examples---

AO3 Questions

- Identify the dependent variable in Peterson and Peterson's study.
- Evaluate the method used by Milgram in his 1963 study into obedience.

Question wording

The wording of the question can tell you what to do. For example, if the question simply asks you to 'describe' or 'outline' something, you know it's an AO1 question. So you don't need to go into evaluating and explaining stuff. Both AO2 and AO3 questions could ask you to evaluate something — but it's what you're asked to analyse that tells you which assessment objective is being covered:

Exam Tip
Underlining key words in the question can help to make sure you keep your answer focused on the right things.

- If the question asks you to evaluate a theory, it's an AO2 question.
- If you're asked to evaluate the method or results of a study, you know it's an AO3 question.

Assessment objective weightings

Each unit has a different weighting of assessment objectives. In Unit 1, there's an equal division of AO1, AO2 and AO3 marks throughout the paper. In Unit 2, there are fewer AO3 marks — there's more emphasis on AO1 and AO2.

		Assessment Objective		
		AO1	AO2	AO3
Weighting (%)	Unit 1	16.7	16.7	16.7
	Unit 2	20.8	20.8	8.3

Figure 2: *Table to show the weightings of the three assessment objectives in the Unit 1 and 2 exams.*

Armed with all your new-found knowledge and by following all the tips and hints in this book, exam success is just around the corner...

Answers

Unit 1

Section 1 — Cognitive Psychology

1. The Cognitive Approach
Page 12 — Summary Questions
Q1 Cognitive psychologists often treat humans as information processors (computers) and explain behaviour in terms of information processing. The brain is described as a processor and it has data input into it and output from it.
Q2 Any two from, e.g. research is often carried out in artificial situations (e.g. laboratories, using computer models), so the results aren't valid in the real world. / The role of emotion and influence from other people is often ignored, which means that the results aren't valid in the real world. / It fails to take individual differences into account and assumes that everyone processes information in exactly the same way.
Q3 Advantage: e.g. they have ecological validity because they take place in a natural situation.
Disadvantage: e.g. there's less control of the variables.
Q4 E.g. natural experiments have high ecological validity whereas laboratory experiments usually have low ecological validity.
Q5 By the end of the project, Washoe had learnt at least 34 signs. The development of language in the chimpanzee appeared to follow the same patterns as language development in children. Washoe learnt language at similar rates to children of the same age. Also, language acquisition seemed to require interaction with caregivers, and communication in everyday situations. However, she didn't learn grammar.
Q6 E.g. the study had ethical issues — Washoe was taken from the wild and deprived of other chimpanzees for companionship. / The study lacked external validity — it is not possible to accurately generalise results from the study of a chimp to the study of human children.

2. Short-Term and Long-Term Memory
Page 18 — Summary Questions
Q1 Sensory memory disappears quickly through spontaneous decay. Because it isn't around for long, it is difficult to study, so fewer studies have been done on it.
Q2 Seven, plus or minus two.
It's the number of items that Miller thought the short-term memory could hold.
Q3 Encoding can be visual, acoustic or semantic.

Q4 STM generally involves acoustic encoding. Encoding in LTM is usually semantic (but can also be acoustic or visual).
Q5 Any one from, e.g. Baddeley / Conrad / Brandimonte.

3. Models of Memory
Page 22 — Summary Questions
Q1 Atkinson and Shiffrin
Q2 The three stores are the sensory store, the short-term store and the long-term store.
Q3 a) The primacy effect is where people are able to recall the first few items of a list better than those from the middle.
    b) It happens because earlier items will have been rehearsed better, so are more likely to have been transferred to long-term memory.
Q4 People with Korsakoff's syndrome have an unaffected short-term memory but their long-term memory is very poor. This supports the multi-store model by showing that short-term memory and long-term memory are separate stores.
Q5 Baddeley and Hitch
Q6 The three components are the central executive, the articulatory-phonological loop and the visuo-spatial sketchpad.

4. Eyewitness Testimony
Page 28 — Summary Questions
Q1 a) Leading — e.g. "Did you see any children?"
    b) Leading — e.g. "Did you see any bikes?"
    c) Not leading
Q2 a) They showed participants a film of a car accident, then asked them "Did you see the broken headlight?" or "Did you see a broken headlight?" There was actually no broken headlight in the film.
    b) Despite there being no broken headlight, 7% of those asked about "a" broken headlight claimed that they saw one, compared to 17% in the group asked about "the" broken headlight.
    Loftus did a lot of work on eyewitness testimony — double check the question to make sure you're talking about the right study in your answer.
Q3 Three groups consisting of either children, young adults or elderly people.
Q4 Young children and the elderly can have less accurate recall than adults. Also, young children can be misled more by leading questions.
Q5 Geiselman et al

Q6 The interviewer tries to make the witness relaxed and tailors his/her language to suit the witness.
The witness recreates the environmental and internal (e.g. mood) context of the crime scene. The witness reports absolutely everything that they can remember about the crime. The witness is asked to recall details of the crime in different orders. The witness is asked to recall the event from various different perspectives. The interviewer avoids any judgemental and personal comments.

Q7 a) In a staged situation, an intruder carrying a blue rucksack entered a classroom and stole a slide projector. Two days later, participants were questioned about the event. The study used an independent groups design — participants were either questioned using a standard interview procedure or the cognitive interview technique. Early in the questioning, participants were asked 'Was the guy with the green backpack nervous?'. Later in the interview, participants were asked what colour the man's rucksack was.

b) Participants in the cognitive interview condition were less likely to recall the rucksack as being green than those in the standard interview condition.

c) An independent groups design was used, therefore the participants in the cognitive interview condition could have been naturally less susceptible to leading questions than the other group.
In an independent groups design, different participants are used in each condition. One group might have been more susceptible to leading questions than the other group purely due to chance.

5. Strategies for Memory Improvement
Page 32 — Summary Questions
Q1 Using word lists that contained words that are highly associated, they found that participants tended to group the associated words together in recall even though they had been separated by other words in the original list.

Q2 The first letter mnemonic helps with learning something's order. The first letter of each word is used to create a sentence using a different set of words.

Q3 E.g. Henry VIII's wives:
"Divorced, beheaded, died,
Divorced, beheaded, survived."
How many days there are in each month:
"Thirty days has September,
April, June and November,
All the rest have thirty-one,
Except February alone,
Which has twenty-eight days clear,
And twenty-nine each leap year."
Spelling words:
"i before e, except after c."

Q4 a) They had two groups of participants — one group were simply asked to learn a word list, and the other were asked to link the words together with a story. Both groups recalled the lists equally well straight after learning them. However, later, recall was much better in the group that had created stories.

b) This links to the multi-store model because the words are moving into long-term memory because they are being rehearsed during the creation of the stories.

Page 33 — Exam-style Questions
1   Maximum of 4 marks available.
HINTS:

- You've got the choice to describe any research method in the cognitive approach, so you could pick laboratory experiments, field experiments, natural experiments, brain imaging, case studies or animal research.

- The question is only worth 4 marks, so that would break down into 2 marks for the description, 1 mark for an advantage of the method and 1 mark for a disadvantage of the method. You don't need to write too much for each point — so don't spend too long on this question.

2   Maximum of 4 marks available.
Short-term memory has a limited duration *(1 mark)* and a limited capacity *(1 mark)*. Long-term memory has a theoretically permanent duration *(1 mark)* and an unlimited capacity *(1 mark)*.

3   (a) Maximum of 2 marks available.
Encoding is the way that information is stored in memory *(1 mark)*. It can be acoustic, visual or semantic *(1 mark)*.

(b) Maximum of 8 marks available.
HINTS:

- As the question is worth 8 marks, it's a good idea to just focus on one study in detail, rather than trying to evaluate more than one. However, it would be fine to bring in other studies during your evaluation.

- Start your answer with a brief description of the method, results and conclusion of the study. You should aim to write enough to get yourself 4 marks.

- The other 4 marks will come from your evaluation. This should weigh up any positives or negatives. For example, you could comment on the methodology of your chosen study, or say how well it supports the theory.

4   Maximum of 4 marks available.
     The working memory model proposes that short-term
     memory is made up of different stores called the
     central executive, the articulatory-phonological loop
     and the visuo-spatial sketchpad *(1 mark)*.
     Speech-based tasks are carried out using the
     articulatory-phonological loop *(1 mark)*.
     The capacity of this system is limited *(1 mark)*.
     This will mean that as both tasks use this system,
     performance on one or both tasks will be reduced
     (1 mark).

5   (a) Maximum of 4 marks available.
         HINTS:

         • Make sure you start your answer by pointing
           out that the question is a leading question.
           Say that this means that a certain answer
           is implied — in this case that there was
           definitely a man pulling out of the junction.

         • The question already implies that this could
           have a negative effect on the accuracy of
           David's recall, so you won't get a mark for
           saying that.

         • Finish off by giving a brief outline of some
           research that has looked into the effect of
           leading questions on the accuracy of recall.
           For example, you could give the results of
           the research by Loftus and Zanni (1975).

     (b) Maximum of 1 mark available.
         E.g. "Did you see anyone pulling out of the
         junction?"

     (c) Maximum of 6 marks available.
         David would be made to feel relaxed by the
         interviewer *(1 mark)*. He would be asked to
         recreate the environment of the scene and to
         remember his feelings at the time that he saw
         the crash *(1 mark)*. He would then be asked to
         recall everything he remembers about the car
         crash *(1 mark)*, and then recall details of the
         event in different orders *(1 mark)*. David might
         then be asked to recall the crash from different
         perspectives — for example, from the viewpoint of
         another driver who was at the scene or somebody
         walking nearby *(1 mark)*. The interviewer would
         avoid any judgemental or personal comments
         throughout the interview *(1 mark)*.

6   Maximum of 8 marks available.
     HINTS:

     • As you'll probably realise, you won't get the
       8 marks by just saying what the effect will be
       — you need to explain your answer.

     • This is a good place to use a study to support
       your explanation of the effect that you think
       you'd see. For example, you could use
       Valentine and Coxon's (1997) study of the
       effect of age on eyewitness testimony.

     • Give a brief description of the method, results
       and conclusion, and then apply them to the
       situation in the question.

     • You also need to give some evaluation of the
       study — that way you're showing how well the
       study supports your answer of how age will
       affect the witnesses.

7   Maximum of 8 marks available.
     HINTS:

     • The two methods could include the method
       of loci, the peg-word technique or narrative
       stories.

     • Break your answer down into parts. The first
       part will describe your first chosen strategy.
       Then go on to describe the second strategy.

     • Don't forget you also need to include some
       evaluation points. You can either give pros and
       cons after each strategy, or you could have a
       general evaluation section at the end of your
       answer.

Section 2 — Developmental Psychology

1. The Developmental Approach

Page 37 — Summary Questions

Q1 Observational studies, correlational studies, case studies, interviews.

If you have examples in mind for each of these methods, you can use them to illustrate your answers more fully.

Q2 Advantage: e.g. they allow us to study variables that would be unethical to manipulate.
Disadvantage: e.g. they don't show causal relationships — results might be affected by a third variable.

Q3 E.g. "Do you feel scared when you see Oliver?"

Q4 longitudinal

Q5 Advantage: e.g. they allow us to do research that would be unethical to carry out on humans.
Disadvantage: e.g. animals and humans are different, so you can't generalise results from one species to another. / It's unethical because animals can't give consent.

2. Explanations of Attachment

Page 41 — Summary Questions

Q1 Attachment is a close emotional relationship between an infant and its caregiver.

Q2 Harlow raised some rhesus monkeys in isolation. They had two 'surrogate' mothers, one made of wire mesh with a feeding bottle and the other made of cloth without a feeding bottle. Harlow found that the monkeys spent most of their time clinging to the cloth surrogate and only used the wire one to feed.

This is a really key study within psychology but don't forget that, as with all studies, it has its flaws. Make sure you are able to evaluate it as well.

Q3 Imprinting is where animals automatically attach to the first thing they see after being born.

3. Types of Attachment

Page 45 — Summary Questions

Q1 a) In secure attachments there is a strong bond between an infant and its caregiver. The infant will typically show distress on separation and will be comforted by being reunited with its caregiver.

b) Infants with insecure-avoidant attachments will not seem distressed if they're separated from their caregiver. They can also be comforted by strangers.

c) Infants with insecure-resistant attachments seem uneasy around their caregivers, but become upset if they are separated. These children show little response to comfort offered from either strangers or their caregivers.

Q2 Observing an infant's reactions to the different stages of the 'strange situation' can tell researchers about its bond with its caregiver, based on how it responds to separation, reunion and stranger scenarios.

4. Disruption of Attachment

Page 50 — Summary Questions

Q1 Deprivation is the loss of something that is wanted or needed.

Q2 Protest, despair, detachment.

Q3 Short-term separation can have very bad effects, including possible permanent damage to attachments.

Q4 Any two from: anaclitic depression / deprivational dwarfism / affectionless psychopathy.

Make sure you know what each of these means so you can talk about them if necessary, rather than just listing them.

Q5 Appropriate good quality care.

5. Failure to Form Attachments — Privation

Page 55 — Summary Questions

Q1 Any one from, e.g. Koluchova's (1976) case of the Czech boys where a pair of twins were brought up by their father and cruel stepmother. They were beaten, locked away and didn't develop intellectually. They were later adopted and developed above average intelligence. / Skuse's (1984) case of Louise and Mary. These girls were raised in a small room and tied to a bed with dog leads. When they were discovered, they hadn't learnt any language and didn't play. They underwent speech therapy and one recovered, whilst the other was sent to a care centre for autistic children.

Q2 Any one from, e.g. Hodges and Tizard (1989) used a longitudinal study of 65 children who had been placed in a residential nursery at a very young age. At 16, those who had been adopted had formed attachments compared with those who remained in care, who didn't form attachments. / Rutter et al (1998) investigated 111 Romanian orphans who were adopted by British families before they were two years old. They caught up developmentally by the time they were four years old.

You don't have to use these examples of studies if you don't want to — just make sure you have a relevant piece of research to talk about.

Q3 Any one from: age / quality of care during and after privation / social experiences later in life.

Q4 a) reactive attachment disorder
b) disinhibited attachment disorder.

Q5 Quinton et al (1985) found that women who had been raised in institutional care grew up to become less caring mothers. They were less likely to form attachments with their children. These children are then likely to become less caring parents, and so on.

6. The Effects of Day Care on Child Development

Page 59 — Summary Questions

Q1 Any one from, e.g. playgroups, nursery schools, nannies.

Q2 a) There was no difference between the two groups — they were both as distressed by the separation from their mothers.

b) E.g. the study lacked ecological validity and so the results can't be generalised to other children.

Q3 Belsky and Rovine's (1988) study used the 'strange situation'. This is a controlled observation, meaning the variables were controlled. However, it lacked ecological validity because the situation was artificial. DiLalla (1998) also found negative effects on children's peer relationships, supporting the findings of their study.

As well as including both positive and negative comments about a study's methodology, evaluations can provide other examples of studies which can either support or counteract the evidence.

Q4 The Effective Provision of Pre-school Education (EPPE) project was a study carried out by Sylva et al (2003). The aim of the EPPE project was to work out what factors were necessary for effective pre-schooling. The EPPE project found that children who went to pre-school displayed better cognitive and social development than children who didn't. The project suggested that high quality pre-school care could reduce the risk of antisocial behaviour too.

Q5 Any three from, e.g. good staff training / adequate space / appropriate toys and activities / a good ratio of staff to children / minimal staff turn-over so children can form attachments.

Page 60 — Exam-style Questions

1 (a) Maximum of 1 mark available.
E.g. ecological validity is high because the subject is in a real-life, familiar setting *(1 mark)*.
(b) Maximum of 1 mark available.
E.g. observer bias may affect the reliability of the results *(1 mark)*.

2 Maximum of 1 mark available.
E.g. since she wants to test how IQ changes with age, it would take a long time and would therefore be time-consuming and costly *(1 mark)*.

3 Maximum of 5 marks available.
Carole may have felt discomfort, e.g. from hunger, which would have made her cry *(1 mark)*. Her mother would then have fed her, which would have removed the discomfort *(1 mark)*. By negative reinforcement *(1 mark)*, Carole would have learnt to associate her mother with food, and Carole would then have wanted to be close to her, producing attachment behaviour *(1 mark)*. This process is an example of operant conditioning *(1 mark)*.

4 (a) Maximum of 4 marks available.
As an insecure-avoidant infant, Jane won't become particularly distressed when she is separated from her caregiver *(1 mark)*. Jane can usually be comforted by a stranger *(1 mark)*.
As an insecure-resistant infant, Antonio is uneasy around his caregivers, but appears distressed when they are separated *(1 mark)*. Antonio won't accept comfort from a stranger, and may even reject it from his caregiver *(1 mark)*.
(b) Maximum of 1 mark available.
Privation *(1 mark)*.

5 Maximum of 8 marks available.
HINTS:

- There are 8 marks up for grabs, so you'll need to include a fair bit of information in your answer.

- Start by detailing the method of your chosen study, making sure you briefly describe what the 'strange situation' involves. You also need to describe the results that were observed and the conclusions that were drawn by the researchers.

- The question asks you to evaluate the study as well as outlining it. So, you need to talk about some pros and cons of the methodology, any problems with the conclusion drawn, etc.

- Evaluating research can involve talking about sampling bias, lack of control of variables, validity of measures, etc.

- Use other relevant research to back up your points if you can. You can also use relevant research to support or contradict the study of attachment you've chosen.

6 Maximum of 6 marks available.
HINTS:

- You can talk about any study which looks at participants from institutional care. For example, it could be Hodges and Tizard's (1989) study.

- The question is only worth 6 marks, so you don't need to go into too much detail. Briefly outline the method, results and conclusion, which should get you a good 4 marks.

- Get the last two marks by evaluating the study. You could either give one positive point and one negative point, or elaborate fully on either one positive or negative point.

7 (a) Maximum of 3 marks available.
Studies have shown that day care causes children to become less aggressive *(1 mark)*. For example, Shea (1981) observed young children playing during their first 10 weeks at pre-school and recorded aggressive behaviours *(1 mark)*. It was found that over the 10 weeks, aggressive behaviours reduced *(1 mark)*.

(b) Maximum of 6 marks available.
HINTS:

- You'll need to outline at least one study into the effects of day care on child development, e.g. Sylva et al's (2003) EPPE project. Talk about the results and the conclusions of each study.

- From this, go on to say what effects the research has had on day care — say what has actually changed. For example, you could talk about the 'Sure Start' initiative.

- Since the question asked you to 'discuss' you could also evaluate the research method and the study itself.

Section 3 — Research Methods

1. Research Methods
Page 65 — Summary Questions
Q1 E.g. laboratory experiments are artificial — experiments might not measure real-life behaviour (i.e. they may lack ecological validity). / Participants in laboratory experiments may display demand characteristics — they may respond according to what they think is being investigated, which can bias the results. / Laboratory experiments may have ethical problems — they can involve deception, making informed consent difficult.

Q2 E.g. you can establish causal relationships by manipulating the key variable and measuring its effect. / Field experiments have high ecological validity — they are less artificial than experiments done in a laboratory, so they relate to real life better. / Demand characteristics can be avoided if participants don't know they're in a study.

Q3 a) E.g. ecological validity is high as behaviour is natural and there are no demand characteristics, as the participant is unaware of being observed. / For theory development — it can be a useful way of developing ideas about behaviour that could be tested in more controlled conditions later.

b) E.g. the situation where you can do a naturalistic observation is limited, as you should only conduct observations where people might expect to be observed by strangers. / Debriefing is difficult. / Observation must respect privacy. / Getting informed consent can be tricky.

Q4 E.g. Milner et al (1957) / Gardner and Gardner (1969) / Curtiss (1977).

2. Aims and Hypotheses
Page 68 — Summary Questions
Q1 A statement of a study's purpose.
Q2 A clear statement of what's actually being tested.
Q3 A variable directly manipulated by the researcher.
Q4 False
The DV is dependent on the IV.
Q5 E.g. if participants were taking heart medication this could affect the dependant variable (heart rate). / Heart medication is potentially a confounding variable in this study.
Q6 It allows others to see exactly how you're going to define and measure your variables.

3. Research Design
Page 72 — Summary Questions
Q1 E.g. in an independent groups design there are no order effects — no one gets better through practice (learning effect) or gets worse through being bored or tired (fatigue effect).
Q2 Differences between the people in each condition.

Q3 A pilot study helps to establish whether the design works, whether participants understand the wording in instructions, or whether something important has been missed out, etc. Problems can be tackled before running the main study, which could save wasting a lot of time and money.

Q4 random allocation

Q5 A questionnaire is randomly split in two — if all participants score similarly on both halves, the questions measure the same thing.

Q6 A measure of external reliability — the test is reliable if the same person always scores similarly on the test.

4. Observations, Questionnaires and Interviews
Page 77 — Summary Questions

Q1 a) Time interval sampling is where you choose to observe for only set time intervals e.g. the first 10 minutes of every hour.
   b) E.g. it's very convenient for the researchers to carry out.
   c) E.g. if interesting behaviours occur outside the time sample they won't be recorded.

Q2 E.g. they give quantitative data that is relatively easy to analyse.

Q3 A question that leads the participant towards a particular answer.

Q4 The data obtained may be difficult to analyse.

Q5 E.g. to ensure that no questions are left out and questions aren't asked twice.

5. Selecting and Using Participants
Page 80 — Summary Questions

Q1 E.g. by giving everyone in the target group a number and then getting a computer to randomly pick numbers to select the participants.

Q2 E.g. it is a quick and practical way of getting a sample.

Q3 If people are interested in something and in the attention they are getting (e.g. from researchers), then they show a more positive response, try harder at tasks, and so on. This means their results for tests are often artificially high (because they're trying harder than normal), which could make a researcher's conclusions inaccurate.

6. Ethical Issues in Psychological Research
Page 84 — Summary Questions

Q1 E.g. children.

Q2 a) Keeping information private.

b) Any three from, e.g. participants should feel safe that any sensitive information, results or behaviour revealed through research won't be discussed with others. / The study's report shouldn't reveal information or data identifiable to an individual. / You shouldn't be able to tell who took part or what their individual data was — these should remain anonymous.

Q3 a) E.g. animal research has provided valuable information for psychological and medical research. / Some research designs couldn't have been conducted on humans.
   b) E.g. some people believe it's ethically wrong to inflict harm and suffering on animals. / Animals can't give consent to take part. / Some argue that it's cruel to experiment on animals that have a similar intelligence to humans, because they might suffer the same problems we would.

7. Data Analysis
Page 88 — Summary Questions

Q1 qualitative

Q2 The researcher is showing researcher bias — it's not okay to make notes only on events that support the researcher's theories, or to have a biased interpretation of what is observed.

Q3 quantitative

8. Descriptive Statistics
Page 93 — Summary Questions

Q1 median

Q2 It can be skewed (distorted) by extremely high or low scores. This can make it unrepresentative of most of the scores, and so it may be misleading.

Q3 The score that occurs most often.

Q4 How spread out the data in a data set is.

Q5 3, 4, 5, 5, 6, 7, 7, 9, 9, 11, 12
   $N = 11$
   Q1 position number = $(N + 1)/4 = (11 + 1)/4 = 3$
   Q2 position number = $2(N + 1)/4 = 2(11 + 1)/4 = 6$
   Q3 position number = $3(N + 1)/4 = 3(11 + 1)/4 = 9$
   Q1 = 5
   Q2 = 7
   Q3 = $(7 + 9)/2 = 9$
   Remember to put the data set in order first. It's an easy mistake to make.

9. Correlations
Page 99 — Summary Questions

Q1 a) The correlation coefficient is a always a number between −1 and +1.
   b) It is a moderate negative correlation.

Q2 There is no correlation.

Q3 E.g. correlational research doesn't involve controlling any variables, so you can do it when (for practical or ethical reasons) you couldn't do a controlled experiment. / Correlational analysis can give ideas for future research. / Correlation can even be used to test for reliability and validity, e.g. by testing the results of the same test taken twice by the same people.

Q4 You compare the result of your calculation with a critical value that you look up in a statistics table.

10. Summarising the Data
Page 102 — Summary Questions
Q1 In a report as a 'verbal summary'.
Q2 Scores before any analysis has been done on them.
Q3 Not to show the full scale can be misleading, because it can make values look a lot higher than they actually are.
Q4 continuous
Q5 Frequency polygons use lines to show where the top of each column would reach. Histograms show the columns.

Pages 104-105 — Exam-style Questions
1 (a)(i) Maximum of 1 mark available.
Volunteer sampling *(1 mark)*.
1 (a)(ii) Maximum of 2 marks available.
Advantage: e.g. if an advert is placed prominently a large number of people may respond, giving more participants to study. This may allow more in-depth analysis and more accurate statistical results.
(1 mark).
Disadvantages: e.g. even though a large number of people may respond, these will only include people who actually saw the advertisement — no one else would have a chance of being selected. / People who volunteer may be more cooperative than others. For these reasons the sample is unlikely to be representative of the target population *(1 mark)*.
1 (b) Maximum of 1 mark available.
A matched pairs design *(1 mark)*.

1 (c) Maximum of 2 marks available.
Mean heart rate of the control group before the stress-inducing event:
$$\overline{X} = \frac{\sum X}{N}$$

$\sum X = (66 + 87 + 88 + 98 + 84) = 423$,
$N = 5$

$$\overline{X} = \frac{423}{5} = 84.6 \ \textbf{\textit{(1 mark)}}.$$

Mean heart rate of the control group after the stress-inducing event:
$$\overline{X} = \frac{\sum X}{N}$$

$\sum X = (159 + 117 + 180 + 99 + 163) = 718$,
$N = 5$

$$\overline{X} = \frac{718}{5} = 143.6 \ \textbf{\textit{(1 mark)}}.$$

These are easy marks if you know the formula — you just have to plug the numbers in.

1 (d) Maximum of 6 marks available.
HINTS:

- As this is an 'outline' question, you just need to briefly state the issues of the study without going into too much detail. For instance, don't talk about what could have been done differently — you just need to highlight the problems with the study.

- When you are given details of a study in an exam, think carefully about everything you're told. It's all there for a reason, so look for anything that could indicate an ethical problem.

- The easiest way to tackle this question is to think about all the possible ethical problems a study could have, and then from these pick out the ones that the study does have. This may sound long-winded, but this way you know that you've covered all the possible issues.

- From this study, you should pick out deception, as the participants weren't told the true nature of the study and what would happen in the waiting room. This also means that they could not give proper informed consent. Also, participants may have been at risk from psychological harm following the stressful events in the waiting room.

2 (a) Maximum of 1 mark available.
Naturalistic observation *(1 mark)*.
2 (b)(i) Maximum of 1 mark available.
E.g. there will be a relationship between the amount of time children spend in day care, and the time they spend playing alone *(1 mark)*.

2   (b)(ii) Maximum of 1 mark available.

        E.g. the more time children spend in day care, the less time they will spend playing alone. *(1 mark)*.

Remember that a directional hypothesis predicts that there will be a difference between two variables and states which way the results will go. A non-directional hypothesis doesn't state which way the results will go.

2   (c) Maximum of 3 marks available.

        As -0.855 is a negative number, the correlation is negative *(1 mark)*. This means that as the hours per week children spend in day care increases, the average time children spend playing alone decreases *(1 mark)*. -0.855 is fairly close to -1, so there is a strong relationship between the variables *(1 mark)*.

2   (d) Maximum of 2 marks available.

        The sample is not representative of the target population *(1 mark)*. The psychologist only looks at one day care centre, which means she can only generalise her results to children who have gone to that particular day care centre. Conducting her study at a different day care centre and with different children may produce very different results *(1 mark)*.

For a representative sample, the psychologist would have to conduct her study across a range of day care centres with children from different socio-economic backgrounds.

Unit 2

Section 4 — Biological Psychology

1. The Biological Approach
Page 108 — Summary Questions

Q1 E.g. human behaviour can be explained by looking at biological things such as hormones, genetics, evolution and the nervous system. / In theory, if we can explain all behaviour using biological causes, unwanted behaviour could be modified or removed using biological treatments such as medication for mental illness. / Experimental research conducted using animals can inform us about human behaviour and biological influences, because we share a lot of biological similarities.

Q2 No. Correlations only show a relationship, not a cause and effect. We can't say that having a stressful job itself causes heart attacks.

Q3 E.g. they rely on the honesty of the person being questioned.

Q4 Certain functions are generally localised more in one of the two hemispheres of the brain.

2. Stress as a Bodily Response
Page 113 — Summary Questions

Q1 E.g. the response that occurs when we think we can't cope with the pressures in our environment.

Q2 E.g. Alex may think she is unable to cope and/or she could be overestimating the demands of the exams. Whether the stress is justified or not doesn't matter. If she thinks that she cannot cope then she will be stressed.

Q3 higher brain centres / cerebral cortex

Q4 Any two from, e.g. blood pressure increases / heart rate increases / digestion decreases / muscles become tense / perspiration increases / breathing rate increases.

Q5 In modern society stressors are more likely to be psychological than physical and are more long-term. Therefore the physical stress response (the 'fight or flight' response) is not really needed, and in the long term it may actually be harmful to our bodies.

Q6 A stress which is positive and exhilarating, e.g. a parachute jump.

3. Stress and Physical Illness
Page 118 — Summary Questions

Q1 After long-term exposure to a stressor our bodies will eventually be unable to continue to cope with the situation. Alarm signs may return and we may develop illnesses, e.g. ulcers, high blood pressure, depression, etc.

Q2 E.g. it can't be said whether having a stressful job itself causes heart disease. Many other factors may also contribute. / The participants were all doctors, and therefore the findings of the study may not be representative of the population.

Q3 E.g. he may develop cardiovascular disease if he continues doing a stressful job.

Q4 The experiment involved giving monkeys electric shocks which is cruel.

These days the British Psychological Society (BPS) has strict ethical guidelines designed to protect both human and animal participants.

Q5 Participants with a higher stress index score were significantly more likely to develop a clinical cold (when exposed to the cold virus) than those with lower measures of stress.

4. Sources of Stress — Life Changes
Page 121 — Summary Questions

Q1 a) More than 2500 American Navy seamen.
b) This group is not representative of the population and therefore the results can only be generalised to American Navy seamen.

American Navy seamen may react to stress very differently to, say, little old ladies — we have to be really careful about generalising the findings of psychological studies.

Q2 E.g. death of a spouse / divorce / retirement / changing schools / Christmas.

Q3 a) Recently widowed individuals scored higher on life satisfaction before the loss of their spouse than afterwards, while divorced individuals scored higher after the divorce than before.
b) Although a big life adjustment occurred for both groups, the recently divorced people may have seen the change as a positive experience.

Q4 E.g. all the 'hassles' Julia had recently experienced may have increased her stress levels, causing a reduction in her immune system function, which caused her to become ill.

5. Sources of Stress — In Everyday Life
Page 125 — Summary Questions

Q1 Daily hassles are linked to stress and health, with a stronger correlation than that found with the SRRS.

Q2 223 first year psychology students at a French university.

Q3 Relationships at work, work pressures, the physical environment, stress linked to our role, lack of control.

Q4 Testing urine samples for stress hormones and measuring blood pressure.

Q5 It was a field experiment as it took place in the sawmill where the participants worked.

Q6 Workplace stress increases as demand increases and control decreases.

6. Stress — Individual Differences
Page 129 — Summary Questions

Q1 E.g. competitive / ambitious / 'workaholic' / hostile.

Q2 Hardy personalities are very involved in what they do, and show a high level of commitment. This means that they work hard at relationships, jobs and other activities in life. They view change in a positive rather than a negative way, seeing it as an opportunity for challenge. Hardy personalities enjoy a challenge and see it as an opportunity to develop themselves.

Q3 a) A strong feeling of control over life and what happens in it.
b) Hardy personality type.

Q4 a) oxytocin
b) Men are stereotypically less open about their feelings than women, which means they're less likely to discuss stressful experiences with others and may use harmful coping methods instead. / Women generally make more use of social support to deal with stress.

'Stereotypically' is an important word here — not all men are the same and neither are all women.

c) controlling anger

7. Stress Management — Biological Approach
Page 132 — Summary Questions

Q1 a) benzodiazepines
b) They can reduce the activity of the sympathetic nervous system.

Q2 a) They found that bus conductors had lower rates of cardiovascular problems than bus drivers.
b) Being physically active reduces the likelihood of stress-related illness.

8. Stress Management — Psychological Approach
Page 135 — Summary Questions

Q1 Control over their lives.
Commitment — a sense of purpose in life.
Challenge — life is seen as a challenge and opportunity rather than as a threat.

Q2 a) E.g. Maddi et al (1998).
b) E.g. the 54 managers who went on the hardiness training programme recorded greater increases in hardiness and job satisfaction and decreases in strain and illness than the other stress management techniques and control groups in the study.

Q3 E.g. psychological methods only suit a narrow band of individuals who are determined to stick to the technique. / Research tends to be based on white, middle-class business folk and so can't necessarily be generalised to others. / The procedures are very lengthy and require considerable commitment of time and effort. / The concepts may be too complex. For example, a lack of hardiness might be just another label for negativity. It could be argued that it's just as effective to relax and think positively.

Q4 A — activating event
B — belief
C — consequence

Q5 To disprove the negativity in a person's thinking. After a while they should be able to use different cognitive processes, leading to a more positive belief system.

Page 137 — Exam-style Questions

1 (a) Maximum of 4 marks available.
Gena's heart rate increases *(1 mark)*.
Gena's muscles become more tense *(1 mark)*.
Gena sweats more/her perspiration levels increase *(1 mark)*.
Gena's breathing rate increases *(1 mark)*.

The question is worth 4 marks, so you need to list four things. Gena's blood pressure would also increase, and her digestion decrease. These are both effects of the initial stress response, however she would be unlikely to feel them, so they aren't really 'unpleasant symptoms' as asked for in the question.

1 (b) Maximum of 3 marks available.
Beta blockers decrease the activity of the sympathetic nervous system, so will act to decrease the effects of the sympathomedullary pathway *(1 mark)*. This will reduce the amounts of adrenaline and noradrenaline in the blood stream *(1 mark)*, and therefore decrease the unpleasant symptoms Gena experiences *(1 mark)*.

1 (c) Maximum of 6 marks available.
HINTS:

- This is an 'evaluate' question — you have to weigh up the good points and the bad points to get the marks. It's no use just talking about the good points, or just the bad points.

- Start by saying why drugs are good, e.g. they are relatively easy to prescribe and use, and are quick and effective in reducing dangerous symptoms such as high blood pressure, etc.

- Then outline the negative points, e.g. they only treat symptoms rather than the cause of stress, they can cause side effects, etc.

- You could outline some studies which show the use of drugs to be effective or ineffective. This provides support for your answer and shows good knowledge.

2 (a) Maximum of 1 mark available.
As the average number of daily hassles experienced increases, the amount of illnesses experienced also increases. / The number of daily hassles experienced is positively correlated with the amount of illnesses experienced *(1 mark)*.

Look at the graph — simply state what it shows. This is all the question wants. Don't explain why hassles and illness are linked — you won't get any marks for it so it's wasted time in the exam.

2 (b)(i) Maximum of 1 mark available.
E.g. using questionnaires results in quantitative data, which is useful for making comparisons. / Large amounts of data can be collected quickly, easily and cheaply *(1 mark)*.

2 (b)(ii) Maximum of 1 mark available
E.g. questionnaires rely on honesty in order for the results to be valid — participants may not be completely truthful. / Questionnaires rely on the participants' recall being accurate *(1 mark)*.

2 (c) Maximum of 6 marks available.
HINTS:

- Make sure you pick a study that's relevant to the question that is being asked. There's no point giving a really good account of a study if it's not answering the question — read the question carefully and check your choice is suitable.

- When outlining a study you need to make sure you cover:
The method — who the participants were and how the experiment was conducted.
The results — what happened in the experiment. You don't have to give the exact figures, but make sure you know the general trend in the results.
The conclusion — what the results showed and what their implications are.

- Don't give any evaluation of the study — you won't get any marks for it because the question doesn't ask for it.

3 Maximum of 4 marks available.
HINTS:

- When you are given a scenario in an exam, think carefully about all the information you are given — it's always there for a reason. It's also a good idea to refer to the scenario in your answer. Make reference to Richard — it shows that you are applying your knowledge rather than just writing generally about a stress management technique.

- Don't just pick any stress management technique — pick the one that applies best to the question. Also, only talk about one method — don't bring anything else into the answer.

- Describe what happens in the technique, but don't include any evaluation of how good it is.

- It's often helpful to write an introductory sentence which links the question to your answer. This can help you get started with your answer, and reads better than if you just launch straight into describing a stress management technique.

Section 5 — Social Psychology

1. The Social Approach
Page 141 — Summary Questions
Q1 Any two from, e.g. conformity / obedience / stereotyping / prejudice.
Q2 Laboratory experiments.
Q3 Any one from, e.g. low internal validity / cause and effect is hard to establish / deception raises ethical issues.
Q4 E.g. 'what are your views on religion?'

2. Types of Conformity
Page 149 — Summary Questions
Q1 Normative social influence is where you go along with the majority, even if you don't share their views. Informational social influence is where you follow the majority and believe in their views.
Q2 In the critical trials, the confederates all gave the same wrong answer.
Q3 The autokinetic effect is a visual illusion where a stationary spot of light, viewed in a dark room, appears to move.
Q4 The study lacked ecological validity because it created a very artificial situation.
In a lot of experiments, the ecological validity is low because they often involve situations that are unrealistic and wouldn't happen in everyday life.
Q5 The participants were male students who had been recruited to act as either guards or prisoners.
Q6 Situational — the participants changed their behaviour to fit in with a social role, even one that had been randomly assigned.
Q7 Reicher and Haslam (2006)
Q8 The participants didn't fit into their expected social roles, which suggests that these roles are flexible.

3. Independent Behaviour and Social Change
Page 154 — Summary Questions
Q1 Confidence could make conformity levels much lower because people will have confidence in their skills relating to the situation. They are therefore more able to resist group pressure.
Q2 They found some sex differences in conformity, but they found that these differences were inconsistent. The clearest difference between men and women was in Asch-like studies where there was a group pressure from an audience.
Q3 Minority influence is where small groups of people and even individuals gain influence and change the way the majority thinks.
Q4 E.g. Nemeth (1986)
If you can't remember the exact date for the study, don't worry. Just try to remember roughly when it took place.
Q5 Any one from, e.g. the suffragette movement / the Civil Rights movement / gay rights movements.

4. Obedience to Authority
Page 163 — Summary Questions
Q1 Any two from, e.g. deception / no informed consent / no right to withdraw / no protection from stress.
Ethics comes up a lot in social psychology and can always be used as a good discussion point in evaluating research.
Q2 Any three from, e.g. used female participants. / Had an experimental set up where the learner's screams could be heard. / Ran the experiment in seedy offices. / Had the learner in the same room as the participant. / Had the authority figure in another room, communicating by phone. / Had other 'teachers' (confederates of the study) refuse to give shocks. / Had other 'participants' (confederates of the study) give the shocks instead.
Q3 The transition from autonomy into an agentic state — people start off acting in an autonomous way but then become obedient, acting out the wishes of another person.
Q4 Participants in the group were asked to sign a petition two weeks before being asked to make a donation.
Q5 He could use the foot-in-the-door technique by asking people to sign a petition about climate change two weeks prior to asking them for donations.
This is based on similar findings by Schwarzwald et al (1983).
Q6 a) Researchers in New York dressed up as a guard, a milkman or a normal citizen. They then approached people on the street and asked them to pick up litter, move up from a bus stop or give money to a stranger.
b) Approximately 90% of participants obeyed the guard figure, but only 50% obeyed the civilian.
Q7 Uniform and presence both have an influence on conformity rates.
Q8 American teenagers from across the USA.
Q9 80%
Q10 E.g. a person may smoke more when they've been told not to, and that it is bad for them.

5. Research into Conformity and Obedience
Page 167 — Summary Questions
Q1 Hofling et al (1966) conducted an experiment where they telephoned 22 night nurses while posing as a doctor. They asked the nurse to prescribe a drug to a patient. This was an order that they shouldn't have followed for several reasons. 95% of the nurses obeyed their orders.
If you can't remember the exact numbers, use words such as 'around' or 'approximately.'
Q2 a) They lose their personal identity and identify with a group.
b) They wore uniforms and mirrored sunglasses.
c) They became aggressive towards the prisoners.
Q3 Any three from, e.g. governments / juries / friendship groups / work colleagues / religious organisations.
Q4 To consider whether the cost to the participants is worth the benefit of the findings to society.

1   Maximum of 4 marks available.
     E.g. she can gather lots of data quickly and cheaply which means she can have a large sample giving more reliable results *(1 mark)*. She can also choose to either collect quantitative or qualitative data. Quantitative data is easy to analyse and qualitative data is detailed *(1 mark)*. However, surveys rely on self reporting so people can lie (desirability bias) / surveys can be time consuming / researchers can often write leading questions which can lead participants towards certain answers *(1 mark for each disadvantage, up to 2 marks)*.

2   (a) Maximum of 2 marks available.
     In normative social influence, someone might conform to appear normal *(1 mark)*. They might feel that going against the majority would lead to exclusion or rejection from the group *(1 mark)*.

2   (b) Maximum of 2 marks available.
     In informational social influence, someone might conform because they're in an unfamiliar situation where they don't know what the correct way to behave is *(1 mark)*. They would look to others for information about how to behave *(1 mark)*.

3   Maximum of 12 marks available.
     HINTS:

   - You've got the choice to describe any research on informational social influence. Make sure you pick studies that you know well, so that you can give plenty of details.
     For example, one of the studies you could choose is Sherif's (1935) study of conformity using the autokinetic effect.

   - The question asks you to do two things — outline and evaluate research. So make sure you do both otherwise there's no way you can get all of the available marks.

   - Start your answer by describing one of your studies — talk about the experimental design and the method, and then outline what the results were. Don't forget to say what was concluded from the results.

   - Next, you need to evaluate the studies. Make sure you weigh up positive and negative points.

4   (a) Maximum of 6 marks available.
     E.g. locus of control is a personality characteristic which indicates how much personal control people believe they have over events in their lives *(1 mark)*. People either have an internal locus of control or an external locus of control *(1 mark)*. Someone with an internal locus of control believes that their own behaviour or actions cause what happens in their life *(1 mark)*.
     For example, if they did well in a test, they might put it down to their own hard work *(1 mark)*. Someone with an external locus of control believes that events are caused by external factors, like luck or the actions of others *(1 mark)*.
     For example, if they did well in a test, they might put it down to good questions coming up *(1 mark)*.
     Including an example is a good way of putting your knowledge in context and shows the examiner you really know what you're talking about.

4   (b) Maximum of 2 marks available.
     People with an internal locus of control feel a stronger sense of control over their lives than people with an external locus of control. This means that they're more likely to exhibit independent behaviour *(1 mark)*. People with an external locus of control may be more likely to conform *(1 mark)*.

5   Maximum of 12 marks available.
     HINTS:

   - Begin your answer by showing that you know what minority influence and social change are — explain that a minority can sometimes affect the majority opinion and bring about change. Include some examples of where this has happened, e.g. the suffragette movement, the Gay Rights movement or the Civil Rights movement.

   - Then go on to say that this phenomenon has been shown in psychological research. This is where you can introduce the studies that you're going to use to support your answer.

   - For each study, give a brief outline of how it was carried out, and then say what the results were. Finish off your answer by explaining how these results, and the conclusion drawn from them, have helped to explain how social change happens.

6   (a) Maximum of 2 marks available.
     E.g. laboratory experiments are highly controlled so the effect of the independent variable can be measured. / It's possible to establish cause and effect. / You can replicate the method. / Participants in different conditions can be compared *(1 mark for each advantage, up to 2 marks)*.

6 (b) Maximum of 2 marks available.
E.g. laboratory experiments create an artificial environment which gives them low ecological validity *(1 mark)*. It's difficult to generalise the results *(1 mark)*.

7 (a) Maximum of 8 marks available.
HINTS:

- In this question you could use Milgram's (1963) study.

- Outline the method, say what the results showed, and state the conclusions of the study.

- You could then go on to talk about the variations Milgram did of his original study. You don't need to outline the entire methodology again — just briefly state what was done differently, and what the results showed.

- You don't need to go into too much detail or list all the variations Milgram did — the question is only worth 8 marks.

7 (b) Maximum of 6 marks available.
HINTS:

- There are several reasons why people might disobey so just choose two and discuss each one for three marks each. For example, you could talk about the situation or about individual differences such as locus of control or moral reasoning.

- Describe how each factor affects obedience levels, e.g. those with an internal locus of control are less likely to obey.

- Use examples to help illustrate your points. For example, if talking about the situation, you could use Gamson et al's (1982) study about people rebelling within a group. Or, if you talk about locus of control you could use Rotter's (1966) research into internal and external locus of control. Kohlberg's (1969) study could be used to support moral reasoning.

8 Maximum of 4 marks available.
E.g. Participant B is less likely to be obedient than participant A *(1 mark)*. This can be explained using the idea of buffers *(1 mark)*. Buffers are things that protect us from the consequences of actions *(1 mark)*. In this case, the buffer was the fact that participant A couldn't see the learner. Participant B didn't have this buffer, which will have made it harder for him to act against his conscience *(1 mark)*.

9 Maximum of 3 marks available.
E.g. Ben will view the teacher as a justified authority figure, and so will be likely to obey the requests *(1 mark)*. Ben could also be acting in an agentic state *(1 mark)* where he feels that he isn't responsible for what he says during the debate because he is simply acting out the wishes of another person *(1 mark)*.
You could also use the idea of Groupthink in your answer.

Section 6 — Individual Differences

1. The Individual Differences Approach
Page 173 — Summary Questions
Q1 A debate that suggests an individual's personality could either be influenced by inherited factors (nature) or environmental factors (nurture).

Q2 Irrational and negative thoughts.

Q3 Any two from, e.g. case studies / meta-analyses / correlational studies / physiological studies.

Q4 a) Seven were diagnosed with schizophrenia and all eight were admitted to a psychiatric hospital.
   b) Rosenhan told staff at a psychiatric hospital that there was at least one pseudopatient trying to get admitted. None actually did appear but 41 genuine patients were judged to be pseudopatients.
If you don't know the exact numbers, don't worry. You could get around it by saying something like, "almost all participants were diagnosed".

2. Defining Abnormality
Page 179 — Summary Questions
Q1 It provides a guide to assess symptoms associated with mental illness.

Q2 Judgements made about abnormality are relative to individual cultures. What's normal in one culture may be considered abnormal in another.

Q3 E.g. native Canadians can sometimes lose their appetite for ordinary food, feel depressed and believe they are possessed by the Witiko, who is a giant man-eating monster. This then can result in cannibalism. This only happens in this culture, so it is a culture-bound syndrome.

Q4 Deviation from social norms — e.g. within our culture, most people would normally wear shoes to class and therefore, James's behaviour might be considered abnormal. However, if everyone else went to the class without shoes, it might not be considered abnormal.
Failure to function adequately — e.g. James's behaviour may be considered dysfunctional (it goes against what is accepted within a classroom). / It may create observer discomfort (his classmates may feel uncomfortable that he's not wearing any shoes). / It may be considered to be irrational (it may not be justified). Therefore, his behaviour may be seen as abnormal.
Deviation from ideal mental health — e.g. James may be considered to not be showing an accurate perception of reality or adaptation to environment, so his behaviour may be considered abnormal.
If there's a question about defining abnormality, it may be disguised in a scenario question. Just remember that definitions of abnormality are often dependent on loads of different factors.

Q5 If people are treated as mentally ill, their behaviour will change and become more like that expected from their diagnosis.

3. The Biological Model of Abnormality
Page 185 — Summary Questions
Q1 Psychological disorders are physical illnesses with physical causes.

Q2 Genetics, neurotransmitters, infection, brain injury.

Q3 E.g. after an explosion in 1848 where an iron rod went through Phineas Gage's head and part of his frontal lobe was destroyed, he became disorganised, impulsive and couldn't plan for the future. His personality also changed.

Q4 Twin studies can show whether mental disorders have a genetic basis. Identical twins share 100% of their genes, so if a disorder is caused purely by genetics, both twins should be affected. Identical twins can be compared against non-identical twins, who only share 50% of their genes.

Q5 SSRIs stop synapses from re-uptaking serotonin in the brain once it's released, making more available to the brain.

Q6 The patient is anaesthetised and injected with muscle relaxants before having electrodes attached to their head. A brief electric shock of 225 volts is passed through the electrodes to the brain, which causes a seizure lasting up to a minute. The patient usually has a rubber stop in the mouth to stop them biting their own tongue. They then wake up about 20 minutes later.
Make sure you are familiar with the procedure in case it comes up in the exam.

4. The Psychodynamic Model of Abnormality
Page 189 — Summary Questions
Q1 The 'pleasure principle' in the unconscious part of the mind. It's our innate drive to do what we want to satisfy ourselves, and appears at birth.
Try to visualise the iceberg diagram to help you remember Freud's different parts of the personality.

Q2 Oral, anal, phallic, latency and genital.
You won't be asked to name these specifically in the exam, but they are really useful in showing you understand the foundations of Freud's theories.

Q3 E.g. she had a conflict during the oral stage, leading to a fixation in later life.

Q4 It aims to allow the patients to access repressed thoughts and unconscious conflicts. Patients are then encouraged to deal with the conflicts.

Q5 a) Any two from, e.g. it's a unique approach linking disorders to biological needs / it offers therapies which allow the patient to understand the cause of their problems, resolve them and release their anxieties / it was the first theory to focus on psychological causes of disorders.

b) Any two from, e.g. it's subjective and hard to scientifically test / psychoanalysis takes time and is expensive / the focus is on the patient's past, not the present problems they are suffering from.

5. The Behavioural Model of Abnormality
Page 194 — Summary Questions
Q1 When Little Albert was shown a rat, he would start to cry. He also cried when he was shown any white fluffy object. They concluded that a fear response to any white fluffy object had been conditioned in Little Albert and therefore, abnormal behaviour could be learned.

Q2 Classical conditioning is about learning associations between things. Operant conditioning involves learning from the consequence of an action.
It's really easy to get these two confused, so try and think of a good way to distinguish between them.

Q3 She has developed a taste aversion based on the principles of classical conditioning. The smell of haggis has become a conditioned stimulus which triggers a conditioned response (feeling ill).
Make sure you know the differences between conditioned and unconditioned stimuli and responses.

Q4 Any two from, e.g. it cannot explain all behaviours because it neglects genetics and biology / it neglects the influence of cognitions / behavioural therapies are not effective for all disorders / the procedures sometimes raise ethical issues / the therapies only treat behaviour, not the cause.

6. The Cognitive Model of Abnormality
Page 198 — Summary Questions
Q1 The 'ABC' model claims disorders have an activating event which leads to a belief about why it happened which then leads to a consequence. If the belief is rational, it leads to an appropriate consequence. If it is irrational, it leads to an inappropriate consequence.
You could illustrate this answer with an example to show you can apply the theory to real life.

Q2 Beck's (1963) cognitive triad identifies negative, automatic thoughts linked to depression. Beck thought that depressed people have negative views about themselves, about the world and about the future.
Picturing the triangle might help jog your memory about how they are all linked together.

Q3 That we can treat psychological disorders by eliminating or changing the original faulty thoughts and beliefs.

Q4 Any two from, e.g. it offers a useful approach to disorders like depression because it considers the role of thoughts and beliefs which are greatly involved in depression. / Cognitive therapies have successfully treated depression, anxiety, stress and eating disorders. / It allows a person to take control and make a positive change to their behaviour. / There is lots of research to support the approach, e.g. Gustafson (1992) has shown that people with depression/schizophrenia and other psychological disorders show faulty thinking processes.

Page 200 — Exam-style Questions

1 Maximum of 2 marks available.
E.g. too much or too little of a particular neurotransmitter / infections / brain damage or brain injuries *(1 mark for each answer, up to 2 marks)*.

2 Maximum of 6 marks available.
HINTS:

- You'll get the first 2 marks simply by saying that behaviour is learnt through two types of conditioning — classical and operant.

- Then get the rest of the marks by giving a brief description of each type of conditioning. Talk about positive and negative reinforcement and punishment for operant conditioning. Talk about learned associations causing a conditioned response for classical conditioning.

- If you find it easier to describe classical and operant conditioning using examples, then that's fine too.

3 (a) Maximum of 2 marks available.
E.g. we can use a normal distribution curve to represent how many times people wash their hands within a day, with the majority washing them five times a day *(1 mark)*. Therefore, it is only the minority who will either wash very few times or wash an excessive amount, suggesting they have deviated from the norms of a society *(1 mark)*.

3 (b) Maximum of 4 marks available.
E.g. this definition does not account for the desirability of the behaviour. Washing hands may depend on what people are doing on a day-to-day basis *(1 mark)*. This definition doesn't give a distinction between knowing whether the behaviour is justified (e.g. for nurses and doctors) or a rare and psychologically abnormal behaviour *(1 mark)*. There is also no cut off point that outlines how many times someone would have to wash their hands in a day to be to be considered abnormal *(1 mark)*. Finally, the definition doesn't take into account the culture that the behaviour happens in. In this country, washing hands is fairly normal as we have facilities to do so — this might be harder in other countries and cultures *(1 mark)*.

4 Maximum of 12 marks available.
HINTS:

- Start your answer by describing the assumptions of the biological and cognitive models.

- Once you've done that, move on to the evaluate part of the question. Give strengths and weaknesses of both models.

- It's really good if you can directly compare a strength of one model against a weakness of the other model, and vice versa. For example, biological therapies are considered as ethical in that they don't blame a person for their illness. In contrast, cognitive therapies could be seen as less ethical than biological therapies because they could make an individual feel like their condition is their fault.

- It's good to finish off your answer by writing an overall summary.

5 (a) Maximum of 3 marks available.
Patients are anaesthetised and injected with a muscle relaxant *(1 mark)*. Electrodes transmit a 225 volt charge to the brain *(1 mark)*. This causes a seizure which lasts up to a minute *(1 mark)*.

5 (b) Maximum of 3 marks available.
E.g. with a therapist, patients identify their faulty cognitions *(1 mark)*. The therapist tries to show the patient that these aren't true *(1 mark)*. Together, they set positive goals *(1 mark)*.

6 Maximum of 8 marks available.
HINTS:

- Systematic desensitisation would be a good example to use for this question.

- Describe the steps which are involved in the method. For systematic desensitisation these include creating a fear hierarchy, developing relaxation techniques and the repetition of each stage of the fear hierarchy until each feared event is only linked with relaxation.

- Try to keep your answer in the context of w fear of dogs.

- Finish your answer with an evaluation of the behavioural approach to treating phobias.

7 (a) Maximum of 1 mark available.
Psychodynamic *(1 mark)*.

7 (b) Maximum of 1 mark available.
Any one from, e.g. it is based on Freud's subjective interpretations of his patients' dreams etc. and is therefore hard to scientifically test or prove. / Psychoanalysis may take a long time and be very expensive. / Psychoanalysis can be inaccurate because a patient's memories are sometimes not reliable. / The focus is often on the patient's past, not their current problems *(1 mark)*.

7 (c) Maximum of 2 marks available.
Any two from, e.g. hypnosis / free association / dream analysis *(1 mark for each answer, up to 2 marks)*.

Glossary

A

ABC model
Ellis's (1962) model that claims that disorders begin with an activating event (A), leading to a belief about why this happened (B), which leads to a consequence (C).

Abnormality
Something that is not normal. Can be described as deviation from social norms, failure to function adequately or as a deviation from ideal mental health.

Absolute
When something occurs in the same way and frequency across cultures.

Adrenal cortex
Part of the adrenal gland that releases corticosteroids.

Adrenal medulla
Part of the adrenal gland that releases stress hormones (adrenaline and noradrenaline) during activation of the sympathomedullary pathway.

Adrenaline
A stress hormone that is released as part of the sympathomedullary pathway. Adrenaline causes various physical changes which prepare the body to deal with stressful situations.

Adrenocorticotropic hormone (ACTH)
Hormone released by the anterior pituitary gland in the pituitary-adrenal system. ACTH stimulates the adrenal cortex to release corticosteroids.

Aetiology
The cause of a disorder.

Affectionless psychopathy
The inability to show any emotion, understanding or feeling towards other people.

Agency theory
Milgram's theory that stated that when we feel we're acting out the wishes of another person (being their agent), we feel less responsible for our actions.

Agentic state
When someone behaves on behalf of an external authority, acting as someone's agent, rather than taking personal responsibility for their actions.

Aim
A statement of a study's purpose.

Alternative hypothesis
See Research hypothesis.

Anaclitic depression
A possible long-term effect of separation, involving appetite loss, sleeplessness and impaired social and intellectual development.

Antibody
A type of protein produced by B-cells as part of the immune response. Antibodies neutralise pathogens in a number of ways.

Articulatory-phonological loop
A component of Baddeley and Hitch's working memory model. It holds speech-based information temporarily.

Attachment
A close emotional relationship between a child and its caregiver. 'Attached' infants will show a desire to be close to their primary caregiver (usually their biological mother). They'll show distress when they're separated, and pleasure when they're reunited.

Autokinetic effect
A visual illusion where a stationary spot of light, viewed in a dark room, appears to move.

Autonomic nervous system (ANS)
Part of the PNS which is responsible for controlling our unconscious activities, e.g. digestion, breathing, etc.

Aversion therapy
Removal of an undesired behaviour by associating it with unpleasant feelings.

B

B-cell
A type of white blood cell that produce antibodies as part of the immune response. B-cells also produce memory cells as part of the immune response.

Bar chart
A way of presenting non-continuous data, where the height of the bars shows frequency.

Behavioural approach
An approach in psychology that claims that all behaviour is learned.

Benzodiazepines
Anti-anxiety drugs used in stress management — these slow down the activity of the central nervous system by increasing the body's reaction to GABA.

Beta blockers
Anti-anxiety drugs used in stress management, which reduce the activity of the sympathetic nervous system.

Biofeedback
Biological stress management technique which gives people information about internal physical processes that they wouldn't otherwise be aware of, e.g. muscle tension. The idea is to give them more control over these internal processes and the ability to alter them.

Biological approach
Explains behaviour as a product of nature. Biological psychologists try to explain behaviour in relation to what's going on in the body.

Boomerang effect
When people feel that they're being pushed too far or a rule restricts them too much, they may react by doing the opposite of what they're told.

Brain lateralisation
The idea that certain functions are generally localised more in one of the two hemispheres of the brain.

British Psychological Society (BPS)
An organisation that oversees psychological research in the UK. The BPS has developed ethical guidelines to help psychologists resolve ethical issues in research and to protect participants.

Buffer
Something that protects us — in the case of social psychology, from the consequences of our actions.

Capacity of memory
The amount of information that can be held in short- or long-term memory at a time.

Cardiovascular disorder
Medical condition associated with the heart and blood vessels.

Cardiovascular system
The heart and blood vessels.

Case study
A research method which involves a detailed description of a single individual or case.

Causal relationship
Where one variable causes a change in another.

Central executive
The key component of Baddeley and Hitch's working memory model. It directs attention.

Central nervous system (CNS)
The part of the nervous system made up of the brain and the spinal cord.

Central tendency
Another way of saying average. Measures of central tendency include the mean, mode and median.

Cerebral cortex
Part of the brain — it is the outer layer of the cerebrum, the largest part of the brain.

Chunking
Grouping pieces of information together into meaningful units to make them easier to remember.

Classical conditioning
A type of learning where associations are made between different things in our environment.

Clinical interview
A semi-structured interview, where the researcher asks some specific questions, but also lets the participant talk freely.

Closed question
See Fixed (specific) question.

Cognitive approach
An approach in psychology that claims that behaviours are controlled by thoughts and beliefs.

Cognitive behavioural therapy (CBT)
A form of therapy which allows a patient to change their faulty cognitions with the help of their therapist.

Cognitive interview
An interview technique developed by Geiselman et al to try to increase the accuracy of eyewitness testimony.

Cognitive restructuring therapy
Psychological stress management technique devised by Beck. The technique aims to disprove the negativity in a person's thinking.

Cognitive triad
Beck's (1963) model which identifies three types of negative, automatic thoughts linked to depression.

Compliance
Where someone goes along with the majority, even if they don't share the majority's views.

Confidentiality
Keeping information private.

Conformity
When the behaviour of an individual or small group is influenced by a larger or dominant group.

Confounding variable
A variable (other than the independent variable) which influences the dependent variable.

Content analysis
A method of turning qualitative information into quantitative data so that it can be statistically analysed.

Continuous data
Data which can be placed on a scale, e.g. height, temperature and time.

Control group
A group of participants who have not experienced any of the manipulations of the independent variable that the experimental group have.

Controlled observation
A study where the participant is observed by a researcher, usually in a laboratory setting. Some of the variables are controlled — e.g. a child might be given a certain toy to play with and observed through a one-way mirror.

Coronary heart disease (CHD)
Cardiovascular disorder resulting in restricted blood flow to the heart. CHD can lead to conditions such as thrombosis, heart attacks and strokes.

Correlation
Correlation means that two variables rise and fall together, or that one rises as the other falls.

Correlation coefficient
A number between −1 and +1 that shows the type of correlation and how closely the variables are linked.

Correlational research
A type of research method which looks for relationships between variables.

Corticosteroids
Hormones released by the adrenal cortex in the pituitary-adrenal system. Corticosteroids give us energy by converting fat and protein.

Corticotropin-releasing hormone (CRH)
Hormone released by the hypothalamus in the pituitary-adrenal system. CRH stimulates the anterior pituitary gland to release ACTH.

Cost / benefit analysis
Consideration into whether the cost to the participants was worth the benefit of the findings to society.

Counterbalancing
A way of 'controlling' variables so that their unwanted effects are minimised. Counterbalancing is mixing up the order of the tasks participants do, to solve the issue of order effects in repeated measures designs.

Critical period
A time in a child's development when certain skills are learnt or attachments are formed. If the child is not exposed to suitable stimulation for these events to happen during this "critical period", it may be hard, or even impossible, for them to happen later in the child's life.

Cross-sectional experiment
An experimental design that assesses a common factor across different people of different ages.

Culturally relative
Something which is specific to certain cultures.

Cycle of privation
A repeating pattern of children who have experienced privation going on to become less caring parents.

Daily hassle
An everyday event that is stressful. It could be something like losing your keys, or getting stuck in traffic.

Day care
Any type of temporary care for a child provided by someone other than the parents or guardians the child lives with.

Debriefing
A way of informing the participants about the nature of the study. It takes place after the study and is an opportunity for the researchers to discuss the purpose of the study and to ensure there are no unforeseen effects on the participants.

Deception
Misleading or withholding information from participants.

Deindividuation
When people lose their personal identity (stop feeling like individuals), and identify with a group.

Demand characteristics
This is when participants form an idea about the purpose of a study which could have an effect on their responses and make the conclusions drawn from the study inaccurate.

Dendron
The branched ending of a neurone which allows it to connect to and communicate with lots of other neurones.

Dependent variable (DV)
The variable that you think is affected by changes in the independent variable.

Deprivation
The loss of something that is wanted or needed. A long-term or even permanent loss is implied.

Deprivation dwarfism
When infants are physically underdeveloped due to emotional deprivation.

Descriptive statistics
A mathematical way of describing the patterns found in a set of data.

Despair
The second stage of the PDD model of how children react to separation. The child will start to lose interest in its surroundings, becoming more and more withdrawn, with occasional crying. They may also eat and sleep less.

Detachment
The third stage of the PDD model of how children react to separation. The child will start to become more alert and interested again in its surroundings. It will cry less and may seem to have 'recovered' from its bad reaction to the separation. However, its previous attachment with its carer may now be permanently damaged — the trust and security may be lost.

Directional hypothesis
A hypothesis which predicts a difference or correlation between two variables and states which way the results will go.

Disinhibited attachment disorder
An attachment disorder, where children have no preference for an attachment figure. They often lack the typical wariness that normal children display of strangers and will approach near-strangers for affection or attention. Symptoms include attention seeking and inappropriate familiarity with strangers.

Dispersion
A way of measuring how spread out the data in a data set is. Measures of dispersion include range, the interquartile range and standard deviation.

Dream analysis
Psychoanalysis treatment that is based on the idea that a certain part of the mind keeps repressed thoughts in the unconscious. Freud believed these repressed thoughts are likely to appear in dreams, so patients' dreams were analysed.

DSM-IV
The fourth edition of the American Psychiatric Association's Diagnostic and Statistical Manual of Mental Disorders. It contains all known mental health disorders.

Duration of memory
The length of time that information can be held in memory.

Ecological validity
A measure of how much the result of an experiment reflects what would happen in natural settings.

Ego
The 'reality principle' and rational part of both the conscious and unconscious parts of the mind.

Electroconvulsive therapy (ECT)
Therapy used to relieve depression in extreme cases and as a last resort. It causes a seizure by passing a 225 volt shock through a person's brain.

Encoding of memory
Encoding is the way that information is stored in memory.

Ethological approach
An approach that involves studying animals in their natural environment.

Eustress
A stress that is positive and exhilarating, e.g. arousal caused by a parachute jump.

Event sampling
A way of sampling behaviour during an observation. You only record particular events that you're interested in and ignore other behaviours.

Experimental hypothesis
A hypothesis accepted when your data forces you to reject your null hypothesis. If your null hypothesis was that two variables aren't linked, then your experimental hypothesis would be that they are linked.

Experimenter bias
See Researcher bias.

External locus of control
A belief that events are caused by external factors, such as luck or the actions of others.

External reliability
When a test is stable over time or between people — it is a measure of consistency.

External validity
A measure of whether the findings can be generalised beyond the experimental setting (e.g. to different groups of people or different settings).

Extraneous variable
Any variable (other than the IV) that could affect what you're trying to measure.

Eyewitness testimony
The evidence provided by people who witnessed a particular event or crime.

Failure to function adequately
Definition of abnormality that states you can't function adequately if you can't cope with the demands of day-to-day life.

Fear hierarchy
A list of feared events, allowing phobic people to show what they fear least through to their most feared event.

Field experiment
A research method where behaviour is measured in a natural environment, like a school, the street or on a train. A key variable is altered so that its effect can be measured.

Fight or flight
An evolutionary response which allows us to quickly mobilise our energy stores, making our bodies as responsive as possible to deal with a stressful situation.

Fixed (specific) question
A precise question used in interviews that can be answered with a short answer. E.g. "Do you get on well with your mother?".

Foot-in-the-door effect
A technique which tries to persuade people to agree to something through small steps. Also known as gradual commitment.

Free association
Psychoanalysis treatment where the patient is given a cue word and asked to say any ideas or memories that come into their mind.

Frequency polygon
A type of line graph useful for showing continuous data.

GABA
Gamma-aminobutyric acid — the body's natural anxiety-relieving chemical which slows down the activity of neurones and makes us feel relaxed.

General adaptation syndrome (GAS)
The three-stage physiological response to stressors described by Hans Selye. It proposes that after long term exposure to a stressor, our bodies will be unable to continue to cope with the situation and we may develop illnesses.

Gradual commitment
Agreeing to something gradually, in small steps where it's harder to refuse the next request. Also known as the foot-in-the-door effect.

Groupthink
What happens in cohesive groups with strong leaders where members of a group converge their thinking so that it falls in line with what they imagine the general view of the group is.

Hardiness
A personality type. Hardy people generally show a high level of commitment to what they do, view change in a positive rather than a negative way, seeing it as an opportunity for challenge and have a strong feeling of control over their life and what happens to them.

Hawthorne effect
Where participants may show a more positive response (e.g. try harder at tasks), if they are interested in something or in the attention they are getting (e.g. from researchers).

Histogram
A way of presenting continuous data.

Hormone
A chemical produced by glands in the body. It is released directly into the bloodstream where it travels around the body in the blood and affects target cells.

Hypnosis
A psychoanalytic technique. Patients are in an altered mental state, involving deep relaxation. Freud believed that repressed thoughts could be accessed in this state.

Hypothalamus
A tiny part of the brain that has many functions, including controlling the physiological activities involved in stress.

Hypothesis
A specific testable statement based on a theory. It predicts what will happen in a test situation.

Id
The 'pleasure principle' in the unconscious part of the mind. It is our innate drive to do what we want to satisfy ourselves.

Immune system
System which helps the body to fight invading bacteria and viruses (pathogens).

Imprinting
A type of attachment, seen commonly in young birds, where they automatically 'attach' to the first moving thing they see after hatching, and follow it everywhere.

Independent behaviour
Actions that people carry out with their own goals in mind and without influences from others.

Independent groups design
A type of experimental design that has different participants in each group.

Independent variable (IV)
A variable directly manipulated by the researcher.

Individual differences approach
The study of how psychological characteristics, like aggression and memory span, differ from person to person.

Informational social influence
Looking to others for information about how to behave, for example, when in an unfamiliar situation.

Informed consent
When participants agree to being studied knowing the full aim of the research. For those under the age of 16, permission has to be given by a parent or guardian to allow them to be studied in psychological research.

Insecure attachments
Attachments where the bond between child and caregiver is weak.

Insecure-avoidant attachment
A kind of attachment where the child doesn't become particularly distressed when they're separated from their caregiver, and can usually be comforted by a stranger. This type of insecure attachment is shown by children who generally avoid social interaction and intimacy with others.

Insecure-resistant attachment
A type of attachment where the child is often uneasy around their caregiver, but becomes upset if they're separated. Comfort can't be given by strangers, and it's also often resisted from the caregiver. Children who show this style of attachment both accept and reject social interaction and intimacy.

Insight
A Freudian term that describes when patients can access repressed thoughts and unconscious conflicts.

Institutional care
Care provided in places like orphanages, hospitals and nursing homes.

Inter-observer reliability
Making sure that the observers are putting each participant in the right category or giving the right rating during an observation. This might involve comparing the data from two or more observers to make sure they're giving the same scores (i.e. that they are 'reliable').

Inter-rater reliability
A test of external reliability. In an observation, if different assessors agree, i.e. both give the same score, then the inter-rater reliability is high.

Internal locus of control
A belief that what happens in life results from your own behaviour or actions.

Internal reliability
If a test is consistent within itself and is measuring the same thing throughout.

Internal validity
A measure of whether an experiment shows that the results were caused by the manipulation of the variables, rather than the effect of something else.

Internalisation
Where someone follows the majority and believes in their views — they've accepted them and internalised them as their own.

Interviewer effects
Where the interviewer's expectations about a study, or the participant's reaction to the behaviour or appearance of an interviewer, affects the outcome of the study.

Investigator effect
Where the actions of the researcher affect the outcome of a study in an undesirable way.

Irritant
A term used by Kanner et al (1981) for an everyday event that is stressful.

Labelling theory
Scheff's (1966) argument that states if people are treated as mentally ill, their behaviour will change and become more like that expected from their diagnosis.

Laboratory experiment
A research method where research is conducted in an artificial setting in a controlled and scientific way. The aim is to control all relevant variables except for the independent variable, which is altered to see what the effect is.

Leading question
A question where a certain answer is subtly implied.

Life change unit (LCU)
Score given to 43 common life events in Holmes and Rahe's social readjustment rating scale, to rank how stressful they are.

Locus of control
How much personal control people believe they have over the events in their lives.

Long-term memory (LTM)
A memory system that has an unlimited capacity and is theoretically permanent.

Longitudinal experiment
An experimental design where the same people are tested repeatedly as they get older.

Magnetic resonance imaging (MRI)
Brain scanning technique which uses magnetic fields to produce a detailed image of the brain that can show up abnormalities such as tumours and structural problems.

Major life event
Events which occur throughout our lives, e.g. death of a close relative, getting married or moving house.

Matched pairs design
A type of experimental design where there are different participants in each condition, but they're matched on important variables (like age, sex and personality).

Mean
A measure of central tendency. It is calculated by adding all of the scores in a data set and then dividing by the number of scores.

Median
A measure of central tendency. The median is the middle score when the data is put in order.

Memory
A process in which information is retained or recalled about the past.

Memory cell
Cell produced by T-cells and B-cells as part of the immune response. Memory cells remember an invading pathogen, which means that if the same pathogen invades the body again, the memory cells will recognise it.

Meta analysis
A study which combines the results of several studies all addressing a related topic.

Method of loci
A memory strategy for remembering a list of objects. The method involves associating the objects with locations.

Miller's magic number
Seven, plus or minus two, which was the number of items Miller thought short-term memory could hold.

Minority influence
Where small minorities, and even individuals, gain influence and change the way that a majority thinks.

Mnemonic verses
Poems that help you to remember facts.

Mnemonics
Internal memory strategies to make it easier to remember something.

Mode
A measure of central tendency. The mode is the score that occurs most often in a data set.

Monotropy
Having one special attachment, e.g. a child to its biological mother.

Multi-store model of memory
This was proposed by Atkinson and Shiffrin. It suggested that memory consists of three stores — a sensory store, a short-term store and a long-term store.

Multiaxial classification
A system where individuals can be rated on multiple axes/dimensions.

Myocardial ischaemia
Lack of blood flow (and therefore oxygen supply) to the heart muscle caused by contraction of vessels around the heart.

Narrative stories
A memory strategy that involves linking together all of the items that need learning by putting them into a story.

Natural experiment
A research method that measures variables that aren't directly manipulated by the experimenter.

Naturalistic observation
A research method which involves observing subjects in their natural environment. Researchers take great care not to interfere in any way with the subjects they're studying.

Nature-nurture debate
The argument about whether an individual's personality is influenced by nature (inherited factors) or nurture (environmental factors).

Negative correlation
A type of correlation in which as one variable rises, the other falls.

Negative reinforcement
When actions are likely to be repeated because they have a good outcome by removing something bad.

Neurone
Cell of the nervous system that transmits information as electrical impulses around the body.

Neurotransmitter
Chemicals released by neurones which allow nerve impulses to be transmitted across a synapse.

Non-continuous data
Data which falls into distinct categories, e.g. exam grades, types of ice cream and names of football teams.

Non-directional hypothesis
A hypothesis which predicts that there will be a difference between two variables, but doesn't state which way the results will go.

Non-participant observation
An observation where the researcher observes the activity without getting involved in it.

Non-specific barrier
Part of the immune system that prevents pathogens entering the body, e.g. the skin and mucous membranes (such as at the mouth, nostrils, genitals, etc.).

Noradrenaline
A stress hormone that causes various physical changes that prepare the body to deal with stressful situations. Noradrenaline is released as part of the sympathomedullary pathway.

Normal distribution
A bell-shaped curve where the most common behaviours or traits lie within the middle.

Normative social influence
Where someone follows the majority to avoid exclusion or rejection.

Null hypothesis
A hypothesis which you assume is true during the study. Any data you collect will either back this assumption up, or it won't. Very often, the null hypothesis is a prediction that there will be no difference or correlation between key variables in a study — and any correlation is due to chance.

Obedience
When people change their behaviour after a direct command.

Observational study
A study where a researcher watches and records the behaviour of an individual. Variables may or may not be manipulated.

Open-ended (non-specific) question
A type of question used in a questionnaire or interview. The wording of the questions means that the participant can reply in any way, and in as much detail as they want. E.g. "how does that make you feel?".

Operant conditioning
A type of learning where an individual learns to associate its own behaviour with a particular consequence.

Operationalisation
Describing how variables will be measured.

Opportunity sampling
A method of selecting a sample of participants where the researcher samples whoever is available and willing to be studied.

Order effect
A problem associated with repeated measures design where participants get better through practice (learning effect), or worse through being bored or tired (fatigue effect).

P

Parasympathetic nervous system
The branch of the autonomic nervous system that calms our body down — it is the 'rest and digest' system.

Participant observation
An observation where the researcher participates in the activity under study.

Participant variables
Differences between the people in each group which might affect the results when using an independent groups design.

Pathogen
A bacteria or virus that invades the body and causes illness and disease.

PDD model
A model that stands for 'protest, despair and detachment'. It outlines these three stages of how children may react after being separated from their primary caregiver.

Peer review
A process used to ensure the integrity of published scientific work. Before publication, the scientific work is sent to experts in the field who assess the quality of the work.

Peg-word technique
A memory strategy for remembering a list of objects. The method involves linking the objects with a set of peg-words.

Peripheral nervous system (PNS)
The part of the nervous system made up of the neurones that connect the CNS to the rest of the body.

Phagocyte
Type of white blood cell that engulfs and destroys pathogens as part of the immune response.

Physiological study
A method such as brain scanning, which can produce a detailed picture showing up any structural abnormalities.

Pilot study
A small scale 'practice' study which helps foresee any problems before running the main study.

Pituitary-adrenal system
This system produces a countershock response to long-term stress which supplies the body with more fuel. It's triggered by the hypothalamus and provides our body with energy by converting fats and proteins.

Placebo
Pills that do nothing at all. They're used to test if any effect happens just because people think they're being treated.

Population
A distinct group of people in society, e.g. children, old people, men, women, British people, French people, students, etc.

Positive correlation
A type of correlation in which the variables rise and fall together.

Positive reinforcement
When actions are likely to be repeated because they have a good outcome through a reward.

Positron emission tomography (PET)
Brain scanning technique that measures brain activity. It uses sensors placed on the head to track a radioactive substance that is injected into the person.

Primacy effect
An effect seen in memory studies where participants can recall the first few items of a list better than those in the middle.

Privation
Never forming a bond with a caregiver.

Protest
The first stage of the PDD model of how children react to separation. During the first few hours, the child will respond by crying, panicking, calling for its mother, etc.

Psychoanalysis
A treatment introduced by Freud. It aims to allow patients to access repressed thoughts and unconscious conflicts. These can then be dealt with.

Psychodynamic approach
An approach in psychology that puts abnormal behaviour down to underlying psychological problems, often caused by past events and experiences.

Psychological harm
Any negative emotion (e.g. stress, distress, embarrassment).

Psychopathology
The study of abnormal behaviour.

Psychosurgery
Brain surgery involving destruction or separation of parts of the brain.

Q

Qualitative data
Data in the form of written notes, audio/video recordings, etc. This data must be quantified before it can be statistically analysed.

Quantitative data
Data in the form of numbers. Quantitative data is easy to analyse statistically.

R

Random allocation
A way of ensuring participants have an equal chance of being placed in an experimental condition. It should ensure groups are not biased on key variables such as age, sex, etc.

Random sampling
A method of selecting a sample of participants where every member of the target group has an equal chance of being selected for the sample.

Range
A measure of dispersion. The range is highest score in a data set minus the lowest score in the data set.

Rational-emotive therapy (RET)
Psychological stress management technique devised by Ellis. It focuses on encouraging people to change irrational beliefs into rational beliefs, for a more positive consequence.

Raw data
Scores from a study before any statistical analysis has taken place.

Reactive attachment disorder
A rare but serious condition, which occurs in children who have been permanently damaged by early experiences such as privation of attachment. Symptoms include an inability to give or receive affection, poor social relationships, dishonesty and involvement in crime.

Recency effect
An effect seen in memory studies where participants can recall the last few items of a list better than those in the middle.

Reliability
If a test is consistent and measures what it's supposed to then it is reliable.

Repeated measures design
A type of experimental design where participants take part in all conditions.

Research hypothesis
A hypothesis proposed at the beginning of a piece of research which is often generated from a theory.

Researcher bias
When researchers' expectations influence how they design their study and how they behave towards the participants.

S

Sample
A set number of participants that are representative of the target group.

Scattergram
A way of plotting points and visualising relationships between variables.

Scientific journal
A magazine that contains peer-reviewed scientific reports.

Secure attachment
Attachments where there's a strong bond between the child and its caregiver. If they're separated, the infant becomes distressed. However, when they're reunited, the child is easily comforted by the caregiver. The majority of attachments are of this type.

Self-fulfilling prophecy
When predicted events, circumstances or actions 'come true' due to a person changing their behaviour to make it happen.

Sensory memory (SM)
A store that holds visual and auditory information as it passes very briefly through our senses.

Separation
Where a child is away from a caregiver they're attached to (such as their mother). The term is used when the separation is relatively short, just hours or days — not a longer or permanent separation.

Short-term memory (STM)
A memory system that has a limited capacity and a limited duration.

Social change
When a society changes over time, e.g. in terms of relationships, behaviours, etc.

Social desirability bias
Where people try to show themselves in the best possible light, and so may not be completely truthful, but give answers that are more socially acceptable instead. This would make the results less accurate.

Social norm
A standard of behaviour and attitude within a society or group.

Social readjustment rating scale (SRRS)
Scale devised by Holmes and Rahe to measure major life events. It ranks 43 common life events from most stressful to least stressful.

Spearman's rho correlation coefficient
A type of correlation coefficient.

Split-half technique
When a questionnaire is randomly split in two to see if all participants score similarly on both halves. If they do, the questions measure the same thing, and therefore have good internal reliability.

Standard deviation
A measure of dispersion. The standard deviation measures how much scores deviate from the mean. It is the 'spread' of data.

Standardisation
Where all conditions are kept the same in a study, to ensure that each participant has the same overall experience.

Strange situation
An experimental procedure, designed by Ainsworth (1978), and used to assess how children react under conditions of stress (caused by separation from the caregiver and the presence of a stranger) and also to new situations.

Stress
The response that occurs when we think we can't cope with the pressures in our environment.

Stress inoculation training (SIT)
Psychological stress management technique devised by Meichenbaum. SIT aims to protect from the harmful effects of stress by preparing people so that they can deal with stress before it becomes a problem.

Structured interview
An interview that follows a fixed set of questions that are the same for all participants.

Superego
The moral part of the mind based in the conscious and unconscious. It balances the id and the ego.

Survey
A method of data collection that includes questionnaires and interviews.

Sympathetic nervous system (SNS)
The branch of the autonomic nervous system that gets our body ready for action — it is responsible for the 'fight or flight' response.

Sympathomedullary pathway
This pathway is responsible for the initial shock response to stress. It's triggered by the hypothalamus and results in various physical changes in the body which make our bodies as responsive as possible to deal with the situation.

Synapse
A very small gap between two neurones that nerve impulses are transmitted across.

Systematic desensitisation
A treatment for phobias based on the behavioural model of abnormality. It involves learning to link a feared event with relaxation.

T-cell
A type of white blood cell that attaches to pathogens and kills them. T-cells also produce memory cells as part of the immune response.

Target cell
A cell which has the right receptors for a specific hormone.

Target group
The part of a population that you're interested in studying.

Target organ
An organ that contains target cells for hormones to act on.

Test-retest reliability
When a person repeats a test to see if they always score similarly. If they do then the test has good external reliability.

Theory
A possible explanation for an observation.

Time-interval sampling
A way of sampling behaviour during an observation where you choose to observe for only set time intervals.

Type A personality
A personality type — people categorised as Type A have characteristics such as being competitive, ambitious, workaholic, hostile, etc.

Type B personality
A personality type — people categorised as Type B have characteristics such as being non-competitive, relaxed and easy-going.

Type C personality
A personality type — people categorised as Type C have characteristics such as being mild-mannered, easy-going people who may not react well to stressful situations and suppress their emotions.

Type D personality
A personality type — people categorised as Type D have characteristics such as being very negative people who worry too much about things and lack social skills.

Universal
Something that is present in all cultures, but not necessarily with the same frequency.

Unstructured interview
An interview which may have a set of discussion topics, but is less constrained about how the conversation goes than a structured interview.

Validity
If the results of an experiment were caused by the manipulation of the variables, rather than the effect of something else, or if the findings can be generalised beyond the experimental setting then the experiment has good validity.

Variable
A quantity whose value can change.

Visuo-spatial sketchpad
A component of Baddeley and Hitch's working memory model. It stores visual and spatial information temporarily.

Volunteer sampling
A method of selecting a sample of participants where people actively volunteer to be in a study.

Working memory model
This was proposed by Baddeley and Hitch. It suggested that short-term memory is made up of several components — the central executive, the articulatory-phonological loop and the visuo-spatial sketchpad.

Acknowledgements

AQA Specification reference points are reproduced by permission of Assessment and Qualifications Alliance.

Photograph acknowledgements

Cover Photo **KTSimage**/iStockphoto, p 2 **Streetangel**/Science Photo Library, p 3 **Antonia Reeve**/Science Photo Library, p 4 **David Parker**/Science Photo Library, p 6 **Patrice Latron/Look At Sciences**/Science Photo Library, p 7 **BSIP, DPA**/Science Photo Library, p 8 **Klaus Guldbrandsen**/Science Photo Library, p 10 **Colin Cuthbert**/Science Photo Library, p 11 **Omikron**/Science Photo Library, p 23 (top) **Rich Legg**/iStockphoto, p 23 (bottom) **Ton Kinsbergen**/Science Photo Library, p 25 **Steve Horrell**/Science Photo Library, p 30 **Muammer Mujdat Uzel**/iStockphoto, p 34 **Sue Baker**/Science Photo Library, p 35 **AJ Photo**/Science Photo Library, p 36 **Thierry Berrod, Mona Lisa Production**/Science Photo Library, p 37 **Sidsnapper**/iStockphoto, p 38 **Photo Researchers**/Science Photo Library, p 39 **Photostock-Israel**/Science Photo Library, p 40 **Time & Life Pictures**/Getty Images, p 43 **Ruth Jenkinson**/Science Photo Library, p 44 **Rich Legg**/iStockphoto, p 46 **Claire Deprez/Reporters**/Science Photo Library, p 47 **Sporrer/Rupp**/Science Photo Library, p 51 © **Bettmann**/Corbis, p 53 **Joseph Hoyle**/iStockphoto, p 56 **Ria Novosti**/Science Photo Library, p 57 **Steve Debenport**/iStockphoto, p 58 **David Clark**/iStockphoto, p 61 (top) **Crown Copyright/Health & Safety Laboratory**/Science Photo Library, p 61 (bottom) **Daniel Sambraus, Thomas Luddington**/Science Photo Library, p 62 **Gustoimages**/Science Photo Library, p 63 **Huchen Lu**/iStockphoto, p 64 **Tom Prout**/iStockphoto, p 67 **Dan Dunkley**/Science Photo Library, p 73 (top) **Avava**/iStockphoto, p 73 (bottom) **Lucas White**/iStockphoto, p 74 (top) **Lemoine**/Science Photo Library, p 74 (bottom) **Martin Purmensky**/iStockphoto, p 75 **Enis Izgi**/iStockphoto, p 76 (top) **Robert Cottrell**/iStockphoto, p 76 (bottom) **Andrew Rich**/iStockphoto, p 78 **clu**/iStockphoto, p 79 **Catherine Yeulet**/iStockphoto, p 81 **Jon Wilson**/Science Photo Library, p 83 (top) **Thierry Berrod, Mona Lisa Production**/Science Photo Library, p 83 (middle) **Philippe Psaila**/Science Photo Library, p 83 (bottom) **Susan Kuklin**/Science Photo Library, p 85 **DNY59**/iStockphoto, p 86 (top) **Willie B. Thomas**/iStockphoto, p 86 (bottom) **Simon Potter**/Science Photo Library, p 89 **Media Photos**/iStockphoto, p 91 **Jacob Wackerhausen**/iStockphoto, p 94 **AJ Photo**/Science Photo Library, p 96 **Chris Hellier**/Science Photo Library, p 106 **TEKimage**/Science Photo Library, p 107 (top) **Arno Massee**/Science Photo Library, p 107 (middle) **James Cavallini**/Science Photo Library, p 107 (bottom) **Hank Morgan**/Science Photo Library, p 112 **Ria Novosti**/Science Photo Library, p 114 Science Photo Library, p 123 **Erich Schrempp**/Science Photo Library, p 130 **Will & Deni McIntyre**/Science Photo Library, p 131 **Sporrer/Rupp**/Science Photo Library, p 139 **Chris Whitehead**/Science Photo Library, p 140 **Lea Paterson**/Science Photo Library, p 142 **Jacob Wackerhausen**/iStockphoto, p 145 © **Philip G. Zimbardo, Inc.**, p 147 Source: **BBC**; permission granted by the researchers, p 150 **Gombert, Sigrid**/Science Photo Library, p 153 **Victor De Schwanberg**/Science Photo Library, p 158 **Suedhang**/Science Photo Library, p 160 **George Steinmetz**/Science Photo Library, p 161 **Johan Sjolander**/iStockphoto, p 164 **AJ Photo**/Science Photo Library, p 165 Science Photo Library, p 166 **NASA**/Science Photo Library, p 170 **TEKimage**/Science Photo Library, p 171 **Mehau Kulyk**/Science Photo Library, p 173 **Ria Novosti**/Science Photo Library, p 174 **Mauro Fermariello**/Science Photo Library, p 176 **Peter Menzel**/Science Photo Library, p 178 **Oscar Burriel**/Science Photo Library, p 180 **Steve Gschmeissner**/Science Photo Library, p 181 **US National Library of Medicine**/Science Photo Library, p 182 **Living Art Enterprises, LLC**/Science Photo Library, p 183 **Will & Deni McIntyre**/Science Photo Library, p 187 **BSIP, Astier**/Science Photo Library, p 188 **National Library of Medicine**/Science Photo Library, p 189 **NYPL**/Science Source/Science Photo Library, p 191 **Dolphin Inst.**/Science Photo Library, p 193 **Lea Paterson**/Science Photo Library, p 196 **BSIP, Keene**/Science Photo Library, p 196 **Romilly Lockyer, Cultura**/Science Photo Library, p 203 **Vladimir Koletic**/iStockphoto.

Every effort has been made to locate copyright holders and obtain permission to reproduce sources. For those sources where it has been difficult to trace the originator of the work, we would be grateful for information. If any copyright holder would like us to make an amendment to the acknowledgements, please notify us and we will gladly update the book at the next reprint. Thank you.

Index of Names

Index

PYTB51